MY REMINISCENCES

My Reminiscences
By Prince Serge Wolkonsky
: : Translated by A. E. Chamot : :

VOLUME I

EIGHT ILLUSTRATIONS

Noverre Press

First published in 1924

This facsimile reprint published in 2012 by
The Noverre Press
Southwold House
Isington Road
Binsted
Hampshire
GU34 4PH

© 2012 The Noverre Press

ISBN 978-1-906830-48-9

CONTENTS

VOLUME I

	PAGE
FOREWORD	13
PREFACE	17

CHILDHOOD AND YOUTH

FALL	27
PAVLOVKA	49
THOUGHTS ON EDUCATION AND ENVIRONMENT	68

LAURELS

ROSSI AND SALVINI	93
SOME RECOLLECTIONS OF THE RUSSIAN THEATRE	107
RECOLLECTIONS OF THE GERMAN THEATRE	117
DUSE, SARAH BERNHARDT, RÉJANE	126
MUSIC IN MY CHILDHOOD AND YOUTH	146
IMPRESSIONS OF THE OPERA	167

WANDERINGS

ITALY	183
RECOLLECTIONS OF THE DUCHESS OF TECK	198
AMERICA	217
ISLANDS	252
ROME	295

LIST OF ILLUSTRATIONS

WOLKONSKY	*Frontispiece*	
FALL, THE CASTLE	*To face page*	48
PAVLOVKA	,, ,,	60
MRS. PATRICK CAMPBELL AS " PAULA TANQUERAY " .	,, ,,	130
SARAH BERNHARDT	,, ,,	140
PRINCESS MARIE WOLKONSKY (*née* BENKENDORF) .	,, ,,	146
ELEONORA DUSE	,, ,,	192
PRINCESS ELISABETH WOLKONSKY (*née* WOLKONSKY) .	,, ,,	302

FOREWORD

Russia has always been a country of contrasts; and foreign, especially English, opinion of Russia has offered a wide field for contradiction.

There were those who knew Russia well, there were those who had no personal experience whatever.

Those who had lived for many years in Russia loved both the country and its people. They loved the character of the people, the beauty and freedom of the country life, that absence of fences, the illimitableness of the horizons; they loved the habits, the ways of living, the cooking. How many English teachers, what a number of governesses I have known, who were inconsolable when they had to leave in order to return home! What lovely letters, full of pleasant recollections, they wrote from England.

There were others, those who had never been to our country, and yet had formed very precise " opinions " of it. These people were critical, more than critical, they were hostile. The hostility manifested itself in a marked preconception and an unwillingness to accept as true anything that did not coincide with their preconceptions. Alas, a system of " two measures and two weights " has prevailed in the estimation of our country. The appreciation, especially of the Imperial Government, was never free from prejudice. I will not enter into polemics (the impartiality of the following will, I hope, plead for justice), but I cannot do less than underline here the fact that, while the unfortunate, meek and humane Nicholas II was so often represented with his legs stained with blood up to the knees, with a sword from which dripped drops of blood, the unheard of atrocities of the present "masters," who have subjugated our country, are scarcely spoken of at all. They are either represented as a sad "necessity" or are spoken of as a "transitory state"; they are almost excused. With a "refreshing" gladness, the "happy" news is being broken to the "pessimist" that an "evolution in Bolshevism" seems at last to have taken ground in Russia. One can only deplore the blindness of those who do not see the universal danger concealed in the sanguinary progress, and the cynical triumph of evil that is offered by Bolshevism.

This book (the author wishes once more to emphasize this point) has no polemic intentions. It is an exposition, and whether of praise or criticism, the author trusts that both are inspired by love of his country and by impartiality for the subjects treated. Those of my English readers who belong to the first category mentioned above, those who have learned to love my country and remember it with kindness, will find in my book many an echo of that which has awakened and determined this sympathy. The reader of the second category, the one who dislikes our country, will find in this book a more conscious foundation for the criticisms he may have built on grounds he has had no opportunity of exploring personally; if some of his criticisms will gain foundations, others, perhaps, will lose their basis; at the same time he will see that there have been many things, many a side of life, worthy of being mentioned with gratitude by him who has known and experienced them.

For the convenience of my English readers, now when time is so precious and a big book so cumbrous, I have endeavoured to be as concise as possible. My memoirs in the original are in two big volumes; at the special request of my publisher, and by the omission of parts that are only of local interest, I have reduced their bulk. I can guarantee that no gaps will be felt, and this is greatly due to the conscientious work and skill of my translator.

S. W.

16th of August, 1924.

PREFACE

I GROUP my reminiscences under three headings: "My Country," "Wanderings," "Laurels." On these three lines do the intellect, the heart and the soul of a man develop, if he loves his country, other countries, and art.

MY COUNTRY

My Country! What a complex conception; and notwithstanding its complexity, how impossible it is now to seize it. We love our country; who does not love his country? But what do we love? What? That which was? That which is? No, that which shall be? We do not know. Our land? Where is it? Nothing but fragments remain. Our people? Where are their faces? In the darkness their faces are invisible. The thoughts of our land? In what are they expressed? The voice of our land? Where is it heard?

Nevertheless I entitle the last part of my reminiscences "My Country." When they are finished it will be seen in what this idea consists. It will be seen, because I shall speak with sincerity. I shall not try to construct the conception of "my country," but I leave it to those who read my book to deduce it.

And if the different deductions of those who read it prove to be in accordance with the soul of each, and are in accordance with each other, then this accordance and the union of these accords will be "our country." It will not be real, but it will be strong in its metaphysics; it will not be outside of us, but it will be all the stronger within us; it will be free from the narrowness of earthly frontiers, and it will acquire the boundlessness of personal judgment.

And if we renounce earthly conditions, the attachment to place, we shall recreate in our creative memory that which is not; and if in those mountain heights, where our soul has hidden itself, our consciousness escapes from the mist of useless regrets we shall say with the poet:

" We *have* no country, we *have* no exile,"

and on the smooth surface of our souls that once bubbled over with agitation we shall find the great equilibrium of the reversed reflection.

Wanderings

Wanderings! Does this word make you feel something of an inner necessity? This is no invention of man, it is in the nature of things. The desire for change of place is not of a very torturing nature. It is of a quite natural virtue. To transport one's ego, to spread one's diffusiveness. Everything living aspires to do so. The animals envy the birds, the plants envy the animals. Nailed to the ground the plants develop, out of a single stem, branches, leaves and flowers. Unable to move about, the flower awaits the visits of winged insects, and at the moment that they sting its heart and drink of its juice it covers them with its dust, that they should bear it to other flowers. The flower dies where it was born, but, in dying, losing colour and scent, changing from the freshness of the blossom to the dryness of the seed, it opens its pericarp and allows the wind to scatter its contents, having provided its seeds with scaly wings or having decorated them with down; it gives them up to the breeze,

> "That the wind may bear them abroad."

Everything living aspires to the experiences of space. Everything living moves and wants to move about; to walk, run, skip, jump, crawl or fly. Everything living knows the meaning of top, bottom, forward, backward, to right, to left; everything knows the meaning of rapidity and slowness, of strength and weakness, of lightness and weight, and everything knows the difference of whence and whither.

Alterations in the conditions of motion are some of the joys of man. Staircases, galleries, bridges, swings are all not only playthings for children, but also for adult men. There is here a victory over space, a victory over the power of gravitation, and we are diverted by our triumph. Why do roofs and belfries and trees have, from our early childhood, such a strong attraction for us? We love to be in a balcony hanging over an abyss; we love the mole that stretches far into the sea; we love the bright lantern shining in the lighthouse, with its foundations fixed in the deep, that mocks the spray of the angry waves. We love embankments, we love subterranean passages. We love to look at nature in a mirror, when what is on the left appears on the right, and the reverse; we love to look through the wrong end of an opera-glass, so that what is small should appear still smaller, and what is far should seem still farther. Yes, we love to play with space and to wander is one of these games.

But the means of locomotion! This is a new sport that is added to the game—on foot, on horseback, on wheels, on rails, on the water, in the air. And in each of these methods what variety there is! To all these victories over space there is added the victory over time: the greatest distance, in the shortest time. This is to what man aspires in his insatiableness—whirlwinds and torrents. That is what he wants to create; that is what he wants to outstrip. To outstrip and leave behind him, and at the expense of the smallest possible amount of personal strength: the greatest repose in the greatest excitement; the smallest motion at the greatest speed; the greatest safety in the greatest danger. To sit at a plate-glass window of a dining-car; to lunch leisurely, while all around is hurrying, while at the side the mile-posts are flying past; what rapture there is in this combination of contrasts! To cheat nature by her own laws, to triumph over her laws; to hurry onwards instead of standing still; to fly instead of falling to the earth—to oppose the horizontal to the vertical, the vertical to the horizontal! Yes, victory over space is one of the stimulants of man's sportiveness.

Wanderings are memory. It is the past in the present. Wanderings! The memory of them peoples our empty moments; no desert is empty when we have memories of it. No recollections are so fresh as the recollections of travel. They do not change—and in this lies the greatest value of recollections. And our relationship to these does not change; we remember that which has been, and we remember it with the same feelings as when it was. Each of his wanderings a man carries with him, carries in himself, because each one alters him. After each one he is not the same; each new wandering is a new wealth, and to these recollections there is never an admission of regret.

Wanderings are the answer to the attractive power of distant invocations. It is the thirst for the new, the different. " La nostalgie de l'ailleurs." Where is it better? Where we are not. Wanderings are the realization of dreams, the appeasement of longings.

> "It dreams that in far distant deserts,
>   In lands first kissed by the sunrise glow,
>   Mid burning rocks, alone and pensive,
>   A beautiful, stately palm did grow."

If it could move the pine would have moved to the

> "Lands first kissed by the sunrise glow."

But longings are not always appeased; appeasement only whets the thirst. The more we know the more we wish to know; the more we see, the more we wish to see. We weary ourselves in the search for its attainment, we sigh in enjoyment, and even satiety is replete with desire. We are always called back to what we have attained. It is not only the pines on the barren heights that dream of palms in the distant deserts; palms, too, dream of frozen dew and of the glow of sunset that rests on the stalactites of hoar-frosted pines.

That is why man has always wandered and will ever wander. That is why as long as he is alive he tramps the earth with the soles of his feet, until at last, like Horace, "lassus maris et viarum"—he reposes beneath it.

LAURELS

Laurels! What can be more enchanting than the images these sounds call up in our imagination! The symbol of all that is high! The symbol of high attainments and of high recognition; the symbol of lofty flights, of soaring beyond the clouds. What pictures arise in our imagination at the remembrance of the hard, green, shining leaves. From the conqueror at the Olympic games to the crowning of Petrarch in the Capitol; from the crowning of Napoleon's frowning brows to the smiling lips of the dancer smothered in wreaths; from the red lipped, passionate chansonette singer nibbling at the odorous leaves, to the motionless face of the dead pallidly reposing in the midst of their dark green; from the dusty, rustling leaves of withering wreaths tied round with faded rags of silenced raptures, to the fragrant odour of the steam rising from a seething cauldron. Leaves! how numerous you are, and how differently you are treated by man! Like the spray of a green fountain flying up into the air, and with trembling wings sinking downwards, returning as rain to the earth, or bending to the ground in twigs lying on gravestones! The whole of man and his spirit and his ashes are under laurels.

And what of the tree itself? How did it happen that man chose just this tree for the expression of his flights, his enthusiasms, his veneration? Another tree would be inadmissible as such a token; the only possible token of peace upon earth is the olive branch; there could be no other token of spiritual peace than the palm, no other token of civic strength than the oak; no other token of grief than the weeping willow. Marvellous tree—vigorous roots, wayward stem, strange branches, mysterious crown, sacred leaves! Their rustle tells the history of man's thought, from the ancient oracles to the end of the world. And their scent! How they break when you squeeze them! Go into an old Italian garden, on to the silent paths between their green walls; go into it just after the gardener has clipped them, and evened with his scissors the dark, smooth vegetation. Do you smell their sharp vivifying odour? It is this odour that the marble statues breathe in their green niches; it is this odour that the audacious fountains cut through, when they force their way out of marble crevices. In the silence of this scent, from their overflowing edges the moss-grown basins drip the lazily bubbling water in a ceaselessly rippling stream. The never silent water—the dumb statues—and the strong odour of the vegetable life coming through wounded leaves.

The physical substance of the laurel immerses you in repose. The scent calms; the salutary juice causes drowsiness; its spiritual substance rouses attention, opens the eyes, and the laurels of Miltiades drove sleep away from the open eyelids of Themistocles. On the other hand, those whom they crown repose on them. The path to laurels is uphill, from the depths; laurels are on the mountains and all around them are lowlands. To reach the laurels—there is work, contest, victory; beyond the laurels there is fame; but not only that; around it there is flattery, and envy and the poison of "intoxicating fumes," all the dregs of humanity swarm under that proud head, and serpents crawl and wriggle beneath the smoke of the incense.

All this rises in my consciousness when I take up my pen to unroll my reminiscences of those workers in art whom it was my fortune to meet and to converse with about the subjects of art to which I gave my attention on my path through life. It will not be only art that will be treated here, and I fear art will be here least of all, but all proceeding from art. Why, it is by the sun that the flowers open out, and the caterpillars are developed. The rays of Apollo burn, and they do not know what they set on fire, and still less do they know what their reflected light also sets on fire. But the laurel was produced by the immediate beams of Apollo.

To escape from the rays of the ardent god the young nymph Daphne could not hide herself anywhere. The burning shafts pursued and scorched her, she was fainting from fatigue, she raised her arms to heaven, she breathed heavily, her limbs declined to obey her, they refused to go on, and stopped—they stopped and took root in the earth. Under the hot pursuit of the amorous god, out of her outstretched fingers green leaves sprouted; her fair hair formed a crown of leaves above her head, with the last beam of light that reached her once passionate eyes, they closed, and the young palpitating god having seized the nymph stopped before a laurel tree.

This is the story of the nymph Daphne and the god Apollo. This, according to Greek mythology—those wonderful tales of man—is the origin of the laurel.

CHILDHOOD AND YOUTH

FALL

FALL, beautiful Fall, resting on the shores of the sea near Reval. Under the banner of Fall my childish soul developed, and all my life the sound of that name—" Fall "—has been for me the symbol of all that is beautiful, pure and free from the burdens of reality. That name revives in me the invigorating caresses of the fresh sea air, the resinous odour of the pine woods. I see before me again the hard outlines of the projecting rocks, the light of the flaming sunsets reflected in the sea; soft green mosses in the moist shadows of the gloomy firs; hard white moss on the dry sand beneath the red stems of the pines; the turbulent river flowing between its high banks, the far outstretched valley and the hillocks of the park; the gnarled and twisted branches of the huge horse-chestnut trees; the thin feathery larches; the murmuring waters and the moss-grown stones, the welcome bilberries ripening in the quiet depths of the forests; the smiling red strawberries; winding paths that disappear from sight; stone steps that mount and descend; summer-houses on the summits of the green mounds that overlook the distant blue sea and undulating bushy thickets over which the pink turret rises with its blue and yellow flag.

Oh! that dear old house, with its odours of carved woodwork, its scents of dried and fresh flowers! It is of a pleasing Gothic style, of a cosy elegance. What splendid views from the terraces, from each of its windows. And all —the air, the light, the scents, the portraits, the books, the quiet, the talks—all were enveloped in the ceaseless noise of the waterfall.

The windows of my grandmother's bedroom look out on the waterfall. The furniture is Gothic, in black and white; the chintz is light with red flowers; portraits, vases, souvenirs. Everywhere in Fall the past touches you and calls to you gently. From the bedroom you go into a small octagon turret chamber—miniatures, a bureau with the initials of the Empress Marie Feodorovna and her portrait in pastel, drawn in Versailles; a splendid view of the noisy and foaming river beneath, over the distant park and through a clearing of the glistening sea. The sea sparkles in the distance, the river roars in the depths beneath, and the window is high up above; between them all are space and air.

Pictures of childhood rise up before me. I am three years old. On the stone steps of the portico an old Englishwoman—Miss Smith—a former governess of my aunts, my mother's cousins, is sitting showing me how to twist my fingers so as to form a house; the forefinger is lowered and represents a counter, the little finger is the shopkeeper and the two thumbs are customers. In the study downstairs, in a wing of the house, an old man with a white beard is seated in a deep armchair, he is wrapped up in a black velvet dressing-gown and is smoking a long pipe, he is my grandfather " the Dekabrist." Uncle Peter Wolkonsky, my mother's brother, has seated me on his horse and is leading me round the circle. I am afraid. After the second round he takes me down and asks: " Well, how was it ? " " Not very comfortable."

And the bathing in the sea! And the drives in the cart, where we sit all crowded together on hay covered with a rug. The cart is drawn by " Fall " or " Hawk," two short-legged, dark sorrel horses with white manes and tails. We drive through the wood. Roots grow across the road; we are jolted, we laugh. A smell of horses comes from the scented wood. This is the last hillock and beyond it we shall hear the sound of the sea. We descend the hill; the wheels sink into the sand. Only grey sea grass grows along the roadside. We undress in the little deal bathing-house, we run barefooted across the sand, skipping over the prickly grass, and jump into the water. The waves are coming in, they break over us. The smooth sandy bottom is even and hard. Now and then the soles of our feet are slightly tickled—it's only a little flounder escaping from under our feet. I could never bathe anywhere afterwards, except in the sea or the ocean. I could never bear to bathe in a river or a pond. I could not bear my feet to sink in soft slimy mud; this was contrary to my early aristocratic impressions.

Once after bathing I felt ill; my brother and our tutor led me out of the little bathing-house into the air. I lost strength; I lost consciousness, but all the time I heard the noise of the sea and the wind. I only recovered gradually, and in this process there was a blissful moment—just before I quite came to. The feeling of indisposition had passed, the sound of the waves grew louder in my ears, the warm wind caressed my naked body, the grass pricked my legs. I felt my unconscious fusion with nature. We returned from bathing on foot; our lips and hands blue from the bilberries. On the way home there is a huge stone in the wood. One day we cleaned it of moss and all the children wanted to cut their names on it. We brought hammers and chisels, but the work proved to be not as easy as we had expected.

The love of inscription is fostered in Fall; several memorial monuments are to be found in the park. There is a large block of stone surmounted by a helmet, a shield and a sword on the high banks of the pond. This monument was raised by the founder of Fall, my grandmother's father, Count Benkendorf, in memory of his brother Constantine. The last words of the inscription are " He ceased to serve when he ceased to live." In Fall you get used to reading inscriptions. There are many cast-iron seats in the gardens ; friends who had stayed in the house presented seats with their crests, and requested them to be placed at their favourite spots. What fun it was to read these mottoes ! Here we had flowers and strawberries, and here too were Latin inscriptions. " Pro fide et patria " were my first Latin words. The spirit of romanticism was early poured into my young soul.

Evening, twilight ! The lamps are not lighted as yet. Grandmother is playing on her Erard—it is sad, spun out and yet somehow soothing. I listen in a blissful semi-consciousness ; the left hand seems to repeat a complaint. Once she said it was a waltz and composed by a man called Chopin. But at that time I did not yet know this, I was not sitting in the drawing-room, but in the next, the " columned room." The twilight evening of the northern spring peeps in at the windows. There is something cold in nature, I have no wish to go there. How quiet it is beyond the windows. Only the upper leaves of the trees flutter darkly against the bright sky. The heavy old horse-chestnut stands out above the abysmal void. They say it had been planted by old Aunt Zakharzhevsky, my grandmother's aunt ; she sometimes stayed at Fall, she is as great and heavy as her horse-chestnut tree ; she smokes quite special cigarettes made of straw, they are called " pachitos " ; she has a nice smell. The red broom-like flowers grow there at the bottom of the precipice. My mother told us that when she was a little girl her grandmother had told her that when she had been a little girl a very, very old woman had said to her: "Every time you see these flowers, think of me." All my life, when I see these flowers, I think of my mother and my great grandmother, Countess Benkendorf, whom I have never seen, and the old, old woman whose name I don't know. Only a short time ago, in June, 1921, when I saw these flowers in the courtyard of a Moscow house, my thoughts flew back from our twentieth century through the nineteenth century to the eighteenth, when the old, old woman had told my great-grandmother to think of her. Those flowers grow at the bottom of precipices or down below near the water; they can only be approached from below, while here in the " columned room " between the columns and in baskets on the window-sills there are hot-house flowers. What pretty ones there are among them; some like deep wine-glasses of lilac and deep crimson colours; they tell me their name is gloxinia. The other day the old gardener took a leaf from the gloxinia, cut it in half and stuck each half into a box of sand, and in a few days each piece took root and sent up shoots. The old gardener has two grandchildren, Wally and Richard, we play with them. One large stone near the pond I named " Wally's Stein," and my mother told me it reminded her of a very famous name.

All is frozen out of doors, all is immovable like glass; only the mist rises from the valley. There, at the other side of the river, in the middle of the lawn at the bottom of the hill, a bronze man is standing, he is called Apollo; you can't see on what he is standing. There is a cloud at his feet; he appears to be in the sky or as one from the sky come to earth. I touch the window, it is cold. The flower terrace is pretty, all looks like glass; all without motion. For how many years the white stone lions have had their motionless eyes fixed on the motionless night. . . .

Grandmother's left hand still continues to complain, but so submissively. A large marble lady in a veil looks at me through the window; beneath her on a bronze tablet is written that she is the Empress Marie Feodorovna, "the benefactress of all and of us."

The lamps are brought in. It hurts; it's unpleasant; all is scattered. But tea is ready in the dining-room. A long, long table and cool junket and Finnish brown bread. In the large dining-room there is much old silver on the sideboards—tankards, cups. On the wall above the sideboard hangs the portrait of an old woman and a little girl in a shift, whose head rests on the old woman's knee. This is the portrait of the woman whom my great grandfather, Count Benkendorf, saved during the inundation, which has been celebrated in Pushkin's *Bronze Rider*, and the girl is my grandmother's sister, who afterwards became Princess Kochubey, the owner of Dikan'ka. At that time I did not know it, but what you hear later has a way of filtering into the past, and even when we think of those no longer there we see them in the past as dead. It is difficult to fix in one's memory the limits where " I don't know " ends and " I know " begin, the point where " to know " commences.

I learnt much in Fall, without trouble, without reading—thanks to Fall; by inner contact with outer objects, by what was produced around us, by slight observations that my grandmother or my mother let fall, their stories, their reminiscences, their sigh or their laughter.

A large, old fashioned, uncouth piano, that tinkled like glass, stood in the " columned room," but it was preserved carefully. It was in keeping with all the other Gothic furniture, and I was told that the celebrated singer Sontag, by marriage Countess Rossi, had sung to its accompaniment; she had once passed a summer in Fall, and there is a seat to her name in the park. Of an evening my mother taught me to play on this clumsy piano, and afterwards we played duets on it together; we went through Haydn, Mozart, Beethoven, Weber—what glass-like sounds, and from what old-fashioned editions! ... On this same piano I once played the "Pastoral Symphony" with the Grand Duke Constantine Constantinovich, afterwards so well known as the poet "K. R." He came to Fall when a cadet, with the other cadets of the Naval School.

The cadets visited us several times. How jolly it was! The corvette *Varyag* or the clipper *Pearl* would cast anchor before Fall; the boats are lowered, we have seen it and run to meet them. Some seventy cadets and officers land with Admiral Brylkin at their head. Then we wander and drive about while preparations are made in the house to entertain them; the cadets dine in the garden under the horse-chestnut trees, while the Admiral in his epaulets, with a ribbon across his breast, leads my grandmother to table in the dining-room. They repaid our hospitality; we went to them in Reval, we lived on the men-of-war; we saw the manœuvres and gun-exercise in Baltic Port. We once returned from Reval in the schooner *Compass*.

I shall never forget one awakening. I was sleeping the sweet sleep of childhood in the cabin of the *Varyag*. I was awakened by a loud rattling, and before I was able to realize that it was the sound of drums, I was wrapped in the sweet blissful sound of the singing of a choir. The crew were singing the Lord's Prayer on the deck, and through the loop-hole of the cabin, in blinding silver radiance, the conquering luminary cast its rays. Oh, what an awakening! Do you like awaking in the morning? The exclamation of Brunhild: "Heit dir, Sonne, heit dir, leuchtender Tag."[1] The awakening! The pledge of the

[1] "All hail to the sun, all hail to the brilliant day!"

future, the pledge that the past is not broken off, the pledge of renewal and revival. I read in some French book: "Les réveils de l'enfance sont triomphants, les reveils de l'age mûr sont moroses, ceux de la vieillesse sont lugubres."[1] No, I have not noticed in myself these changes; even now I am triumphant when I awake in the morning, even now I jump out of bed because the joyful day is beginning, especially when the weather is fine or I have on my table some commenced MS. that is awaiting me. But another such an awakening as I had that morning on the *Varyag* I cannot remember.

Life on the sea is picturesque; where this picturesqueness of the sea blended with the picturesqueness of Fall what beauty was produced!

When the cadets put to sea again what a void was left . . . I sat in the "columned room" and counted the squares in the parquet floor made of oak and some black wood. Grandmother used to tell us that when she was a little girl, Lvov, the celebrated composer of the Russian National Anthem, "God save the Tsar," used to stand near this door and play upon his Maggini; his violin sounded just like an orchestra. He was my great-grandfather Benkendorf's aide-de-camp, and he was as good an engineer as he was a musician. In Fall there is a bridge over the river called Lvov's Bridge: a single arch supported on iron bars, whose ends go into the banks. When Nicholas I saw this bridge he said: "Lvov has thrown his bow across the river."

To the north of the house on the meadow there is a clump of trees, every tree of which is surrounded by a railing with an inscription. These trees were all planted by members of the Imperial family, beginning with Nicholas I.

---

[1] "The awakenings of childhood are triumphant, the awakenings of middle age are morose, those of old age are lugubrious."

In the year 1871 the Cesarevna Marie Feodorovna paid a visit to Fall. How well I remember all the details of that visit. It was six o'clock in the morning when two Barons, Meyendorf and Buxhowden, came to announce the Cesarevna's visit; she was to arrive about twelve o'clock from Hapsal, attended by a suite of six. My mother got up at once, and, with her, all the inmates of the house rose, too. Everybody began to bustle about and to work; when grandmother awoke she was only informed that everything was ready for the reception of the guests. I remember that an Esthonian workman was sent to the tower to watch for the arrivals, and to give notice as soon as the carriages came in sight. But this blockhead did not understand the duty confided to him, or, rather, he understood that he was to wave his hands when he saw them coming, so there he was waving frantically on the top of the tower while my mother and grandmother sat calmly conversing in the drawing-room. The calash, with the Cossack on the coach-box, followed by another vehicle, was already at the yard gates, when I ran into the "columned room" quite out of breath, and shouted, "They're coming!" My mother appeared on the lowest step at the front door when the Cesarevna alighted from her calash. They kissed; then the Cesarevna kissed my grandmother. The suite consisted of the governess of the Court, Princess Julia Kurakin; the maid of honour, Countess Apraxin; the maid of honour of the Empress Marie Alexandrovna, Miss Zhukovsky, the daughter of the poet; General Stürmer, Prince Suvorov, and the Cesarevna's secretary, Oom. I remember very well the Cesarevna's dress, it was of grey linen, trimmed with red velvet under lace insertion. I also remember my mother was in a white summer dress and a white lace hat with black berries and leaves; my grandmother was in grey silk.

While the guests were having tea we children remained in the garden near the house, waiting for them to come out: is it possible they will go for a walk without calling us? They all came out on the terrace; first my mother and the Cesarevna; my grandmother remained in the house; "Serge! Peter!" my mother called. In an instant we had run up and followed the Cesarevna like two pages. We went along the paths down the garden, crossed Lvov's Bridge, went up to the old ruin which stands on the steep bank of the river; we went down to another bridge, which we children called the "long bridge," though it was no longer than the other, only narrower; we went to the "Imperial Summer-house," where there was a bust of Nicholas I in memory of his visit, and then went to the gate that leads into the wood, where open carriages were waiting to drive us round the park.

The Cesarevna was amiable and gay, in almost childish spirits. She plucked flowers on both sides of the path; but suddenly she noticed strawberries—then she rejoiced like a child. We saw this, and my brother and I began to pluck the strawberries and gave them to her. We were very much surprised that she ate them all, even the unripe ones. . . . As we were going down the steep path from the "Imperial Summer-house" I heard her ask my mother:

"Vous ne l'avez pas vu?" (You haven't seen him?)

"Mais non, pas encore." (Not yet.)

"Je vais vous le montrer." (I will show him to you.)

She stopped and began trying to open a locket she had on her neck. In gloves and without a mirror it was difficult; my mother assisted.

"Vous permettez?" (Will you allow me?) She opened the locket and exclaimed: "Quel beau garçon!" (What a fine boy!)

"Mamma, who is it?" I asked.

"Eto moy syn" (It is my son), the Cesarevna said.

"C'est les premières paroles que je vous entends prononcer en russe" (These are the first Russian words I have heard spoken by you), my mother said.

When we came to the carriages my mother and the Cesarevna stepped into a two-seated basket-carriage, the rest of the party seated themselves in three chars-à-bancs. Mother took the reins and made a sign to me to get up behind on the dicky. We drove off. The park of Fall is enormous; there are fifty-four kilometres of roads in it, and how varied it is! The roads go along the sea-shore, through pine woods, by green meadows, on the banks of rivers, up hill and down dale. I know nothing to equal the beauty and charm of the Fall park. . . . The Cesarevna was enchanted; she constantly asked that we might stop to enjoy the view, or to gather flowers. When we started she had on her knees a blue jacket with bronze buttons with anchors on them. My mother took the jacket and gave it to me to take charge of. I noticed in the pocket a closed envelope with a pretty coat of arms; I wanted awfully to see her handwriting, and also—to whom the letter was addressed. I was troubled with this wish the whole time we were driving; but I did not dare to turn the envelope over. I have seen the Empress' handwriting since then, but to whom that letter was addressed remains for ever an unknown secret. . . . When we reached home dinner was served. That day we children were sent to dine in the bailiff—old Lilienkampf's house. . . . After dinner the Cesarevna planted a chestnut tree with the same spade that Nicholas I had planted a birch tree. When she cleaned her gloves from the earth mother took a handkerchief out of my pocket and wiped her hands with it.

This is all I can remember. After they had gone there was, of course, much talk about the visit, and exchange of the impressions the day had left. I noticed when they spoke of Miss Zhukovsky, somehow my mother lowered her voice; she said: " Poor thing, she had to sit down and rest on every bench." Many, many years afterwards I learned that at the time she was pregnant by the Grand Duke Alexis Alexandrovich, and only a few days before they had asked the Empress to allow them to get married, but they did not obtain the permission. She gave birth to a son, Alexis, who received the title of Count Blêvesky. Although at that time I did not understand anything, this I did understand, that one must not ask one's elders about what they are speaking, when they speak in a certain tone. But why can't the elders wait till the children have left, if they want to speak of things that children have no right to ask about? . . . On the evening of that day— I have just remembered it was the 10th of July, 1871— when my brother and I were going to bed, our old major-domo came into our room to tell us his impressions of the day. He spoke in a low voice, a sort of tragic whisper:

" Oh, what negligence ! "

" What was it ? "

" It's entirely Edward's fault " (he was the second manservant).

" And what has happened ? "

" We had settled with him that he was to look after the knives and forks, and he has proved so inattentive."

" Well, how ? "

" I had served the peas round, I look to see if all is right. The Cesarevna does not eat ; she has peas on her plate, but does not eat them. What's the matter ? I

Childhood and Youth 39

think. I look again—she has no fork. And she never asked for one—how delicate!"

This was the only hitch in the ceremonial of that complicated day.

In the bright and cosy house at Fall there was one room into which we children went with a certain awe—it was a gloomy and silent room in which nobody ever sat. It was the study of my great-grandfather, Benkendorf. In front of the writing-table there stood a large high-backed armchair; on the writing-table were bronze busts of Nicholas I, Alexander I, and Benkendorf's forefathers. There were many bronzes—models of cannon, small reproductions of the statues of Kutuzov and Barclay de Tolly; a paperweight made of a piece of wood of Alexander I's coffin, set in bronze and surmounted by a crown. There were many portfolios with engravings and plans; high bookcases with books, medals in remembrance of the year twelve and " Tsars' portraits on the walls." Kohlmann's celebrated water-colour of the December revolt on the place before the Senate; it represented the boulevard; generals with plumes making commanding gestures, soldiers with white straps across their dark uniforms, and the monument of Peter the Great enveloped in cannon smoke. How interesting it was to think that my grandfather, the Dekabrist, had stood before this picture and looked at it when on his return from Siberia he had passed the summer of 1863 in the house of his son's mother-in-law. In this room everything was silent, quite in a special manner. The room smelt of olden times, of greater antiquity than the rest of the house; in that room one always felt one ought to ask: "May I?" But there was nobody there whom one could ask. Through the only window the waterfall could be seen; on the other side of the river, in the wood at the top of the hill, was the " izba," the log cottage which an old lady, Baroness Milinka Sacken, called " das Schweizerhaus im russischen Stil."[1]

In that wood on the top of the hill are the Fall graves. A lovely place. Half-way up the hillside on a sort of natural terrace ; in front lies a sloping meadow, on both sides are woods, in front beyond the meadow are also woods, and beyond these woods the sea. Behind is a hill, and on the summit of the hill an enormous wooden cross. My grandmother said that the cross had always been there, and that once, when taking a walk with her father, she had said : " I would like to be buried there at the foot of the cross." Count Benkendorf died on a steamer on which he was returning from Amsterdam to Reval. His last words were : " There, at the top of the hill." Those who were present did not understand ; when his body was brought to Fall my grandmother explained. One other detail. My great-grandmother, Countess Benkendorf, had been looking through a telescope from the tower when the steamer passed Fall on its way to Reval. She saw the steamer, but it bore only a corpse.

I remember hearing how they got married. A certain Marie Dmitrievna Dunina, née Norova, lived in a house on her estate called " Old Vodolagy," in the Kharkov Government. Although she herself was the mother of a numerous family, she had brought up two nieces, the daughters of her sister, Madame Zakharzhevsky. Like an old brood-hen, Marie Dmitrievna spread wide the patriarchal dominion of her soft but strong wings. Her daughters and her nieces got married, but the apples did not fall far from the tree ; with each wedding a new house sprang up. However, for dinner, all assembled in the big house. They lived grandly there ; an ox was often slaughtered for dinner. The whole of Kharkov paid their respects at

[1] The Swiss cottage in the Russian style.

"Old Vodolagy." One day a young aide-de-camp of the Emperor's, Alexander Benkendorf (he was not a Count at that time), arrived in Kharkov on a special mission. Somebody said to him:

"Surely you will call on Marie Dmitrievna Dunina?"

"On Marie Dmitrievna Dunina?"

"How is this? Don't you mean to call on Marie Dmitrievna Dunina?"

He noticed such an expression of amazement on the faces of all around that he hastened to answer: "I shall certainly call on Marie Dmitrievna Dunina."

He paid her a visit. They were seated in the drawing-room, when the door opened and a young woman of such unusual beauty entered the room with two little girls that Benkendorf, who was as absent-minded as he was amorous, upset a splendid Chinese vase. The lady was a young widow, Madame Elizabeth Bibikov, née Zakharzhevsky, Madame Dunina's niece. Her husband had been killed in the wars of 1812.

When the position of affairs became clear to her, Marie Dmitrievna found it necessary to obtain information about Benkendorf. As a former Maid of Honour of Catherine the Great, she was in correspondence with the Empress Marie Feodorovna, and in order to procure this information she addressed her inquiries to the highest Imperial source. Instead of information the Empress sent an icon. She knew Benkendorf very well; he was a favourite of the Imperial family. His mother, who was a Schilling von Kanstadt, had come from Würtemberg with Marie Feodorovna. Catherine did not like her, and wanted to send her back, but Marie Feodorovna arranged a marriage with Benkendorf for her, and she remained in Russia. Her son, Alexander, the future Count, Chief of the Gendarmerie, and the founder of Fall, was from his youth a favourite of the Imperial family. He was the Empress Elizavesa Alexievna's page; at Fall there was a snuff-box with her portrait and the inscription " To my little love."

His father was famous for his forgetfulness. He was the Governor of Riga. My grandmother used to relate that once Paul I came there. Benkendorf quite forgot to order dinner. He sent to his friends to ask them to help him out of his difficulties; they all hastened to send him a dish. The dishes were brought covered with dish-covers —when the covers were removed they found on each dish a goose. It was in the autumn, and every friend thought to send the dish that was best at that season. When grandmother had finished her story I asked, as all children do when a story is finished, " Well, and what then ? " but I received no answer. Is it only children who ask questions ? Is it only children's questions that remain unanswered ? " The rest—is silence," Hamlet said, and the rest is much more than what has been said. . . .

My great-grandmother had two brothers Zakharzhevsky; I have but a faint recollection of them. One was a general; he died during a parade in front of the Winter Palace. His wife was that aunt who smoked pachitos. She was a Thisenhausen, and spoke bad Russian; her knowledge of the language went no farther than the notices she received from the Palace, and she had a curious way of repeating them. The other brother was unmarried and lived on his estate in the Kharkov Government. His throat was cut while he was in bed. His nephew, Nicholas Pokhvostnev, was suspected of the murder, and died under the suspicion, but at the trial his innocence was proved—the valet confessed to the deed.

The Benkendorfs had three daughters; my grandmother was the second. The eldest, Anna, married the Hungarian Count Apponyi. I visited the old lady twice in her estate,

Lengel. She left Russia in 1842, and lived in her new country surrounded with family portraits and with her former recollections. In the distant plains of Hungary she retained the memory of the undulating valleys, the sea-coast, of the pink turret in the bushy woods, and the neversilent waterfall. In her stories there were of memories of a strange Russia, that was centred in the Winter Palace, Peterhof and Fall. At that time Petersburg was a large, smart plaything. All that was built then had the character of a plaything and of carelessness. All that is left of that time—monuments, palaces, pavilions—were adapted for luxurious life, behind which one feels somehow the absence of practical care. Nicholas' drill was a sort of military screen that partitioned off life and insured its even flow. The whole of life was a parade, and I never felt the presence of this parade so closely as I did when listening to my aunt's stories. She knew the Petersburg of that time very well, she had been wonderfully beautiful, notwithstanding that she had a squint, and she possessed a rare voice. She was the first to sing Lvov's " God save the Tsar " in public. It was in the Hall of the Nobility at a concert given for the Patriotic Institute. The hymn was executed for the first time; it was sung by a choir, but first she sang each verse as leader of the choir. My aunt Apponyi only survived my grandmother a short time. I paid her a second visit in 1898, a year before she died. She was blind, but in her eighty-fourth year as courteous and lively as ever. . . .

Benkendorf's third daughter was called Sophie. She was married to Prince Kochubey, the owner of Dikanka. I never saw her.

The image of old Benkendorf soars over Fall, but together with his image a certain architectural officialdom—the pipe-clay of Nicholas' days. Behind the romantic unconstraint of country life, you feel the official turnpike; while the muslin-clad ladies and girls sat at their canvas-work, aides-de-camp came and went to and from the study and couriers hurried post-haste along the Reval high-road. On that road, a kilometre and a half from the mansion, stood a tiny pink house where the aides-de-camp redressed and refreshed themselves after their journeys. Punctilio was never relaxed and it regulated life even in its daily minutia. . . . All this, all this Fall of Benkendorf's time lives within me, somewhere far down in those depths of man's consciousness, where things abide that we have never seen, in those crannies of our being where things of real non-existence find the subjective confirmation of their metaphysical existence. Do not say that this is subjective—yet no, rather say that this is subjective, but confess also that subjectiveness is the best ornament of the object.

And after that there was another Fall; the Fall of my grandmother, Marie Alexandrovna. That Fall lives in those near, those upper strata of consciousness, where things live that we have seen, known, loved, loved so dearly that it will only be with life that this love can be extinguished, and its freshness will only be extinguished with this love itself.

My grandmother was the most aristocratic being I have ever met—thin and frail. I see her before me in a plain white dress, with a white muslin handkerchief under her straw hat, clipping the roses or the bushes. I date my love for trees and bushes from that time. She was well versed in the names and the habits of the plants. How many firs, how many chestnuts she sent to us in Pavlovka, in the Tambov Government. To all these natives of Fall my mother gave the Latin epithet: Fallensis. How much love and tender care there was of the trees and flowers. Whenever my grandmother found a heap of horse-droppings on the roads, she would stick the end of her parasol into them and carry this valuable fertilizer on the end of her parasol to a flower-bed and spread it out there.

She spoke Russian badly. She belonged to the generation that had been brought up on French, and only picked up Russian from the nurses and maids when she was a young girl. In consequence my grandmother, this fine flower of the aristocracy, often used unexpectedly vulgar expressions when speaking Russian. Yes, she was very aristocratic, and sometimes this showed itself with a certain narrowness with regard to others; questions of outward forms often had an estranging influence. But this was only in little things of no importance to the real conditions of life; in large, important occurrences she approached others with that broadness of soul which is the highest manifestation of real aristocracy. Another's sorrow, another's illness found her like a soldier at his post.

One year, when she arrived in Fall, where we had come before her, she announced to us that from that day she would only talk French with us. Oh, how thankful I am to her now for that decision, which alarmed me so much at the time! What a great thing it is to know foreign languages; by it we not only enrich our speech, we enrich our reason with new ideas, new correlations, new logical categories. At the same time we began to read with our mother the old French writers. The first thing was Racine's *Athalie*—what a world of beauty; not only the words and the sound of those words, but the thoughts, and the form of those thoughts. The sense of form was taught me not only by those with whom I lived, but also by the place where I lived and from what I lived by. The large library at Fall was remarkable for its fine editions and fine bindings of books up to the beginning of the eighteenth century. I began to take a book with me when I went into the woods. In this way the beauties of style were joined to the beauties of nature; some scene of a tragedy was blended with the rays of the sun that fell through the trees on the green carpet beneath them. It was there I read all Racine, Corneille, and Molière.

When my brother and I arrived at Fall after having passed our examination to enter the sixth class of the Gymnasium, we were greeted by a triumphal arch of fir branches at the post-office bridge near the exit of the Kaesel Wood. My grandmother, mother, brothers, sister, nurse, in a word all were waiting to receive us under the arch, which bore on a scroll of white linen the inscription which we afterwards heard had been chosen by our little brother, Alexander, it was the one with which Paul I greeted Suvorov after the campaign in the Alps: " Worthy of the deserving." Our younger brothers presented each of us with a wreath of laurel, grandmother gave us each a gold pocket-pencil.

I passed one summer in the " Izba " that peeps out of the woods on the other side of the river above the waterfall. I was pleased with the independence and the beautiful solitude. The joy of morning, the morning hubbub of the woods, and the first rays of the sun that pierced through the dewy branches of the trees surrounded me, when I descended the stone steps to cross the chain bridge, on my way to the big house. The meditative, resinous odour of the pine woods embraced me when in the twilight of evening I mounted those stone steps to regain my abode. When I left to go into the eighth class, and went to take leave of my grandmother and laid the key of the " Izba " on the table, I said :

" May I have the use of it another time ? "

" Whenever you wish, as long as I am in this world."

But it was the last time. The next summer I passed in travel, and did not go to Fall, and the following autumn she died. In September, 1881, she went to Rome. In October we received news that she was ill. My mother and I started at once. I had just entered the University; I am grateful that my father allowed me to go.

My grandmother lived for twelve days after we reached Rome. Her excellent elder sister, Aunt Apponyi, was with her. My grandmother died in horrible torture of a contraction of the intestines; but she displayed the greatest bravery, and that frail, delicate creature showed us how one should die. She died on the 4th of November at six o'clock in the evening. She lived in the Palazzetto Borghese, which is just opposite the Borghese Palace. The daughter of her sister was married to Prince Borghese. Her sister was living there and my grandmother joined her. We conveyed her coffin to the station and placed it in a luggage-van; we covered it with a red pall and surrounded it with palm leaves; the van was sealed up. The seals were only removed in Reval. Thus in the midst of frost and snow the coffin of the Princess Mary Wolkonsky, covered with a red pall, and surrounded by Roman palms, arrived at Fall and was placed in the family chapel, in the so-called " Church House." It was a mild winter's day. The hill was covered with white snow, and the white valley stretched out beneath; the fir branches looked black where they peeped out of the white snow cushion, as we laid the green palms in the grave. Twenty years of life were abstracted from real existence and passed into the thin smoke of memory. At the moment that the pitiless earth levelled the bourne between the present and the departing past, I saw beyond the white shroud that covered the valley, over the tops of trees, the distant line where the sea blended with the sky.

That is how I remember Fall, beautiful Fall. I have not mentioned—but perhaps it is of no interest—that I was born there on the 4th of May, 1860, at 6 o'clock in the evening, in the large bedroom above the " columned room "; there were cretonne curtains with a pattern of passion flowers in that room. I may mention that. I do not like reminiscences which begin " I was born there and then." Every man was born somewhere and at some time. But I can end this chapter as

> " To classic usage now I pay
> All due respect, though with delay,
> And a beginning thus is made."

Now, of the old house at Fall nothing remains but the bare walls; in 1918 our Red Army was quartered there; bare walls remain. What a pity!

> " Combien j'ai douce souvenance,
> Du beau lieu de ma naissance."[1]

[1] " What happy memories abide
  Around my native countryside."

FALL, THE CASTLE

PAVLOVKA

Can you remember your feelings when, having passed your examinations with distinction, you took your place in the railway-carriage? Do you remember the huge vault of the station roof? The arch that opened into the world, before which the engine puffed impatiently, and beyond it space and nature? And do you remember, two days after that, your arrival at the estate? You must remember it—such things are unforgettable.

It is already long since the caressing, sweet-scented air of the steppes is wafted to us through the open windows. On each side of the railway-line stretch endless fields of softly waving rye and oats. The sun is setting, it is no longer painful to look at it; what gratitude, free from care, seems to spread out between the sky and the earth. The train goes slowly. You can count the soft and even rotation and the regular stroke of the wheels. Larks fly up, soar, descend, and disappear. The sounding air circling around almost intoxicates with its ringing cadences.

It is delightful, but long; the train goes on slowly—too slowly; too slowly it puffs along, and with what indifference it sends out behind it whiffs of smoke that gradually fade away. A whistle. There's the red watering station—and then at last is our dear old station, Wolkonskaya. We must get down on the left side.

Quick, quick, through the dirty waiting-room to the porch. The old grey *troïka* with its tinkling bells drives up; the old coachman congratulates us on being home again. Quick, quick, huddle all the things into the calash.

We are off. The bells tinkle again. We rattle over the pavement of the station, we clatter over the rickety wooden bridge, we are now on the black earth road. It is soft, and quiet. The whistle sounds behind us, the train puffs, shakes, puffs more energetically; the rattle becomes more regular, feebler, dies away. . . . There's a quail somewhere. . . .

How far away is all I love! How far! Florence, Venice! Is it possible that these very rails on which the train has disappeared behind me into the distance of the steppes leads to you? How far all that is, all that magnificence of marble and . . . ! Yes, how far away is all I love, yet how I love all that is around me! My country, oh, my country! Here everything is soft, earthy, strawy. The historian Soloviev divides Europe into two parts: the stony and the woodeny.

The calash drives on, the off-horse catches at the rye growing along the roadside, Evening is darkening. The evening air is full of rye flowers. The last sounds of day are heard; the weariness of constant motion overcomes us. There is a scent of straw, smoke, manure. The disappearing horizon is not intersected by anything if it be not the arch over an approaching horse's head. The conflagration of the setting sun has faded away. The sound of bleating seems to hang in the clouds of dust; an occasional crack of the long whip. And again silence; all fades more and more away, and the gloom becomes more intense. An unexpected bark comes out of the darkness, an unexpected horse's sniff, an unexpected flash from a distant bonfire.

We drive on. The bells tinkle; is it as a lullaby, or to wake us up? There is a smell of horse sweat. The side horse strikes one hoof against the other loudly. We drive on and on. There seems to be no space—we do not know how time passes.

Suddenly there is a smell of verdure, of the dampness of a wood; we are approaching the park. Darker than night, the dark oaks darken the dark sky. Suddenly, like a sea of sound, the song of the nightingales fills the night air; we are driving along the avenue. There is a light at the end of the avenue. Somebody has run out of the front door. The light flashes through the dining-room window. They have long been awaiting us, and have suddenly heard the regular sound of horses' hoofs in the stillness of night, and somebody cried: " They are coming ! " And somebody repeated : " They are coming ! They are coming ! " and all run out on the doorsteps with lights. The avenue is at an end, we have driven into the spacious courtyard; we have driven round the green lawn. The horses have stopped in the strip of light.

Oh, the first supper with dill from our own kitchen-garden!

" Formerly," Gorgol says, " long ago in the years of my youth, in the years of my childhood, that can never come back, I was joyful when I arrived." I must own that at every age and not only in my youth I was joyful when I arrived. Even when I neared my seventh decade this joyfulness has never deserted me. And now, when I am beginning my seventh decade, and when nothing is left of that past, when in the corners of the soul, where the choicest flowers bloomed, even wormwood does not grow, even now I cannot think of those arrivals in our dear Pavlovka without feeling joyful emotions at the recollections.

I remember that the hours of those arrivals varied; I find it difficult to say which I preferred—the arrival at night or by day—to guess at, or to see. If it were by day we usually arrived at about six o'clock. What a lovely hour on the estate ! The hour when the earth is still hot; and coolness descends from the sky. I stop at the porch. The long shadows of the trees stretch out over the lawn; the flowers near the house are being watered, there is a sound of watering pots and pails; bees are humming over the petunias and the mignonette. Each year they lived behind the boarding of the wooden house. From the porch I look back along the road by which we had come. There is a green round before the house; in the middle of this grass plot we have one of those enormous brick-coloured pots which we had brought from Florence. To the right a huge three-stemmed oak has stretched its branches over the road; it is an enormous tree; if you were to measure the circumference of its crown on the earth, it would be about two hundred paces. When we were children we used to prepare our lessons in the branches of this oak. Our old coachman used to wait in their shade with the carriage on a hot day. Beyond the grass plot I can see the avenue by which we arrived; it is called the "Count's Avenue," in memory of the former owner of the estate, Count Koushelev. In the early seventies we had a bailiff who tried to rename the avenue and call it "Prince's Avenue," but the old name stuck to it. It is an avenue almost a mile long; the trees are clipped like walls, only the tops hang down; a closely clipped hedge borders the road; and two white posts are on each side of the exit into the open steppes. The sun sets there, its warm rays creep along the whole avenue and fall upon the Florentine vase in the middle of the grass plot, making the geraniums burn like fire. During fifty-two years, how many have arrived along this avenue; how many have driven away down it. What can be more delightful than hospitality in the country. To send to meet the guests at the station, to prepare their rooms, to order the dinner for them, to think of their favourite dishes. With joy the white posts receive them, and they joyfully see them depart, as the guests depart without solicitude. Handkerchiefs are waved from the porch, and from the calash a lady's handkerchief is waved in return; the *troïka* has grown quite small, it can hardly be seen, till at last, in the bright spot between the white posts, a lady's umbrella waves or a man's hat is hoisted on a walking-stick for the last time.

In front of me, to the left of the avenue, is the white house that goes by the name of the " Dairy," not on account of its colour, but because at some previous time it had served as a dairy. It is a pretty little house with a high gabled roof, and has a certain Gothic look about it, and a weathercock upon it. Beneath the cock there are four letters, and around are the four quarters of the earth, but he is like the cock in Alexis Tolstoy's poem, " he does not know which way to turn," it is so still in the air. The cock has no reason to turn specially in any one direction, but he looks to the west, through the avenue, where the sun sets and the village of Kriusha lies, and from whence the rain always comes ; he has probably remained in that position since the last rain. Below the cock, on the frontal, is a large clock which points to two minutes to six. A stone-paved pathway leads to the white house across the grass plot, between two borders of flowers that glow brightly in the farewell caressing rays of the departing sun. A peacock all glittering in golds and emeralds, with unfurled tail, struts proudly along that gay pathway. To the left, half-way down the path, is our pretty little storehouse. It is an old-fashioned construction, built in the " Empire " style, with a portico and four columns. How dear to me is the memory of the creaking door of this house. The clock on the " Dairy " strikes six. It is hot on the perron from the walls, which had imbibed all day the relentless heat of the pitiless sun. I had built this large portico with a balcony above it for the purpose of having breakfast there on hot days; but it is hot now, let us go to the other side.

A pleasant coolness greets us in the hall; the shutters have been closed all day; they have only just been opened, and in the hot rays of the sun the brick-red walls seem on fire. An oak staircase with a dark-green carpet leads to the portrait-gallery. On the wall is a large painting by Pannini representing a seaport, ships, a tower, and also a sunset; a brass lamp, like the lamps in Venice in the Cathedral of Saint Mark, hangs from the ceiling. Here is the oak-panelled library, with two plate-glass windows; from these windows there is a view of the meadow, you see the great oaks, the distant valley, and farther still the grey willows, behind them a strip of the pond sparkles, and beyond the pond, again trees that form the distant outskirts of the park. I have left behind me on the perron the dry steppes; on this side is the green sap of the woods. Dear old library! Here three generations have abridged rainy days and the long autumn evenings. Passing through the two-windowed drawing-room I pass out on to the balcony; it is decorated with flowers, and I can guess by the pungent scent that tuberoses are among them. In front of the balcony there is a circle of ten giant oak trees; they are plunged in reflection 'mid the rising shadows, only the very uppermost leaves on the tips of the summit still glow in the sunlight that lingers on the other side of the house. There are seats under these trees—a second drawing-room, where we loved to dine or sup when we were children. To the right of the balcony, through a cutting in the trees, you can see our church; it is on the other side of the ravine, a mile and a half away. It is a very beautiful building in "Empire" style; it was built in 1806. It is quieter on this side of the house, the evening has come, nature is preparing for the night. . . . There is the sound of wings, but no cawing, as a flight of rooks pass over the house ; they have flown to the pond to drink. The meadows stretch beyond the oaks to the edges of two ravines that intercross ; at that point there is a seat, with a parterre in front of it, and two huge agaves placed on stumps of trees. They had been brought by my mother, as quite small plants, from the Villa Wolkonsky in Rome.

What beauty is there in all this ? Why do we love it so much ? I have seen many more beautiful places ; the country around is ugly, the climate is dry, and the only water there is in the park is found in two ponds. What is the cause of this attachment ? Why are the roots of our nature so firmly fixed in the earth, fastened to each tree, blossoming in each flower, embracing the limitless, monotonous steppes. I do not know what others think, but I can answer for myself. For me it represents unceasing work. To plan, to execute, to see at each return to the estate improvements, and the growth of that which was done in previous years—what an endless satisfaction that is. Yes, our part of the country in the steppes is dismal, but the house is surrounded by an old park of two hundred and fifty acres. When my parents bought the estate in 1863 everything was neglected and in bad repair ; only large old trees gladdened the eye, but nettles, burdock, and brushwood grew everywhere. Now it is all clean, fresh, and smart-looking. There was not a single coniferous tree in the park ; the two first fir trees arrived with us on the roof of the carriage ; in 1868 the railway did not go farther than Tambov. We brought two fir trees—they were not ordinary ones, but balsam-firs—and my mother planted them in the yard at either side of the entrance gate. They are now big and emit fine aromatic resin.

My mother never ceased planting, and I continued to do so, too. It was not easy for her; it was much less difficult for me. First, because I worked on already prepared ground, and secondly, as in my time the labourers had already acquired a certain amount of skill and respect for what was planted. But how difficult it was for my mother at the beginning! The calves were let out to graze in newly planted ground, the young firs were mown down. I may say that the work of the first ten years was more educational than constructive. Shevyrev said that in the "Lay of the Regiment of Igor" is expressed in a poetic form our endless task—our struggle with the desert. The struggle with the desert was my mother's work in Pavlovka, and of course it is not only a "natural" desert that is to be understood by this, but also that desert the men make of nature, and that desert that they make in themselves. It was not easy for her. A certain elemental opposition, caused by man's incomprehension and also of his derision, swept away the work of her hands. She did not despond; but it was only when the people saw the results that they began to see the value of that which produced those results. Gradually a period of careful work commenced. In the ravine near the brook I planted ferns, such as had never grown there before; they grew very well—the mowers took care not to cut them down.

We planted groves, whole woods, and so many pines and firs that in the evening sometimes you could notice their scent, and many varieties of mushrooms began to grow that had not been known there before. It had been impossible to go through the deep brushwood and wild hops of the valleys, even on foot; now you can drive there in a char-à-banc or an auto.

How beautiful the park is, where the soft green roads

wind about amid clumps of trees, or go along straight architectural avenues. There is the oak avenue that looks like the interior of a Gothic cathedral, and is a mile in length, and the maple avenue, where three carriages can drive abreast and the branches form a vault overhead. You cannot imagine the effect of these avenues at night. You seem to be in another world. The park is interesting for its trees; we have more than twenty varieties of coniferæ. During the last thirty years we extended our plantations of trees far beyond the boundaries of the park. Groves were formed of larches and firs in the bare steppes. The change from the steppes to the park became gradual. Those who have not been to Pavlovka for a long time would not know it again; it used to be bare, now there are clumps of trees and groves along the roadside.

This is the work that attaches you to a place. I have often been asked: " Do you like farming ? " " No." " Are you a sportsman ? " " No." " Then what do you do on your estate ? " I can assure you my day is fully occupied.

And my house, my little white house, our dear " Dairy," so irregular, so patched up, but so interesting. My bedroom is upstairs. The whole of the upper story is a remembrance of childhood, a remembrance of Fall, got up in the Gothic style of the thirties; there everything is an imitation, rather cold but very cosy. The chief room is the one with the balcony, the one above this is the clock-tower; this is called the Nicholas room, as it has a portrait of the Emperor Nicholas I on its walls, and also portraits of my ancestors. Nobody would say it has been arranged; everybody would say it had been inherited as it is; my great-grandmother might ask: " Where is my work? I left it here yesterday." A corridor leads to this room; it is the " Siberian corridor." There are the souvenirs of the " Dekabrists," portraits, views, documents, things that have been in Siberia. It is instructive: everything tells a tale, they speak to you; there we have the Blagodatsky mine, Chita, the Petrovsky works, Angara, the Amour, views of the prison cells, my grandfather and grandmother in their cell, No. 54. A tale of suffering and endurance, of eminence and humility. All this has been collected and hung in this small passage, which is lighted from above by a dormer window. All this is fresh, and white; only the Gothic glass door casts patches of colour on this whiteness. How few people know of its existence. How few have interest for it. It has never once occurred to any town school to make an excursion here. Why not show the school-children such a " Siberian Museum," to say nothing of the park, of the trees, of all the arrangements of the farm? Why are they never given a holiday in the midst of nature, to pick flowers, to catch insects, to sleep on the hay? No, instead of this the unfortunate children are taken in July to see a railway-workshop! This is all that class difference, over which man is unable to step in spirit.

In the lower story there is a room that you would scarcely expect to find there. The former cellars and dairy I have transformed into a hall. The architectural plan resembles more a swimming-bath than anything else, with columns and a gallery round it. Below round the whole hall there are shelves with books, and it is arranged like a sitting-room, with soft, comfortable seats. There is no ceiling, but the rafters of the roof are seen as in old Italian churches. In this hall at Christmas, in the first year of the war, we arranged a Christmas-tree for all who worked on the estate. The tree was seven yards high, it stood below and was tied to the rafters; round the room between the columns are lustres made by our own smith. We had recitations, we had singing, we had presents, and it was very gay. Ten days before in that very hall a Catholic service had been held for the prisoners of war; one hundred and twenty prisoners stood below, in the gallery behind the columns our own "rank and powers" were stationed. Of these prisoners of war I shall have more to say later on.

I never cared for farming or the management of the estate; I was always more interested in the expenditure than in the receipts. In my childhood I had an aversion for farming. Notwithstanding all the attempts my father made, he was unable to interest me in the management of the estate. Oh, those expeditions with the bailiff to the farms. How they bored me! We drove on these rounds in a cart, in the heat. All that my father talked of with the bailiff was so uninteresting, and was so far removed from what interested me. They talked about corn, about the alternation of crops, of the rate of rents, and I drove beside them looking at the fields and admiring the cornflowers and even the enemies of the corn—the red chrysalids. I was enchanted by the drooping oaks, and they talked of sawing and felling. I did not listen to what my elders were talking about behind my back, but I looked ahead on the endless billows of the endless fields of rye. It is hot; a gadfly hovers over the horses. Lassitude influences the whole of nature, it affects me, too. I was very much interested in the sweat-stained breeching of the off horse. In passing the horse caught at the ears of rye and the ripe grain fell on the footboard of the calash. I look down at my feet. The grains of rye are dancing about there. They are cunning; they have cheated man; he wanted to take them and grind them down, but from the footboard they again jump down to the earth and will take root there. I watch them, I follow them with my eyes until they fall on the earth. This dance of the grains interests me more than any conversation about the management of the estate. . . . But now we have arrived at the farm; we drive up to the office. Oh, those visits to the office! That overseer with a wedding-ring on his forefinger! The flies on the windows, the pictures from illustrated papers on the walls, hens on the threshold, sucking-pigs under the porch. . . . Oh, that fatal necessity—office books, reports! I see and hear all this—but do not look or listen. While all the time at home a commenced road, a freshly planted tree, a picture that the joiner has just framed, is waiting for me. . . . Thus from my very childhood life was divided into the necessary and wearisome, and the unnecessary and pleasant. From my childhood I felt the inimical encounters of Beauty and Usefulness. It was only much later I understood that you need not be ashamed of not taking interest in things that do not interest you. This leads to another question, which, by the by, Schiller has formulated. He said that you must judge of a man's tastes not by his work, but by his leisure. Much later I found out that it is possible to convert the occupations of one's leisure into the object of one's work. Of course not every hobby is worthy to be transformed into work, and on the other hand not every man is in a worldly position that enables him to unite his inclinations with his duties. But for him who is able to do this the path of life offers the rare privilege of the union of peace and concord.

And so I preferred expenditure to income. But it never appeared to me that I was spending on myself when I spent money on Pavlovka. I had a feeling that it was my duty, my mission, to make of Pavlovka that which in this time of revolution is called a " cultural value."

My relations with the peasants were good. They wrangled in the office with the bailiff and the overseer, but they

PAVLOVKA

Childhood and Youth

were always polite to me. On Sunday mornings I had a sort of reception in the portico. One came to ask that his rent should be decreased, another asked to receive corn before he had paid his rent, this one's cow was dead, another wanted straw for his thatch, a fourth osiers for his fence, or bricks for his stove. Sometimes it was difficult to settle such questions with justice and sincerity; in such cases the village priest was a faithful counsellor. It was also difficult because the condescension of the owner did not please the bailiff; this diminishes the revenues. But I told him to book charity as assets, and say no more about it. Others came only to ask advice: how they were to act in this or that case; in the division of the land or the affairs of the commune; questions I knew little about, but I always valued their confidence. Special cases of education or illness always brought them to me. One blind man I sent to Petersburg. I placed him in an asylum for the blind; he became a chorister, and learned how to make baskets and brushes. For this I became very popular among the blind. There were a good many blind people in our district, and it was a strange thing that at a distance of five or six " volosts "[1] they all knew each other. One of them said to me, laughing, " A blind man sees another blind man from a distance." In one family in the Pavlovka village there were two blind brothers, the third, Egor, who could see, served in our house; he was a most faithful fellow; he went to the war and was taken prisoner by the Austrians. After a year no more news of him was received. How many times his old mother came to ask me " to write just once more."

I had quite a correspondence with the Red Cross and with a certain institution in Geneva. God preserve us when news arrived! Then there came such a shower of

[1] A district including several villages.

petitions of all sorts. I even received requests from the Saratov Government to make inquiries. What a wonderful power of generalization there exists in hopelessness; one successful case arouses a thousand hopes. . . . Poor, faithful, jolly Egor, all who lived in my house remembered him well.

I remember one man called Menshikov, from the Posevkin village. It was in the second year of the war. He came to me and fell at my feet. After fifty years they were still not able to unlearn that! However, it was only those who came for the first time who did so. I asked what he wanted. There was to be a new levy, and he was a widower with five young children; he had neither mother nor mother-in-law with whom was he to leave them?

" I have come to you to ask for a letter?"

" To whom?"

" There's a Grand Duke who's come from Petersburg to recruit."

I had heard already who the recruiting officer was.

" No," I said, " not a Grand Duke, but Prince Engalychev."

" Do you know him?"

" Yes, I know him."

" Well, then, give me a letter to him, please."

" Listen to me. You'll believe me?"

" Yes."

" Well, then, my letter will not help you at all. When is the conscription?"

" We must appear on Sunday in Alabukhi."

" Very well, take all your five children, load them into a cart and drive off to Alabukhi, and take them all with you to the recruiting point."

" But the youngest can't even walk."

" Take it in your arms."

"Well, thank you for the advice!"

He did what I told him, and he was exempted.

And so on Sundays the peasants came to me. I went up quite close to them. Those who did not know me were surprised. I noticed that this surprise in its turn seemed to raise a sort of barrier between us, but it soon disappeared. Our relations were good; I always felt there was a certain condescension on their part; they seemed somehow to forgive my superiority. Perhaps, however, this also did not exist, but I simply appeared an oddity in their eyes. It is difficult to understand another's appreciations; that is the psychology that directs another's appreciations. One old woman told a neighbouring landowner that the peasants treated me well because I took care of the poor. I did what I could, but it is hard when you know that you are pouring into a bottomless barrel.

Yes, the help the landowners can give to the peasants is a stick that has only one end; or we may say, the impulse given is one thing and the result quite another. On the one side there is the desire for improvement, on the other emptiness. All this was of no avail, and I always had the feeling that on my side it was a sort of ransom—a ransom for the impossible, the unworthy state of things. But I never felt that I was responsible for it. The futility of all help given to the peasants is caused by his only wanting to receive, he does not understand what it means to invest. When the understanding of returns is replaced by the idea of gain, there remains only one step for the idea of gain, in its turn, to be replaced by the idea of roguery. The destructive principle of "assistance granted but once" has eaten into the peasant mind and has sunk deep. Roguery is one of the forms of this kind of assistance; and roguery is for him one of the conditions of husbandry. During forty years I can only remember one case that can really be called assistance given to farming and not a present. What an intelligent, upright man Alexey Davydov is. Every year he borrowed from me, and each year more than the last; he always returned the money on St. Nicholas' Day. He has bought cattle, implements, and, by my advice, he has roofed his house with tiles. Each year he is gayer. But all the others are but bottomless barrels—an eternal refusal. It is hard, from my childhood it was hard, to feel this difference between myself and the vast sea that surrounds me. There always was a feeling that sooner or later there would be an upheaval. But I never felt that when the upheaval came it would be better; and still less did I feel that *they* would become better. Alexey Davydov does not require my Italian hall, and he is quite happy without it.

When I have such thoughts I go to a far corner of the park. Everything is far when there are two hundred and fifty acres, but when I say far I mean the point that is farthest from any human habitation. This point is the summit of one of our gorges. We call it the Chumakov Summit. It is in the western side of the park, a young part of the park, and at that point the gorge divides into two, and there are promontories on all sides. I had had fir trees planted on the slopes, and at the top of the promontory that divides the two chief gorges I had planted a large Siberian cedar. It is a strong tree now, and its velvety green can be seen from afar; it seems to rule over the firs. To that corner of the park I love to go when my reason foresees something and my soul prefers not to know of it.

The firs on the slopes stand straight and their shadows fall evenly; they are planted in stories so that their tops form a sort of wavy carpet. Here a large hare has made his home, and is sure to jump out from some corner. But he is the only living thing in the place, if you do not count a red velvety bumble-bee, who hovers over the clover, settling down on a flower from time to time, hastily sucking up the honey, and then leaves the empty flower, humming indignantly, and flies on to another.

I walk past the young firs. The trees give me an affable welcome; they have no different moods as men have; they have misfortunes, illness, but they have no nerves. They are always affable. I like to go up to young firs, to such that are not too high for me to touch their tops. I always feel that there is something affable, something forgiving in this western corner of our park. I examine the trees, and I think how they will be in thirty years. I have planted so many fir trees here where

> ". . . above the firs, above their prickly summits,
> The golden sunset shines through evening clouds."

I go round the trees, and remove encroaching creepers. Have I the right to love all this, and to enjoy all around me so deeply? Can love be considered as a right? No, love cannot have any *rights*, love can only cause the envy of others. But envy does not give it to him who does not possess it, and envy cannot take it from him who has it.

I had planted a few poplars in the hollows; I clip them that they should have pyramidal shapes. Here I had also planted some silver willows; I examine them, they have taken root. Why, there's a fir that has thought good to decorate itself with green cones; at its time of life, too! What imprudence! I must take them off. Why does the tree want to wear itself out? The cedar looks splendid! Will it continue to thrive? It is hot and dry here; it must sometimes be watered, and the pond is far off. It is taller than all the others; the young trees that surround it are no protection. It can easily be broken by a gale. It was tied with wire to posts in three directions, the wire was stolen; it was then tied with ropes, the ropes were stolen; it was tied with bast, the bast was stolen.

The sun has set; I go home through the ravine. To the left the ravine grows deeper and deeper and more and more gloomy; large oaks grow higher and higher on the slopes and at the bottom. I don't want to go down, it is damp and already dark there; it smells of rooks in that hollow. Here above, it is dry, it is still light, there is a smell of honey and of hay up here. . . . The park has lost its wildness; the lawns are well mown and tidy, the bushes properly clipt; the roads are green, the soft places have been made hard with broken bricks. Here are the well-trimmed hedges that lead to the house, and there is the flower-garden, and here we are at the porch. The stone floor is like a chess-board; there are comfortable wicker chairs. . . .

Calm. They have finished watering. The avenue is dark, and the hot geraniums are extinguished in the Florentine vase that stands in the middle of the grass plot. It is hot!

" Marie Gavrilovna! "

My old housekeeper had only just closed the squeaking door of the larder and had turned her tottering and hurried steps towards the kitchen.

" Can I have some junket? "

" In a minute! "

How often when she brought me the cold, delicious junket I thought, " Perhaps this is for the last time." It was not the last time. But I always finished by saying some day it will be the last time. . . . And the last time came. . . . It *was* the last time.

I see that all these reminiscences I have written in the present tense. Forgive me and correct it. Wherever I have written " is " write " was, was, was." Of all I have described, do you know what I have saved, and now, while I am writing these lines, what still lies before me? A cedar cone from the cedar that grows on the Chumakov Summit.

THOUGHTS ON EDUCATION AND ENVIRONMENT

THE IV Larin Gymnasium was in the 6th Line of Vassili Ostrov; we lived in a lovely house in the 4th Line, at that time No. 17. It had a garden and a fine verandah.

The examinations took place at the most beautiful season of the year.

> "The love of earth, the beauty of the year,
> Sweet-scented spring around us."

We prepared for the examinations, working together with some of our schoolfellows in the verandah. Lilacs were in full bloom in the garden. The day was over, but the night did not come; it was the strange twilight of the northern *white* night. We close our books and run all together to the river and take a ferry-boat to the islands.

The Petersburg sea-shore! How softly the low earth stretches out under the water; the white sand can be seen through the clear water, and the gentle current seems scarcely to touch the white sand. The outlines of the prickly firs are marked sharply against the sky. The gentle ripple of the water is blended with the song of the nightingale. On the white sky there are white stars, moist like tears. . . . How tasty sausage, cheese, and a glass of foaming beer seem after a day of cramming! We glide along the smooth surface; streams of water drop from the oars. There are no sounds except our voices and the songs of the nightingale. How marvellous is the dark wood, unknown to the mist-hidden sunrays.

I owe more to the Gymnasium than to the University, in the sense of acquired knowledge and even with regard to methods of reflection. What is the most important in instruction? Some will say " to know how to teach." I think the instructor is least of all a teacher; he is, first of all, an arouser. There are three men I must mention with gratitude as arousers.

Victor Ostrogorsky, our teacher of the Russian language and literature. He was a typical " man of the sixties," with all the unbearable narrowness and prejudices of that decade, and all the beauties of their theoretical idealism. He had a large flow of civic concern and some bitter drops of sarcasm. This appeared in his teaching in a very reserved form, but for those who knew how to hear, they could find his meaning between the lines, and his soul beneath his undress uniform. Notwithstanding that many of his ideas were not congenial, he was very useful to me. I did not follow him through the door he invited me to enter, but by his criticism he helped me to recognize the door to which I was drawn. Literary tendencies, artistic literary forms, questions of the correlation of form and subject, of ethics and æsthetics—all this he knew how to touch upon, like a gardener who loosens the earth round the roots. "Thought once awakened shall not again slumber," Carlyle said. It is for this I am grateful to Ostrogorsky, not because he pointed out the path along which I should go, but because he indicated the existence of paths. He was a mild, kindhearted teacher; he was sometimes the worse for drink, and then he was specially sarcastic. He neglected the practical side of teaching; lessons were not prepared for him, compositions were not produced. One unwritten composition on Zhukovsky lay heavily on our consciences, and we were always afraid that he would suddenly remember it. One day he was looking through a note-book where the whole course of instruction was registered when he suddenly said :

" By the by, have you given in the composition on Zhukovsky ? "

" We gave it you ; of course, we gave it."

" Yes, and it was very superficial, too."

What could be more superficial, we thought. Twenty-two years later, when I was the Director of the Imperial Theatres, and had asked him to come to some meeting, I told him the story of this composition while we were having tea. He burst out laughing and choked over his tea.

Our teacher of Latin, Vladykov, was a fanatical grammarian. I can't say that I owe him a love for the antique world ; I can't say that he aroused in me enthusiasm for the ancient poets ; but he kindled in me respect for grammatical precision ; and taught me that grammar is the nearest approach of word forms with the subjects of thought. I owe to him the consciousness of my own verbal reflective apparatus. He was dry, imperturbable, and repeated the rules of the Latin grammar rapidly, requiring the same dryness and rapidity in our answers, and he gave us " ones " for the slightest inaccuracy. I am very proud of a copy-book I had in the eighth class for Latin exercises, in which there was only one " four," all the others were " fives."

His dryness proved to be a form of disease ; a malignant form of consumption carried him to the grave in less than three months. I visited him in the hospital ; he did not know his end was so near. With feverish enthusiasm he developed the principles of the Latin grammar he intended to publish, and with a voice that seemed to come from the grave, and flaming eyes, he spoke of the gerunds of the verbs *utor, fruor, fungor, potior* and *vescor*. . . .

The third teacher whom I remember with gratitude is

Vladimir Belozerov; he taught history. He prepared my brother and me for the Gymnasium, and we sat a whole year on the Greek mythology. I had a copy-book in which I had written the genealogical trees of the gods and heroes. All this was alive with epithets, comparisons, and the whole of it was permeated with the true breath of classicism. In truth this was the only classicism that the "classical" Gymnasium gave me. These are the three men whom I can remember. All the rest was pipe-clay routine.

I have said that the University gave me less than the Gymnasium. Of course I mean relatively; that is to say, if I compare what I knew when I entered the Gymnasium and what I left it with, and in the same way compare my knowledge when I entered the University and when I left it, there certainly will be a considerable plus on the side of the Gymnasium. On leaving the Gymnasium I wrote to Professor Veselovsky, under whom I intended to study, to ask him to advise me what books to read, and, in general, how to prepare for his lectures; I was specially attracted by the Romanic literature. My letter remained unanswered. I cannot explain what the reason could have been that this charming man, who was so responsive, who was so ready to assist any student who might apply to him, took no notice of my request; but this affected the whole course of my University studies; I was never able to approach any of the other professors. My interests remained beyond the University; the University became a sort of duty that had to be performed and got over. And I got over it without any inner enthusiasm. It was necessary to go through the University and take a degree. Even this did not appear to me to be an inner necessity, it was merely indispensable, to satisfy my father's demands. My father had finished his education in the Irkutsk's Gymnasium, and he was not able to go to the University. This, however, was not his fault. He had requested to be allowed to go, but when Nicholas I saw this request of a convict's son laid before him he said, " The Gymnasium is enough for him." But my father, who himself had never been to the University, would have been heart-broken if any of his sons had failed in taking a degree. I worked to satisfy his wishes, but even now I sometimes dream that I have still to pass the last University examination. The dream grows more troubled, and I become horrified at my insincere efforts to satisfy my father's wishes; when, suddenly, I remember in my sleep that my father is no longer alive, and that I can grieve him no more, I chuck up the examination, breathe freely again—and awake.

Those were unpleasant times. A wave of political fermentation poured on the University; the professors did not check it, many of them encouraged it. It was the scholastic year of 1880–81. It passed in never-ceasing excitement, in endless meetings. In the second half of this year, on the 1st of March, the most infamous of all political crimes, the assassination of Alexander II, was committed. A brutal feeling seemed to possess the University. The position of men of our circle was very hard, and for my brother and me it was still more aggravated by the fact that our father was the assistant of the Minister of Public Instruction. What scowling glances we had to endure. How strange it is that just those people who preach equality are the very first to sin against that principle. One of my fellow students, called Kryzhanovsky, a dishevelled young fellow in a red Russian shirt, used to distribute among us lithographed notes on the lectures given by Yagich and Lamansky. I usually received my own copy and one for my friend, Nicholas Struve (the brother of Peter Struve, afterwards so well known as a writer), because he gave lessons and was not able to wait for their distribution. However, it happened somehow that twice he was free and I was occupied, and he took mine for me. The third time he was also free, and in going away I said to Kryzhanovsky in the cloak-room, where he was distributing the papers:

"Kryzhanovsky, give my share to Struve, please."
"I won't."
"Why not?"
"Because you are playing the fine gentleman."

By the looks on the faces around I noticed that he would regret his words, and his own expression showed me that he would comply with my request. It was in this way that those people had in everything, however small they might be, two measures and two weights. The professors connived at it. At Minaev's examination on philology I answered well. I got up and asked:

"May I ask what number you have given me?"
"Three."

At the corner of the table Kryzhanovsky was sitting preparing his paper. I don't know if Minaev saw it, but when he heard Minaev say "three" Kryzhanovsky jumped up; his whole figure seemed to say "Is it possible?" Two or three days later one of my fellow students was at Minaev's house; the conversation turned on the examinations.

"You say that you are just, and yet you gave Wolkonsky a 'three.'"
"Well, I only abated one for his title."

And thus all my life, at school, in the provinces, later in the criticisms of my works, in the appreciation of educational work, I have always had "one abated for my title." My whole life I have felt that the reproach of being "a prince" weighs heavily upon me, and now, in these days

of Bolshevism, I have it thrown in my face that I am
"a former prince." A sin that cannot be washed off,
in the eyes of those people who preach the doctrine of
equality.

I would like to note here another recollection, as it is
in connection with the subject of this chapter, though the
occurrence took place at a somewhat later date. It is
about the student disturbances of 1899, which were
important and serious in their consequences. Strictly
speaking, from that time the agitation has never calmed
down.

At that time Bogolepov was Minister of Public Instruction; he had been curator of the Moscow district and had
been recommended as Minister by the Grand Duke Sergei
Alexandrovich, who was at the time Governor-General of
Moscow. Shortly before the 8th of April, the date on
which the University celebrates its speech-day, the
Emperor expressed to Bogolepov his hope that the students
on that day would not pass over the Palace Bridge singing
or making a noise, as the Empress was ill and it would
disturb her. Bogolepov transmitted the Emperor's wish
to the Provost of the University, Sergeevich. Sergeevich
found nothing better to do than to hang out a notice in
the University warning the students not to make a noise,
as those who transgressed this order would expose themselves to the action of the police. This did not prevent
those who wished to make a noise from doing so, but it
offended those who had no intention of taking part in any
sort of demonstration. Our University life had long
suffered from the constant interference of political protests
that disturbed the peaceful work of the students who
wished to work. The authorities took measures against
revolutionary manifestations, but at the same time, owing

to their deeply rooted mistrust of youth, they did not permit the healthy elements to have the possibility of uniting to counteract this movement. In the eyes of the authorities the word " student " had a generic meaning, and therefore when the minority were treated with strictness the majority were offended. Feelings became heated, and the authorities, in the persons of the minister and the curator of the district, Zverev, decided not to be present on the speech-day. There were, however, honoured guests —the Minister of Finance, Witte, the Metropolitan Anthonius—but the masters of the house were not there. The only disorders that took place were whistles when the Provost took his place on the platform, and the whistlers were walked out of the hall. After that all proceeded smoothly. The Metropolitan Anthonius distributed the medals. He afterwards said that when a student came up he asked: " Which one do you get ? " He answered: " The gold one." " Well, so I gave him a gold one. But who knows if it was right ? " It was in this spirit that the speech-day, which had been so much dreaded by the authorities, went off. Afterwards there were strange, contradictory accounts circulated in town. Some said that when Bogolepov came to make his report to the Emperor, the Emperor asked him:

" Were you at the distribution of prizes in the University ? "

" No, Sire."

" Oh, you were not there ? "

The Emperor turned his back on him and went away.

Another report said that Bogolepov had explained to the Emperor why he had not gone—that he had foreseen a row, and he did not wish to increase the culpability of the students by his presence. It appears that the Emperor found his action correct. Such contradictions are typical of Petersburg. This was not empty gossip, but the reports came from good authority. The first was from the lady governess to the Court, Princess Golitzin, and the second from the Grand Duke Serge. Who was to be believed? However, such conversations are not interesting, but it was followed by facts, distressing facts, whose consequences spread to all the educational establishments of Petersburg and the whole of Russia. When the students left the University at the conclusion of this function, they were met by a company of mounted police. They were pressed back towards the Neva; disputes arose, the mounted police charged into the crowd; mutual abuse followed, then came the crack of a whip, a stone was hurled—and in the end there was a general "disturbance," and they were all arrested and driven into a *manège*. The behaviour of the mounted police towards the students was disgraceful on this occasion; this I heard from witnesses and from the sufferers.

After this the disorders changed into a clearly political-revolutionary movement, that embraced all the higher scholastic institutions, and spread to other towns. Much was said at the time of the participation of instigating agents. Stormy meetings were held; they were dispersed, the scholastic institutions were closed down. In search of a place to hold their meetings, it is said that the students of Moscow once assembled in one of the public baths and held their meeting in the swimming-bath; when they left it they were arrested. All this was the beginning of the great and terrible movement that, with interruptions and periods of calm, like the one before the opening of the Douma, or the patriotic enthusiasm that was aroused during the first months of the war, continued, ever increasing in strength until it culminated in what we all know. . . .

The Ministry of Public Instruction was the only Government department that I had the opportunity of observing closely. It was musty. My father was the curator of the Petersburg educational district during the last years of Alexander II's reign, the minister was Count D. A. Tolstoy, and he was the deputy minister during the early part of the reign of Alexander III, when Delyanov was minister. I therefore knew much about this department. Nowhere and never have I felt such an utter stranger as I did when I had occasion to go to that ministry, or to have to speak to the officials in their undress uniforms. In those days the Gymnasiums realized Tolstoy's ideal of the " classical system." It was well ordered, but dry, and not at all classical. The chief spring of this system, old Alexander Georgievsky, would look at his watch with self-sufficiency and say, " At this minute in the fifth class of all the Gymnasiums in the Russian Empire they are learning the Latin irregular verbs." This was called classical education. Of course, I personally will always be grateful to my parents for having sent me to a classical Gymnasium. But what a preparation I had had at home for it, what a store of information, and of impressions. What I brought to the Gymnasium, as regards the direction of my mind and spiritual training, was certainly not less than what I received from it. The Gymnasium only completed it ; I might say that the Gymnasium provided the state text to my home-made and not at all state-like illustrations. But what did the Gymnasium give to the ordinary run of schoolboys, to those who had not homes, nor parents like mine, nor such reminiscences ? Nothing but a formal execution of a programme ; and, I may add, a detestable programme ; as not only did the scholars look with indifference on the programme, they regarded it with hatred ; we hate every effort of which we do not see the expediency nor experience the benefit it can produce. In Petersburg, in spite of all these regulations, a new spirit showed itself from time to time, when the teacher was possessed of a certain amount of brilliant individuality; but in the provinces! What a sleepy kingdom the Gymnasium represented! How unnecessary all this was! Afterwards I became the honorary trustee of the Gymnasium in Borisoglebsk, the district town of the Tambov Government. How much against my conscience it was to sit on the platform and praise for correct answers. The day before I had bought some chintz in a shop, the shopman had measured it out for me, and the next day the son of this very shopkeeper told us about the hoplites and quirites, or of the participles $\mu\epsilon\nu$ and $\gamma\alpha\rho$. Exhausted by the heat of June, the unfortunate boys are sweating over Greek aorists, while three hundred furlongs away the rye was coming into ear. What a lie there was in all this; it was as little suited to the natural inquiring instincts of the child as it was to his station. After having finished such a course, all this only led either to a breach with the paternal home or a rupture with all that the man had been learning for so many years; it proved itself inapplicable and unnecessary for life. The same thing applies to the townspeople as well as to the villagers. These youngsters, whom their parents had given their last drop of blood to make men of! How many such-like have I seen. In the village they walk about with a walking-stick; they sprinkle foreign words around them; if you ask them the time of day they are sure to answer with the addition " according to Moscow time." The unfortunate parents do not know whether to be proud or ashamed of them, to rejoice or to grieve. Their contemporaries call them " white collars," the old men shake their heads and say: " They have ceased ploughing."

Thus education, instead of improving their condition, only deprived the villages of their mental strength, and inspired class hatred. How much we heard in our time about the obscurity of the village. Can you enlighten the village because five or six of its men, who had been at a Gymnasium, are afterwards in some Government department in Saratov, in some banking-house in Kharkov, or in the post-office of Tambov. It seemed understood that education was not wanted for the village, but in order to get away from it. Thanks to these exceptions something worse was produced: education gradually assumed the character of something appertaining to a class. And at last this side of the question found its expression in that terrible word "intelligentsia." I remember very well when first this ugly word, that was invented in accordance with foreign forms and really does not exist in any foreign language, began to be used. At first it had a definite polemical character and denoted the opposite of " aristocracy." Our class was not recognized as " intelligentsia "; the " intelligentsia " was a class that stood between the " higher classes " and " the people "; it was hostile to the " higher classes " and friendly towards " the people." Now, after all the upheavals of the revolution, when all that is in any way cultured above a certain standard feels in a like manner that it is beyond the boundary—now the meaning of the word " intelligentsia " has been enlarged to the limits of a sort of spiritual brotherhood, which has levelled down even the memory of the former oblique glances. Those who formerly cast hostile glances upwards and friendly glances downwards now look downwards with hostility and upwards with offers of alliance. The community of worldly and social conditions has caused a tendency to arise for the recognition of a kind of union, and the indivisibility of that in which formerly, at the very best, there was mistrust and estrangement.

In my district I was the only " prince," and I was the owner of ten thousand acres of land. The S.R.s[1] never lost an opportunity of showing me up before the eyes of the populace in the light that according to their views was suitable to a prince, a landowner, an aristocrat, etc. One day, at a meeting concerning some questions of rural economy, one of them, with all the ardour that is adherent to those gentlemen and with the passion that the subject demanded, thundered at the landowners of our district for the destruction of the forests. I was sitting among his listeners, and after the meeting I wrote him a letter, in which I said that in his speech he might have made one exception—for our estate, where during more than twenty years there had been a systematic felling of trees with a seventy year rotation, and where during the last forty years the estate had been rewooded by the plantation of young trees on an area of at least sixty acres of bare steppes. When we next met he apologized for having " forgotten." A strange forgetfulness in a man who was specially occupied with the statistics of forestry in our district. But the effect had been produced. *Pereat mundas, fiat—injustitia.* This was their inner unspoken system.

The denunciation of two drunken peasants was sufficient to cause an official paper to be sent stating " that on Prince Wolkonsky's estate armed prisoners were going about and preventing the peasants from gathering in the corn " ; the paper concluded with the request " to take immediate measures." Fortunately, before the " immediate measures," an investigation was made which proved the absurdity of such accusations. But, all the same, excitement had been

[1] Social Revolutionists.

caused, and instead of "what is necessary to be proved," people might say "what it was necessary to attain." By all this I only wish to show that these same people, who had been able to give such detailed information about my personal affairs, said afterwards, and quite sincerely too, that the only house in Borisoglebsk where their souls were able to get rest was mine. And he who had "forgotten" to mention the system of forestry practised on my estate, and he who demanded "immediate measures," came to me in Tambov to ask for four hundred roubles in order to escape from the Bolsheviks. I do not know if it is possible to place any positive value on such a connexion? Why, during an inundation even wolves will take refuge on the same mound with lambs. Does it mean that they are friends? . . .

Such a fortuitous, I may even say forcible, union of heterogeneous elements I see under the cover of the word "intellegentsia." Not only the above reflections on the moral and social orders, but also considerations of a purely intellectual character—considerations that might be supposed must, more than any others, play a part in such a word as "intelligentsia," cause me to see the falseness of their union under one term. Indeed, when I hear the same epithet employed for the professor of philosophy, Il'in, and the girl who taps a typewriting machine in some Bolshevisk institution and at night frequents a ballet studio, I must confess I cannot understand such a union. *He* belongs to the "intelligentsia" and *she* belongs to the "intelligentsia"? Excuse me, but what have they in common? Why, the word indicates qualities of mental capacity, although we often hear such expressions as: "Judging by his clothes he must belong to the 'intelligentsia.'" Then, in what way are Professor Il'in and the typewriting-ballerina alike? They both are *not illiterate*.

F R

But really that is not sufficient to make them birds of a feather.

Let us return again to the Ministry of Public Instruction. This apparatus, which was organized in the reign of Alexander II by the iron hand of Count Tolstoy, never satisfied anybody, incensed everybody, and under Alexander III passed into the soft hands of Delyanov. Ivan Davidovich Delyanov was an extraordinary phenomenon in the annals of the Russian Civil Service. What caused him to succeed? Why did he get on and receive the order of Saint Andrew, and the title of Count? He grew up as a tree grows up—not by virtue of any merits, but by the power of vegetative inertia. His softness, weakness and impotence—I don't know how to call it—is impossible to describe. My father used to say that if compromises did not already exist Delyanov would have invented them. It was always hard for us children to know that our father was the assistant of such a minister. I remember, as if it were yesterday, when my father received the offer of that post. We were at dinner " under the oaks " in Pavlovka, when a telegram was brought. My father opened it, and, saying, " From Delyanov," handed it to my mother. I remember there was somebody dining with us, and therefore I asked in French : " Des offres de camaraderie ? " (an offer of comradeship?). My father nodded. He did not hesitate long. He occupied that post twelve years.

It was a sad time—little satisfaction and very questionable respect. My father felt it, but for him the discipline of service occupied the first place and he never spoke about it. It was not sad that Delyanov was a muff, that he could not stand up for any question, that he dozed at the meetings, and when he received at home he had to pull his eyebrows to keep awake, but it was sad that Delyanov was a typical representative of the mentality that was created during the reign of Alexander III under the protection of the all-powerful Procurator-General of the Holy Synod, Pobedonostsev. The Uvatov formula, "Orthodoxy, Autocracy and Nationality," that at first was trumpeted about, so to speak, with outspread banners, gradually became less noisy—was simplified ; from a political hymn it changed into a school exemplar. The intermixing of the principles of nationality and religion attained the last degrees of abnormity. Only the orthodox were looked upon as real Russians, and only Russians could be truly orthodox. A man's political fidelity was measured by his religious tenets. It is clear that such relations with the most important questions of a man's spiritual life degraded them to the level of something like service regulations, in which the development of individuality found no place, and where an immense field was opened out for hypocrisy. Therefore I can only call the whole system of those days a school for hypocrisy. Nobody really believed in his own heart in this political bigotry. It was extraordinary how the false representation of these questions led directly to a sort of distortion of the mind.

I remember the following case : The inspector of the Larin Gymnasium, Constantine Blumberg, was proposed for the post of director. He was a splendid Hellenist, an excellent pedagogue, and a most honourable man, one would suppose all that could be required. Suddenly there was a hitch—he was a Lutheran ; officially this was called " heterodox." This difficulty caused long delays. I remember he said to me once, when conversation turned on this point : " Surely I can't be expected to change my religion in order to get a better post." At last he was appointed. Just at that time my former Gymnasium celebrated some jubilee. I was going up the stairs with Blumberg, when we were caught up by a functionary from the Ministry ; he was a man who stood in close connexion with the Minister's office, knew which way the wind blew, and which way to turn his nose. He shook Blumberg's hand warmly and congratulated him on his appointment in a loud voice, and after complimenting him, he added, " Well, of course it was impossible to count *you* among the heterodox." If he could speak in this way, it was impossible that he could believe in what he said; still, the formula of political fidelity of those times, and the desire to satisfy its demands, caused men such mental aberrations, such deviations from the truth. Compliance became the nerve of activity. Imagine the moral level of such men ! There is a close connexion between the reason and the conscience. I think it is impossible to support that which is absurd without giving a twist to the soul, and he who wilfully sins against logic will also inevitably sin against his own conscience.

I said that Delyanov was the most typical representative of the political mentality of that time. Here is a little case, a tiny case, but even in tiny indications the symptoms of serious maladies can be found. I was appointed commissary of the Ministry of Public Instruction at the Chicago Exhibition in the year 1893. I was assisted in the collection of the necessary material by an employee of the Ministry, old Saint Hilaire. When I began this work he showed me a vignette that had already been approved of by the Minister, which was to be used as an ornament for the binding of the school-books that the Ministry was sending to the exhibition. The vignette was quite pretty ; in the middle there was a shield surrounded by a wreath of oak and laurel leaves, with a blank left for the title of the book at the bottom, a globe of the world on which Russia was seen, and above, the two-headed eagle surmounted by a radiant cross. This cross on the bindings of Latin and Greek grammars, manuals of chemistry, mathematics, and natural history, gave me no peace. At the same time the design had been approved of by the Minister; had I the right to change it? To ask permission might lead to a row. At last I took courage and went to the printing-office.

" Have you the design for the cover of the books that the Ministry of Public Instruction is sending to the Chicago Exhibition ? "

" Yes, we have it."

" Is it already printed ? "

" No, not yet."

" Is it possible to make a slight change ? "

" If you please."

" Then please replace the cross by the Imperial crown."

When I told old Saint Hilaire of the instructions I had given he shook his head. " It had pleased Ivan Davidovich so much. He said the cross was so appropriate—Orthodox Russia." Why, this is what results : The cross, the symbol of universal Christian unity, was monopolized as the symbol of an exclusively chosen nationality. I felt, as always when speaking to a *chinovnik* (Government official) of foreign origin, that at that moment there were two creatures in Saint Hilaire : a man and a Russian *chinovnik*. The first approved of what I had done, the second shook his head at my too light-hearted veracity. That same evening I told my father how I had overstepped my powers; he only said " *nichevo* " (no matter).

What Delyanov would have said, I can't even imagine. He was so indifferent to everything ! When anything was told him, or any report made, he only pulled his eyebrows and repeated with a nasal voice, " Yes, yes ; yes, yes."

The time about which I am writing—the eighties of the

last century—was a difficult one for a man with a clean, unviolated conscience. How will it be looked upon by the future? How will it be judged, and will it ever be judged? It is difficult for one who did not live at the time to understand the side of life of which I am writing. It is doubtful if the mental process by which the men of that time defined and justified their outlook on the world in the domain of civil education has ever penetrated into any serious books. The serious men of science did not share it, but to criticize it was impossible. Only in an inverse sense, so to speak, "from the contrary," is it possible in certain writings to form a picture of what was considered necessary by the thinkers in the ruling spheres of that time. This we see by the involuntary polemical character which pervades them, by the persistence with which they prove the evident. All the works of Vladimir Solovev on questions of nationality and nationalism are nothing more than polemics in the name of spiritual, scientific and worldly verities in opposition to the officially sanctioned forms.

The idea that the Russian people was chosen above all others; national self-conceit; the loss of all national objectiveness in judging, replaced by nationalistic subjectiveness; the blending of religious with national principles, and by this the justification of political persecutions in questions of faith; the gradual emergence of the idea of the "people" not as the aggregate of the nation, but as an individuality that had not been touched by culture—the bearer of certain gifts that inspired caution, on account of the very reason that it had not been touched by culture, and lastly the sacred idea of a God-inspired nation, and a sort of spiritual cult, of a spiritual want of culture: this is what was gradually evolved, this is what moved the conditions of that time in questions of social and political life. All this penetrated into the official theories of education, the measures that were taken, and even into the legislation of the times. A great sin rests on the souls of the men of those days—they played with dangerous toys. It is evident that such principles could not lead to any kind of serious work; they were the confessions of men who were incapable of serious reflection. Therefore it is not in books that future researches will find the formulas of the official outlook on the world, but in pamphlets, in jubilee orations, in minutes of meetings and in circulars.

I have called it a time of toys—of dangerous toys. I wish to say a few words of one of these toys—a little toy, but a typical one, one which was looked upon in Government circles, however, as being of serious importance.

There was in Petersburg a certain General Bogdanovich. He was churchwarden of the Isaac Cathedral, and had become famous, thanks to pictures for the people, which he invented to commemorate certain events of political importance, and distributed under the cathedral portico after the liturgy, and also sent to other churches in other towns. He was a devout man, and, one may say, he had grovelled into a visible position in the circles of the Government officials and clergy. They came to his house; they consulted him. He lived in Myatliv's well-known red house at the corner of the Post Street and the Isaac Square, and often the carriage and four-in-hand of the Metropolitan could be seen standing before its columned porch. "General Bogdanovich's pictures" were documents of the annals of the times. I will describe one—it was to chronicle the foundation of the Peasants' Bank. A peasant following his little horse is ploughing a field with a small plough; in the distance a village and a church. Above, in the blue sky, the Russian Imperial coat-of-arms is hanging, attached by a string to the outstretched wings of a white dove—the Holy Ghost. The peasant is making the sign of the cross. Below there are some appropriate verses about the Tsar taking care of the peasant. The verses are in the style suitable to such literature—unctuous, sweet and tender. Such like pictures were sent all over the country, and their distribution acquired the character of an important event. Such telegrams appeared in the newspapers: " After the liturgy so many thousand copies of General Bogdanovich's pictures were distributed under the portico of the Cathedral to the people, who examined them with interest and read the verses with emotion." It is difficult to believe it, but great importance was attached to this plaything. I said to one of the assistants of the Minister of the Interior:

" How can you encourage or even tolerate such a thing ? "

" What can we do ? " he answered, " it is the only means we have of combating the occult literature."

What weakness to think that this is strength. . . . But General Bogdanovich was a big man, his lunches were famous ; on the occasion of some sort of jubilee he received an Imperial Rescript. It was well known to all that he was a shameless taker of bribes, he traded in his intercessions with the strong ones of this earth.

One of his wife's relatives told me as a positive fact the following anecdote: Bogdanovich was expecting a petitioner, a very rich man, who required his intercession very much. He instructed his son (I think he was an officer) to enter his study and in the presence of the visitor to tell him that he had seduced a young girl and that the girl's father demanded compensation from him. . . .

Bogdanovich was one of those extraordinary apparitions in which the last years of the Tsardom is so rich. In one of Ostrovsky's plays a matchmaker says, " It is possible now to become a general without serving." A number of people who never occupied any official position attained the high title of counsellors; some enjoyed official acknowledgment; others found compensation for the absence of notoriety in their close proximity to the person of the Tsar. Such men were Prince Meshchersky, the editor of the *Grashdanin;* General Bogdanovich; the occultist, Franz Papius; the foreteller of the weather, Demchensky; the obscure Prince Andronnikov, and lastly Rasputin. An interesting gallery of portraits for the future historian. These were the steps by which the autocracy descended into the grave.

LAURELS

ROSSI AND SALVINI

I WAS a schoolboy when the celebrated Italian tragedian, Ernesto Rossi, came to Petersburg. It was in the year 1877, and I date my interest for the theatre from that time. I shall never forget his first performance; it was *Othello*. I am unable to describe the impression it made on me. It was something new, something immense; a new side of life, new forms of humanity, a new world on our earth. I remember all around me grew dim and perished; everything real became fantastic—this only was reality. During the whole of Lent, while these performances were taking place, I lived in a dream, I was in a mist. We had a subscription box; but we also took advantage of every opportunity of getting to the Marie Theatre. Our parents were on very friendly terms with Countess Adlerberg, the wife of the Minister of the Palace at that time, and we often were able to go to the large Minister box. From that box a small door opened on to a corkscrew stair; this stair was the passage by which I first entered the coveted land of the stage.

One evening I gave the attendant a letter and begged him to take it to the great artiste. I must confess that during the next act I listened but badly, my heart was beating so strongly. In the following pause the attendant returned me my envelope, and I displayed with pride to my parents and brother Rossi's photograph with his signature on it. This photograph I had bought at Daziaro's shop, and I had sent it to Rossi with a letter in French, which had taken me three hours to write. At the next performance my brother and I plucked up courage and asked the attendant to conduct us to Rossi's dressing-room. We found our divine Hamlet smoking a cigar. We introduced ourselves, and I said I had come to thank him for the signature. I remember the singular impression that his sonorous voice, which had just spoken Shakespeare's words to Ophelia and Horatio, made on me, when it spoke to me in ordinary, everyday small talk. We looked with reverence at the costumes hanging about, on the pots of vaseline, paints and pencils, on the laurel wreaths tied with ribbons. There was bustle and confusion in the dressing-room, people running in and out, oft-repeated questions, and unheard answers. Korsov, our celebrated baritone, an intimate friend of Rossi's, was also there. A pretty, stout, fair-haired woman was standing at one side. " Voilà, madame," Rossi said. She was a Frenchwoman. As I heard afterward, he always travelled about with some temporary lady friend ; this one was called Madame Gachet. She looked at us and smiled ; she was holding a bunch of laurel leaves in her hand, she pressed them to her red lips, bit them with her white teeth, and said with a wink, " Ça fera une bonne soupe ! " (They will make a good soup !)

One night, when my brother and I left the theatre on foot, we noticed a small crowd near the stage-door ; we went to see what it was, and found a number of adorers, both male and female, awaiting *his* exit. Here I made the acquaintance of a terrible phenomenon—the theatrical psychopath—the enthusiast of art. To wait in the frost or the dirt, with hearts palpitating whenever the door opened, to examine *his* carriage ; to talk to *his* coachman— what joy ! I was astonished at this union, this friendship, this public expression of feelings ; this entire absence of jealousy ; these mutual confessions, this " collectivity "—

a sort of communism in love. And all this hanging about in the frost or standing in puddles was for the sake of a single minute. The door opens—a moment of silence; *he* appears wrapped up in furs. A rush forward; cries and squeals in all imaginary languages; wafted hand kisses; a few flowers flying through the air—a bouquet is thrown after *him* into the carriage; Madame Gachet is embraced twice or thrice; as rapidly, as passionately, the door is slammed—and the carriage drives off. The enchanted admirers remain spellbound. Such ovations were repeated every evening. I have never seen the like of this in any other country. This phase of insanity was especially prevalent among the female frequenters of the Italian Opera. The celebrated tenor, Masine, had a long queue of admirers who always waited to see him. The real " Masinists " did not wait at the stage-door, but at his house, with flowers, sweets and bottles of wine. He alighted from his carriage, and as he went proudly past his female worshippers, looking with contempt at their offerings, he would say, " Donnez ça à Antonio," and disappear into his apartment. Yes, even the contact with the laurels of others evidently seems for some an indispensable complement of an artistic existence.

Our privileged position behind the scenes was not of long duration, the Director of the Imperial Theatres, Baron Küster, reprimanded me and my brother severely, and told us not to go on the stage again. In this way I was driven away from the place where, twenty-two years later, I was master. We had to submit; we no longer went down the corkscrew stairs, but we opened the door and peeped out with sinking hearts and bated breath, as we watched kings and queens passing by with raised trains amid the dark stage dust, and saw them come in contact with various gentlemen in lounge jackets, workmen in red shirts, and firemen in sparkling helmets. . . .

To Rossi's visit I owe not only my love for dramatic art. Through him I got to know Shakespeare—he acted in *Othello, Macbeth, King Lear, Coriolanus, Romeo and Juliet,* and the *Merchant of Venice.* Through him I learned the Italian language, that is, I became sufficiently familiar with it to understand it, and to feel acutely its beauties. Besides, it was through his acting that I saw and understood the meaning and the artistic power of dramatic technicalities. From that time it was surprising how my attention was drawn to the methods by which certain effects were attained. In the moments of the greatest excitement I did not lose interest in the technicalities of the art; my feelings were overcome by *what* he did, but all the time I was watching *how* he produced his effects. In *Macbeth*, in the scene after the murder, when he stands bewildered in the middle of the courtyard, and knocks are heard at the gate, I remember how he stood motionless, and at each knock only his wrists trembled. I remember in *Hamlet*, when he tears from his mother's breast the portrait of his uncle—step-father—and flings it on the floor, he cried three times, " A terra ! " I remember that before the third exclamation he stamped his foot on the ground and stopped as if spellbound. I remember how clearly I felt that all the power was obtained by the momentary pause after the movement. I also remember in *King Lear*, when the old repentant man presses Cordelia to his breast, his hand, with outspread fingers and the palm firmly pressed on his daughter's back, moved about it with pointless efforts. How much love, solace, and bewildered feebleness there was in that movement. In Casimir Delavigne's tragedy, *Louis XI*, he was admirable in his combination of cruelty and piety. Crosses were hung all round his cap, and in one scene, just after having condemned somebody to death, he took off his cap and kissed one of the crosses.

One other thing I clearly understood—the superiority both in oratory and plastic art of the Latin races, their astonishing truth to the laws of nature. What others have to learn with difficulty, they have in their blood. Our Russian theatres seemed to me very imperfect and far behind, and this feeling I still have. Even more than ever now, after the three years I have passed in teaching declamation and acting, I am convinced of the low artistic standard of our Russian material. It is only after long education that this material can be developed. But where is this education? Now, when the fashion is to have everything " short-dated," when in four months they want to produce instructors, actors and diplomatists, an old anecdote I once heard recurs to my mind. A very rich American, who had acquired his wealth rapidly, came to England to visit his friends in their mansion, and one morning, going out for a stroll, he saw a gardener working on the lawn. It is only those who have been to England who can know what an English lawn really is like—it is a smooth green carpet. The American asked the gardener how he succeeded in producing such a lawn? He had everything in America—houses, gardens, flowers, fruits—but he could not have a lawn. " There is nothing easier," the gardener replied, " you must plough and sow, and when the grass comes up, mow it twice a week with a mowing-machine and water it twice a day. If you continue to do this, in three hundred years you will have similar lawns." Yes, this is the meaning of culture. But to resume.

We became acquainted with Rossi; he came to our

house. My mother spoke Italian like a native. He often read Dante aloud to us. Once he left his gloves; we kept them for a long time. . . . He came to Russia again in 1881. He had added to his repertory *Kean*. He was splendid in this part; I especially remember the scene in the tavern when he is smoking a cigar, and smokes the Duke out of the room. Another novelty was *Christopher Columbus;* I remember one scene, a monologue. Columbus is in prison. I remember the wonderful tale of his endless and perilous voyage, and suddenly he sees—land on the horizon! I shall never forget that shout, " La terra!!" The tone of the voice was high and distant, producing at the same time the effect of the high masts of which it gave expression, and of the horizon of which he spoke. The third novelty was Giacometti's *La Morte Cevile*. This is the story of a convict who returns home and finds his wife married to another man and his daughter adopted by another man. The splendid monologue about his escape from prison: the screaking of the saw as he sawed through the bars, and when they were removed—liberty. I shall never forget the words, " La libertà! " In that whisper there was all the horror of the prison discipline, and all the strength of the enticing liberty.

His second visit was broken off by the catastrophe of the 1st of March—the assassination of Alexander II. All the theatres were closed, and he went away. In his autobiography, which appeared about fifteen years after this event, he wrote in the headings of the chapters, " Assassinio di Alissandro II—consequenze fatali per me."[1] Alas, from the sublime to the ridiculous there is but one step, especially in the life of an actor. Some years afterwards I saw him in his home in Florence. It had been better if I had not seen him there. His wife, a presumptuous, snappish

[1] " Assassination of Alexander II—fatal consequences for me."

Jewess; his daughter, like her mother; and her husband not much better; and a little grandson—a little scamp of eight years, who, in honour of his grandfather, was called Ernesto. All these stuck to the great artiste, pumped money out of his greatness, while by their conduct towards him they only abused it. At that time I was helping him with his translation of the *Death of Ivan the Terrible*, by Count Alexis Tolstoy, and advised him about the costumes, restraining him from giving them too much of an Oriental character. I also helped him in the pronunciation of the Russian names. All this was difficult, especially in his domestic surroundings, and I often thought of Flaubert's words: " Il ne faut pas toucher aux idoles—la dorure en reste aux mains."[1] He took upon himself the task of removing the gilding: in his autobiography he showed himself without his make-up and costumes. It would be impossible to imagine anything meaner than the constant shoving forward of himself—his words, his conversations with various kings, in which the most important part was not what had been said to him but what he had said.

I also knew the other Italian tragedian, Salvini. He and Rossi were rivals, and the whole of the theatre-lovers in Italy, and not only in Italy, were divided into admirers of one or the other. There was a certain coolness between them, but on great occasions, such as the jubilees of poets, they acted together; and then the managers, not knowing to whom to give precedence, printed their names crosswise on the play-bills. Each was admirable in his own way. Rossi had a wonderfully sonorous voice; Salvini's voice was wonderfully deep. Rossi's best part was Hamlet; Salvini's Othello. He came to Petersburg after Rossi, in 1882. His repertory was smaller than his rival's, but in

---

[1] " Do not touch your idols—their gilding sticks to the hands."

none of his parts did he come up to his Othello. He admitted that he had the greatest success in this part, and explained the reason of this " as not all can understand the torments of Hamlet, not all can understand the sufferings of Lear, but all understand the love of Othello." These words explain his interpretation of the part. He enacted not the jealousy but the love of the Venetian Moor, and therein was its whole charm; the scene with Iago was not a duel, but the sick heart of a child under the knife of an operator. In *Hamlet* he was unpleasant, rational, dry. However, he had a good piece of business in the play scene. Lying at Ophelia's feet he held some loose sheets of paper in his left hand, as if it were the text of the play. He turned the pages over and arranged them nervously with his right hand, and when the king rose and left the hall, he jumped up, raising his arms above his head, and the pages fell around him like rain.

Tommaso Salvini's son, Alexander, wanted to go on the stage; his father opposed this wish, they quarrelled, and Alexander left his home. I saw Alexander Salvini act in Chicago in 1893. He acted in English. He was an excellent actor, clever, refined, brilliant, passionate; he had a great success. I remember a truly American advertisement that was given him. Little flags with his name on them were hung on all the tramway cars that went past the theatre where he was acting. With his growing fame his father's anger melted away; he took his son again into his favour and invited him to come home; Alexander returned to Italy, but after two months he fell ill and died. Tommaso's second son, Gustavo, was quite a bad actor, and his name was scarcely known beyond Florence.

Rossi's visit to Petersburg aroused in me an interest for the theatre and the art of acting. My brother and I, and our friend Victor Bariatinsky, knew by heart whole scenes in Italian out of the pieces he acted. We began to act ; we arranged home-made costumes and scenery.

We acted Hamlet's scene with his mother. I was Hamlet, Bariatinsky acted the mother, my brother the father. From *Macbeth* we acted the last scene, the duel with Macduff. From that time our interest in the theatre continued to increase. In the summer, while staying with my grandmother on her estate Fall, near Reval, we arranged a stage in an empty conservatory, where we acted Molière's *Le Medecin malgré lui*. Later on, in my father's house in Petersburg at the corner of the quay and Gagarin Street, there was a real stage. Here we acted long plays both in Russian and French; among others we gave, in 1889, *Feodor Ivannovich*, by Alexis Tolstoy, which at that time was prohibited. Our example proved to be infectious ; private theatricals became the rage in Petersburg society. *The Power of Darkness* and *Boris Godunov* were acted in different houses. In the Hermitage Court Theatre *Tsar Boris* was given. This performance was most brilliant for the eye—there were more diamonds than talents on the stage.

I have mentioned that in Petersburg at that time (it was in the 'eighties) we also acted French plays. When I think of them one image always rises to my memory, one voice always rings in my ears. Madame Mary Hartong, née Countess Stenbock-Fermor, was the ingénue-comique of our company. Small, round—we used to call her " the bun "—with a charming little mouth from which the words dropped like pearls ; with a voice which was alike sonorous and well modulated, she was one of the most extraordinary phenomena I have ever seen on the stage. Our manager was Andrieu, one of the French actors of the Michael Theatre. He often said to me that if Madame

Hartong had gone on the stage she would have become a celebrity. The first time I saw her act was at my parents' house in a play by Meilhac and Halévy, *L'Ingénue*. It produced continuous laughter; and the most amusing part was that she did not appear to want to be funny. She did not *represent* naïveté, she *believed* in what she said; and it was just because you saw that she believed it that it was so funny. She was splendid in *La Bataille des Dames*, by Scribe and Legouve; in *La Papillonne*, by Sardou; and also in the *Barbier le Séville* she made a bewitching, child-like Rosine. Afterward she tried dramatic parts, but that was not the same thing.

I owe to the actor Andrieu my first initiation into the actor's art; then I understood the meaning of pauses, of breathing. He was an excellent instructor; he went through each part separately, and only joined us all together when we knew our parts, and then began the interesting work of general orchestration. We often heard " Begin again at such a point, please," and then came demands for more emphasis, a lower tone, more rapidity, slower, etc. I early understood the power of dynamics in theatrical art. I have seen the work of managers on many stages and in many languages, but the work of none has satisfied me as Andrieu's did.

He was a very charming man, and he knew how to behave in Petersburg society, where he was very much liked. Here is a trait characteristic of him: A certain lady lived in Petersburg; I don't remember her name; she was very rich, and kept open house. Artists always received a warm welcome from her. Afterwards her circumstances changed; her sons, guard officers, squandered away her fortune and she was ruined. She went to live somewhere at the end of the Sadovaia, on a back stairs in a dirty yard. Every year at Christmas and Easter Andrieu went to call on her and took her a magnificent bouquet, worthy of an empress.

He also had many adorers; among them an English girl, Miss Night, the assistant superintendent in one of the girls' schools. She was very devoted, and succeeded in gaining Andrieu's gratitude. But her stupidity was equal to her devotion. A circumstance occurred in which these two qualities were united. We were dining at Andrieu's; he had to act after dinner, and was in evening dress as his part required. Somebody spilled some wine on the table-cloth, and as always on such occasions somebody else said, "That's for luck." "For luck?" Miss Night asked. Suddenly she took up a glassful of claret and emptied its whole contents on Andrieu's starched shirt-front and evening dress. For the summer he returned to France. How often when staying in Paris I have visited him in his villa at Rueil, Malmaison. On Fridays he had luncheon parties, where artistes forgathered. A charming little house, small garden, pond with goldfish, roses, radishes, strawberries, and a good French cook, old Marie. After coffee, endless stories kept the guests sitting round the table; as the French say, "On ne vieillit pas à table."[1] You did not meet celebrities at his house, they were all people whose names were not known beyond the French frontier; but what talent, what literary culture, what love for their art; what great names appeared in the stories: Fréderic Lemaitre, Bressan, Marie Dorval, Madeleine Brohan. What respect for their teachers, what reverence for their heritage! Let me try to say a few words about those I knew; not the celebrities all know, as they have visited every country, but of those to see whom you had to come to France.

I no longer found the great names in the Comédie Française which I have just mentioned, but those I saw

[1] "You do not get old at table."

were never to be forgotten. Old Mlle. Joissan rises in my memory—in old maid parts. I saw her in the part of Armande in *Les Femmes Savantes*. How can I explain the severe piety of that boniness, the high exaltation of that scragginess. Every movement was art, every intonation perfection. And bewitching, laughing Samary, brilliant and captivating by her gaiety. She acted in Pailleron's *L'Etincelle*, and, of course, she took the part of the servant in *Le Bourgeois Gentilhomme*, a part that Molière wrote for his laughing maid. What life there was in it; a spring bubbling over. I also saw her in Pailleron's *La Souris*, a long three-act comedy with only one male part, all the others were for women. The man's part was acted by Worms, a marvellously clever actor, and among the women was Céline Montalan, who had once been celebrated for her beauty, but now took the mother's part; it was impossible to forget the brilliancy of her eyes. Enchanting Bartet also acted in this play. Svelte and graceful, she was the personification of elegance, with wonderful moments of tenderness caused by the deep fall of her voice in the lower register. I see her still, and will always remember her in *Allain Chartier*. She crossed the whole stage with a white lily in her hand and laid it at the feet of the Holy Virgin. The whole audience sat spellbound, watching her movements; the silence of the auditorium was as profound as the silence on the stage while she crossed it.

Of the actors of the Comédie Française I will only name two, Delaunay, the most elegant figure I have ever seen on the stage; he was a Duke from head to heels. I don't know what was more elegant—his appearance or his speech. The finesse of the irony with which he holds up Trissotin in *Les Femmes Savantes* was so full of venom that it appeared as if Trissotin could never rise from under its weight;

he crushed, he annihilated his rival, and how? By saying, as if with the tip of his tongue, a shrug of the shoulders, a slight smile, and an ironical pause between each of the five syllables, "Monsieur Trissotin . . ." In *Les Femmes Savantes* he also had the scene with Mlle. Joissan that has already been mentioned. He asks the spare old maid to say a good word for him to her niece Henriette, but the old woman cannot admit that the handsome youth can love anybody but herself; subtile and inventive, she understands that the name of Henriette is only a mask, and that the whole of his ardent speech is addressed to her; and prizing highly the discreetness of the young man who had hidden under the name of her niece the real object of his passion, she asks him to continue to burn, but never to tell "Henriette" of his flames. What a long labour of historical culture was required to create such a speech, such a scene, and such people.

Delaunay was a pupil of Bressan's, and he left a pupil, Le Bargy—a good actor—but how could he be compared with Delaunay? When I spoke to people older than myself about Delaunay they only shook their heads and said, "How can he be compared with Bressan!"

The other actor I wish to mention is Got. Of this wonderful actor what I chiefly remember is the hands. In *Le Gendre de M. Poirier* he has two scenes before the fall of the curtain; without saying a word, with his hands he proves, he refutes, he shows perplexity—it is impossible to enumerate all that those eloquent hands expressed, but after both scenes the whole house burst into applause; he had not spoken; the applause was for his hands. Got was perhaps the greatest mimic I have ever seen on the stage. Unfortunately he was goggle-eyed, and for this reason I give the palm in mimicry to the Italian actor Novelli. But even he sometimes failed; at least, I can remember once—it was his appearance in the part of Tartuffe. I remember how severely the critics treated him then, but I also remember with what respect; and it was on account of this very respect that the condemnation appeared so severe.

SOME RECOLLECTIONS OF THE RUSSIAN THEATRE

FOR thirty years Mme. Savina reigned supreme on the stage of the Russian dramatic theatre at Petersburg. Yet I am very sceptical about our "greatest actress," though she had doubtless great talent. I knew her at her most brilliant period. In every part there was always something unfinished, unseized, there was always at the last moment an effort that missed fire—but talent? Yes, she had talent; she was an exceptional phenomenon in Russia, but can you, who have seen anything besides the Russian theatre, tell me if it is possible to compare Savina or even to place her next to any of those French women I have mentioned? And I have not mentioned celebrities. You will say I am partial? To whom, and why? I remember the testimony of a man who heard, with his own ears, Savina say at a French performance in the Michael Theatre, "If we only had one man like these in our Alexandra Theatre," and Sazonov[1] answered, "If we had but one woman like these in our Alexandra Theatre."

I remember another case that was told me by Nicholas Popov, the well-known manager, theatrical worker, and a man of fine taste. He was talking to a member of the German theatre, if I am not mistaken it was one of the Meiningen Company. In reply to the remark that they knew nothing about the Russian theatre in Germany, Popov said, "But our Savina has acted in Germany." " Nu, wissen Sie, die gute Dame hätte auch zu Hause

[1] One of the best Russian actors at that time.

bleiben können,"[1] was the German actor's answer. As an element of the company, Savina was a plague; she was the personification of spite. During the last years, she did not act when she appeared on the stage; in all the parts she acted she only expressed her dissatisfaction. And her dissatisfaction extended to everything: to her colleagues, to the manager, to the director, to the theatre office, to all. Besides, there was the contagion of ambition. I remember when old Madame Alexandrova celebrated her 50th jubilee she received from the Emperor a bracelet with his monogram. Savina received the same thing for her 25th year jubilee. She was furious. By the bye, I have transposed these events. It was Savina who had her jubilee first, and when Alexandrova received the same thing that she had, she could not stomach it. "Who is Alexandrova? She's nothing but an old woman!" Yes, Alexandrova was an old woman, but a charming old woman. On the occasion of her jubilee she was presented to the Emperor, and when she left she retired backwards as far as the middle of the room and then she said, "Well, Tsar golubchik (darling), I don't excel in walking backwards." The Emperor hurried towards her and conducted her to the door. So Savina could not stomach that Alexandrova had been given the same thing that she had received. She petitioned the Minister of the Palace that she should be allowed to remove the monogram from the bracelet and to wear it on a ribbon of the Order of Saint Andrew. I don't remember if she succeeded in obtaining the permission to do so.

Whatever part Savina played she always acted as if she had been wronged; by her expression she always seemed to say to the audience: "Now, is it possible to act under these conditions." The audience were attracted

[1] "Well, you know, that good lady might have remained at home."

by her name for a long time, but gradually their interest in it waned. Savina used to send to the box-office of the theatre in the morning to find out if many tickets had been sold, and if it proved to be few, she sent to say she was ill. Then a red lantern was hung out at the entrance of the theatre. This denoted that the piece had been changed.
. . . I knew her at the time of her full bloom; she had brilliance; she had the gift of irony. The best that I can remember was *Belugin's Marriage;* the scene with the husband, acted by Sazonov, was admirably carried out. A charming representation of a muslin young girl she gave in *The Inspector*. Her Marie Antonovna ought to have become classical and a confirmed tradition. But—traditions exist only where there *is* a school.

The two columns of our dramatic theatre were Davydov and Varlamov. Davydov was one of the greatest actors I have known; he possessed astonishing versatility, ranging from the wildest comedy to the most restrained pathos. He and Varlamov were the only two actors of the Alexandra theatre who could draw tears. Varlamov had more external appearance; he was huge of stature, with a loud voice, and he struck off his words accurately in spicy conversations; he conquered the attention as soon as he appeared on the stage. But he was careless, he never knew his part, added his own words, and he took advantage of the methods he had once found successful and relied on his name to secure the adoration of the audience. They were delightful when acting together, when a scene or the whole play rested on them as in *Krechinsky's Wedding*, or in Tchaikovsky's *Wrestlers*. *Krechinsky's Wedding* was given, among other things, in Yaroslav at the jubilee celebrations in memory of Volkov, the founder of the Russian theatre. The building was beautiful; a fine town with its scale-covered cupolas on the steep banks of the Volga, a holiday mood, the hospitality of the inhabitants, excursions on the Volga with a band, all this is blended together in delightful recollections of spring. It was in the year 1900, and the second year of my directorship. The Governor of Yaroslav at the time was that unfortunate Stürmer, who afterwards became Minister of the Home Department and later the last but one Minister of Foreign Affairs of the Imperial Government. He had commenced his career in the ceremonial department of the Ministry of the Court, and therefore loved and knew how to arrange solemnities. Well, I remember that during the performance of *Krechinsky's Wedding*, at the most touching moment, when the whole hall was kept in a mood of pathetic emotion, Varlamov drew an enormous coloured silk handkerchief out of his pocket, in order to wipe his own eyes and blow his nose, and produced a sound like a motor horn, so that the whole theatre, although in tears, burst into laughter. Always and in every part Varlamov had some such sally. Davydov never did it, he was always serious when necessary, he always kept within bounds.

Davydov was the only Russian actor of whom I can say that he read verse beautifully. You felt in his elocution a deep love for the beauty of words, for the beauty of the text, he always maintained the picture of the thought, and never destroyed the temperament required by the art of reading and logical clearness. He was the best Famusov[1] I have seen, and besides him I have seen in the part Lensky and Stanislavsky. Lensky was dry, he had not the Moscow geniality and sociability. Stanislavsky was noisy. Davydov was a real " barin,"[2] with charming geniality, and at the same time the official reserve in all his movements ; he had a well-cultivated wrist and eloquent

---

[1] A character in Griboiedor's *Gore of Uma*.
[2] Master, gentleman.

fingers. His cordiality was so sincere that no other actor on the Russian stage has ever appealed to me to the same degree. My father was not a sentimental man, but after a performance of Turgenev's *Bachelors*, he said, "One can kneel down before Davydov." He was a splendid "Town Provost." During the last monologue he made you feel quite creepy—"At whom are you laughing? You are laughing at yourself!" but when he came to "quill-drivers," etc., there was no limit to his irony, to his contempt. What wonderful effects he produced with his hands and fingers! Like a conjurer who makes a heap of a large handkerchief, squeezes it together, rubs it between his palms, presses it into his hand and at last—there remains nothing of the handkerchief, so he treated the "quill-drivers." He kneaded, turned them inside out, twisted, poked them about, and turned them into nothingness. But he was too fat, he lost his breath, and that greatly weakened the impression. To what a state they had brought themselves, these two coryphæi of ours! From excessive fatness Varlamov could no longer walk, he rolled along. Davydov was even worse; when last I saw him he had put on so much flesh that he was quite breathless and had no longer any expression in his face. His face was a sort of mass of fat—his eyes and nose were surrounded with flesh, and his cheeks and chin were also a flabby mass of flesh. In this lump of moving breathlessness, the sparks of the former flame were dying out, quickened and supported by the habit of long years, and I must add the routine of a repertory that became more and more narrow, simplified, and even vulgarized. Correctly speaking Davydov, the real Davydov, had long since left the stage. In him departed the last real original actor. Yes, *departed*, as our actors do not know how to transmit their art to others. Davydov taught in the theatre school, but he did not know how to teach that with which he had been so largely endowed; and the simple reason why he did not know how to teach was that he, as all our players, acted by inner inspiration that was not enlightened by judgment. You can teach only what you *know*, not what you can do. With us there is no knowledge, therefore there is no school, and there is no transmission. I will say further, only he can *teach* who himself has *learned*. It is vain for a talented actor to think that under his talent it is not perceptible that he has not learned. Nicholas Popov, whom I have already mentioned, told me another delightful story. When Savina acted in Berlin the Emperor William went behind the scenes, and after greeting her he asked, " Where did you learn ? " " Nowhere." William turned to the aide-de-camp who accompanied him: " You see! I told you so!" And nevertheless she taught others. Who does not teach with us? What teaching it is, too! When one of our actors teaches, he only shows how he himself would act a certain part. He is incapable of giving instructive rules for acting in general, such rules as would be of use for every part. I remember the words of Saint Augustine, " Teachers place themselves as examples, and they call this teaching." Thus the few born geniuses are swept away from the Russian stage, leaving no traces behind them except a name. Like smoke the impression is blown away, like a shadow the glory departs with the man, and memory is unable to retain it. The French song says :

> " J'ai perdu la mémoire
> De cette ombre illusoire
> Qu'on appelle la gloire
> Et qu'emporte le vent."[1]

[1] " I have lost all memory
Of that illusive shadow,
That is called glory
Which the wind bears away."

In the midst of all this a silver lily blossomed—Komissarzhevskaïa. Far removed from intrigues, indifferent to the criticism of the Press, she lived in her parts, concentrated in her art. Of a soft, pliant character, inoffensive in that theatre world, where in whatever you touch you find the painful wound of self-love, she herself was quiet, bright and simple. Small, thin, frail, not very pretty, with a somewhat crooked face, with an enchantingly bright smile, a beautiful voice, and, what is so seldom to be found in the voices of the women on our stage, without a trace of vulgarity—these were the natural gifts that Komissarzhevskaïa possessed. But when we speak of art, as always, and even more than always, I must be inexorably strict. Why, the more a man has received, the more he must give; the more that has been given him, the more he must cultivate. And I cannot call that art, where I see no cultivation ; I cannot call it art when a man takes on to the stage his natural gifts and nothing else. In her, as in all our actors, there was no consciousness of her resources ; and when there is no consciousness there is no guidance, as you can only guide that which you know. I never felt that she had control of her powers ; I never felt that from the diversity of her resources she had consciously made her choice. She had a beautiful voice, very diversified, but it was evident she did not know her own voice ; I remember very well that in the beginning of each part when she opened her mouth the first impression was an unpleasant one—a false note ; and it was only when she had somewhat warmed to her part that she gradually found the suitable tone. The technical weakness of the voice was often perceptible and disturbed ; she had no low notes, and she was wanting in fullness ; and all this might have been acquired, but our actors disdain technique. But for that, in the moments of involuntary passion in the part she attained wonderful depths, and then it became clear what she might have become if she had enlightened herself with the light of consciousness. Is there anything in the world more incompatible, more incongruous than art and chance? And yet the acting of our Russian players is full of chance—to-day it succeeded and to-morrow it did not. Nobody notices this, and it is called art! But why is it that when on the billiard table a ball falls into the pocket without the intention of the player it is called a fluke, and not scored by him? And on the stage such flukes are called art. Of course, I do not say that all that was good in Komissarzhevskaaï's acting was only by fluke; but when I find with an actor a phrase that is said not badly or not well, but simply not correctly, when whole scenes are acted not in the right tone, then I involuntarily begin to doubt his consciousness of what is good in his acting. An actor can only answer for what he does with discrimination, as a player at billiards only scores the balls he has pocketed intentionally.

With this reservation, which I make regarding Komissarzhevskaïa, but which extends to the whole of the Russian theatre, in so far as the theatre consists of the actor's elocution and the actor's mimic art, I will award Komissarzhevskaïa the first place among the Russian actresses of her generation. The first time I saw her was in Sudermann's play, *The Destruction of Sodom*. She was an apparition such as had never been seen before on the Russian stage; she acted a girl of fifteen, naïve, bright, without a shadow of vulgarity, without the slightest design. Such truth to *life* I have never seen on the Russian stage before or after her. She had two rare pre-eminences; her wonderful lightness in passing from one mood to another, and the power to give to words quite another meaning than the one they express. As an example of the last quality I may cite a scene in the *Lights of St. John's Eve,* also by Sudermann. She remains on the stage alone with her lover; they have just found out that they love one another; they must hurry to the train, but she does not want to go, she finds it so nice there! It is already late, they have missed one train; to his arguments she answers, " Never mind, we can go at eleven "; they let that time pass; she says, " We can go at two." They miss that train also, and sitting down on the sofa, squeezing into a corner, wrapping herself up in a shawl, and pressing close to her lover, she says " We can go at four." All those three phrases from her lips expressed not at all the meaning of the words; they expressed, "I am so happy! I want nothing more. I am in the seventh heaven." And all three were transpierced with but one thing, " I love you so much!" Just this facility to give words another meaning than the ones they are given in the dictionary she possessed in the highest degree: she abolished the word as such and drowned it in an ocean of feeling. Only great talent can do that. She could do it, but—there is always a " but " when one speaks of Russian actors—but she was able to produce everything that was naïve, not complicated, simple; in real drama it was different, and in tragedy something was wanting; it might not have been so, but there was no study, there was no mastery; she perished under the difficulty of the task, she was not wanted—not in her place. Thus she was pale as Ophelia; and her Desdemona, which she acted with Salvina, was quite insignificant; and notwithstanding this she wanted to go along this path. She left the Imperial Theatre and placed herself in the hands of Meyerholdt, a manager who was much talked about at the time. That theatrical mountebank, who knew how to spoil and poison all he touched, took Komissarzhevskaïa in hand, he got up a company for her and toured the whole of Russia. At that period I did not see her, but I was told that she was not to be recognized; she was broken—distorted. In Meyerholdt's hands the lily faded. . . . Soon after Komissarzhevskaïa died.

RECOLLECTIONS OF THE GERMAN THEATRE

THE first time that I saw German acting on the stage was when the Meiningen company came to Petersburg. They acted Schiller and Shakespeare; and in the company there was such a prominent power as Barnay. It is unnecessary to speak of the important place occupied by the Meiningen company in the history of the theatre; the part they played is too well known, their name has become appellative. To stage a play in a "Meiningen style" denotes at once the intentions. I will only say that after the flagrant lies of which the stage properties in the theatres of that time were composed, the real, the authentic which the Meiningen showed us, the real rusty swords, real heavy wooden doors, with real locks that snapped, real crockery, the clink of crystal goblets and silver beakers, was all so new, so magnificent, so full of life, that just on account of all this reality it produced the impression of another world. However, it was not in all this materiality that their force lay; it is not true, as some say, that the success of the Meiningen company was due to their manner of mounting plays; no, man was stronger than properties, and all this "practicable" was transpierced by the spirit; the people who moved in it, that were in touch with it, were real live people, with but very few exceptions. It was not in lifeless objects that the novelty which they brought was to be found, but it lay first and foremost in the scenes in which crowds took part. There was an astounding impression of novelty in these pictures of popular excitement; the blustering crowds in Wallenstein's military camp; the stormy crowd of the Roman Forum, around Cæsar's body; the bowing, obsequious crowds of Queen Elizabeth's courtiers. The most wonderful part of these crowds was not that it knew how to render all sorts of extremes, from the heights of tension to the last degree of weakness or the reverse, but that it was impossible to catch the various degrees of these transitions; there were no shocks here, it was all flowing, unbroken like life itself. None of the " popular scenes " that I have since seen could be compared with these; and I do not think that the novelty was the cause of this. Here there were evidently principles, strict observance of the apportionment of growth and decline. The work was accomplished in this way. The chief manager (I think his name was Kroneck; I may be mistaken, it was so long ago) had his own delegates, whom he had trained for certain scenes; these took in hand small groups of figurants, and showed them what they were to do at certain moments, and they were instructed during the performance to watch their leader and do what he did. For the performance these groups were scattered, and the figurants that composed them were placed at different parts of the stage. In this way precision was obtained in diversity, and by intense attention exactitude and simultaneousness. The most perfect of all these scenes of crowds that I saw given by them was the Roman Forum in *Julius Cæsar*—the speeches of Brutus and Mark Anthony; that is to say the life of the masses during these speeches. In the sense of the reaction of the crowd, I have never seen anything better since, or even equal to it. The much-vaunted scenes of the populace in *King Œdipus*, arranged by Reinhardt, cannot be compared with the Roman mobs of the Meiningen company, they are as far-removed from them as a herd is from art. I must add that both speeches were splendidly delivered, Barnay was Brutus, I don't remember who was Mark Anthony.

Besides the admirable principles of growth and decline in separate scenes the Meiningen company knew how to develop the whole piece, that is to say, the gradual growth of interest from act to act. This skill in staging left the audience, when the curtain fell at the end of an act, wondering what would come next. The understanding of how to leave the audience in suspense during the *entr'acte* is, of course, the most important quality of a manager with regard to the piece, as it is the most valuable quality of the actor with regard to his part.

Of Barnay I can say he was the essence of nobility. I remember him best in the part of Wallenstein; his low, deep tones, his splendid elocution, his admirable deportment. He represented a real Commander-in-Chief; one felt the whole camp lay behind him, the whole army; he appeared as the bearer of historical responsibility; and with this high impression—what simplicity. One can test the actor by Wallenstein's last significant words. He leaves to go to bed, and we, the audience, know that it had been decided to kill him in his sleep; when he leaves the stage he says to those around him that he has the intention of sleeping for a long time. All the actors of the old, bombastic type pronounced these words with such solemn emphasis as if they wanted to say, "I am going to sleep, but I am really going to enter the life beyond the grave." Barnay said them in a tone that seemed to imply, " I am going to sleep; I am tired; don't wake me, please."

It is regrettable that Barnay's simplicity has found no followers in Germany; tragedy, costume, verse, seem to have the unfortunate result of raising the German actors on to stilts. Only great talent understands the majesty of simplicity; but great talent is rare, and that is why I say one must judge of the theatre, not by the actors of talent, but by those who are untalented. The theatre is as little answerable for talents as the earth is for an aerolite fallen from heaven ; it is only in the untalented you will see if education and tradition acts in him, or if he is left to his own devices. Finally, I would say that in the clearness of the tasks they had set themselves, for the sincerity with which they regarded them, and for the conscientiousness with which they executed them the Meiningen company is certainly one of the most highly estimable apparitions in the history of the theatre.

In the year 1885 I passed two of the summer months in Vienna. I went to the theatre almost every evening ; I was often in the Grand Opera, where I saw the whole of Wagner's cycle. I went to the Theatre An der Wien, where I saw the comic operas of Strauss and Zuppe with that charming and unique singer Gerardi ; I was also in the Erzherzog Karl Theatre, where I saw that enchanting Jennie Gross, who afterwards came to Petersburg on a visit. But the most precious were the evenings I passed in the Burg Theatre.

The celebrated Vienna dramatic company was still acting in its old home, the theatre in the Burg, the Imperial Palace. Afterwards it removed to the theatre that was specially built for it on the Ring opposite the town hall. The new theatre is sumptuous and rich, but those who have seen the old theatre will always remember it and will regret the simple, old-fashioned hall. The Vienna Burg Theatre is for the German theatre what the Comédie Française is for the French. It is the history, it is the academy, of eloquence. There is something wonderfully attractive in this theatre, and notwithstanding the enormous diversity of their repertoire there is a character of uniformity in the style that rests on them all. The similarity of the manner in which they all looked upon their work, the extraordinary accord, and sureness, which inspired the audience with confidence that they would be good from the moment they appeared on the stage, all the " respect " and seriousness, with which even the lightest comedy was staged—all this called forth esteem, communicated a sort of incontestability, and put a stamp on them that I have not seen in any other theatre. They impressed themselves on the memory with an extraordinary power; why, this was thirty-six years ago, and I remember them as if I had seen them yesterday.

Anybody who is well acquainted with the history of this theatre will at once know of what period I am speaking when I say that at that time the great Wolter, the extraordinary Sonnenthal, were still acting, and young girls were being played by " little Hohenfels."

Without the slightest hesitation I employ the epithet of " great " to Wolter, although she was not known beyond the frontiers of Germany. She was the last representative of the great tragic art. Deportment, movements, voice, pronunciation, she had all the requisites, and such a tragic instinct, that she was able in a single flight to sustain a long scene. In this I can only compare her with Sarah Bernhardt. Her voice did not possess those soft upper tones, " la voix d'or," of Sarah Bernhardt, but her lower tones were deeper and fuller. The intonations of her voice still ring in my ears in that scene of Schiller's *Maria Stuart* in which, contrary to history, he makes the two queens meet in the garden. I remember the intonation of Wolter's voice, when she says to Elizabeth, that she has borne *all* that a human heart can bear—" Alles hab'ich ertragen." Seldom has an intonation of a human voice given me the impression of the cup having been drained to the dregs as this " Alles." It was really all to the very last drop. Her pronunciation was delightful ; it was the most noble German I have ever heard. Goethe's and Schiller's verse from her lips was like music ; I have never heard such a sonorous and tragic " R." I saw her in many and varied parts ; she was always admirable even in such pieces as Sardou's *Fedora*, but of course her real forte was the classic repertory.

In Goethe's *Götz von Berlichingen* she has a striking scene. She is alone in her castle and is awaiting her lover ; he is long in coming ; at last a rider appears in the distance ; he approaches and her joy grows stronger. But suddenly —a doubt—it appears not to be he ! Misgiving, uneasiness, fear ; the rider jumps off his horse ; is mounting the stairs— a terrible foreboding. The door opens—there enters and stops, like a ghost, a knight with a veiled face. She understands that this is her judge come to execute on her the sentence of death. He casts a noose round her neck, and having killed her, strikes his sharp dagger into the lintel of the door ; he hangs the cord on it, and goes away. The corpse is lying on the floor. It is difficult to find in the whole of dramatic literature a scene of such psychological diapason. This one scene was a whole tragedy. It was in such pieces that this wonderfully rich nature was at home. She acted in one tragedy—*Messalina ;* I don't remember by whom it was ; but in no other part was the entire power of her gifts so completely displayed. She was a moving Roman statue. In seeing this play I regretted that the old Frenchmen Racine and Corneille were not included in the repertory of that theatre. To see Wolter in the parts of Athalie or Camille would have been the extreme of artistic perfection ; however, who knows what the German translation would have made of the marvellous French verse. Wolter was already old at that time, but she suffered from the general infirmity of celebrated actors—in the second part of *Faust* she acted Helen the beautiful! And *Faust*—Paris—was acted by old Sonnenthal! I remembered the words of dear Salvini when speaking of some private theatricals, and I wanted to say, " Why did they do it ? "

Sonnenthal was an excellent actor, but it was not in classical pieces that he displayed his greatest value ; he was better in a frock coat than in costume ; his costume raised him on stilts. In drama in ordinary dress, and in comedy, he was exceedingly simple, with an entire absence of the actor's mannerisms. I remember him in a piece called *Der Hüttenbisitzer*, an arrangement of Georges Ohnet's *Le Maître de Forges*. I have seen this play in French, and I must say the Vienna actors were better. With the French, one often notices, especially when there is much movement, their sole endeavour is to realize the appointed form ; here each one develops his own understanding of life. The honours of the piece were shared between Sonnenthal and the enchanting, though somewhat cold, Schratt, who was the mistress of the Emperor Franz Joseph. Handsome, showy, with a clear voice and a sonorous laugh, she was specially good in pieces where she played peasant parts. In short skirts, with a large black bow at the back of her fair head, she was brilliant in irony, she was cutting in her rebukes. Her chief triumphs were plays in the Viennese dialect ; the whole of charming Vienna seemed to speak through her, Vienna with its kind-hearted smartness. All the blood of Vienna seemed to boil in her, the whole of the " Wiener Blut " with its delicate, unmerciful smile. Another of his great successes Sonnenthal scored with little Hohenfels ; the piece was called *Frau Susanne*, but I don't remember by whom it was written.

Little Hohenfels was quite an extraordinary creature.

Imagine a creature that you could not listen to without emotion, and whom you remember after thirty-six years with the same fresh emotion you felt at the time you heard her then; whose voice will never be silent for those who have once heard it, even once; and this voice was *quite hoarse.* Just think what talent she must have possessed, as she was deprived of the chief means of effect. The first moment I heard her I was puzzled; what is this? Is it possible to produce such an actress? But afterwards! What she was able to do with that voice of hers, and afterwards how one's whole being was drawn to hear it again and again. I remember Delsarte's precept, "If you are not able to rid yourself of a defect, cause it to be loved." Yes she was loved. How she was received, how she was reconducted! How each of her words was greeted with involuntary roars of laughter in the stalls. In *Frau Susanne* she acted Sonnenthal's wife. She has heard that the husband she adores suspects, and is even certain, that she is unfaithful to him. Her husband has not said a word about it to her, but he is about to fight a duel. Here Sonnenthal has a splendid scene when seated at his writing table. He is arranging his papers and opening and shutting the drawers of his writing table. I remember very well while he was doing this a servant came in and announced that somebody had come, and he, without stopping in what he was about, said with inimitable simplicity, "Ja, lassen Sie ihn herein,"[1] and continued to lock the drawers, and then put his keys in his trousers pocket. After this business talk he remained alone, the door opened and Susanne came in. She knows all, but she must not show that she does; she also knows that for the whole business to be cleared up he must remain at home that evening. And so it is her task to interest him, to bewitch him, to

[1] "Yes, let him come in."

keep him until nine o'clock, only till nine; after that it is not important, but she must manage to prevent him from looking at his watch. She was seated at the other side of the writing table. Well, but how can I describe this scene for you after thirty-six years? I only remember that after his first cold words in answer to her question whether she is bothering him he took out his cigar-case and asked, "Du erlaubst doch?" "Na, gewiss." "Du bist ein Engel." "Nun, so umhulle mich mit Wolken."[1] What can be more difficult on the stage than the heroical jokes of a suffering soul? And the whole time she makes jokes, diverts him, prevents him from thinking; and when at last he looks at his watch, he is dumbfounded; she understands he is too late, that her great effort has been crowned with success—she can do no more, and loses consciousness.

These are the most precious names in my reminiscences of the Vienna Burg Theatre.

---

[1] "You permit?" "Oh, of course!" "You are an angel." "Then envelop me in clouds."

DUSE: SARAH BERNHARDT: RÉJANE

No actress who is known to our generation has succeeded in conquering so many hearts as Duse. It is not the love of man for woman that I refer to here, I mean the appreciation of her spiritual being, the appreciation of a human being by a human being, regardless of sex. The best people, the people who are far removed from the life of the theatre, people whose interest in the personality of an actress never oversteps the footlights, honour Eleonora Duse as one of the most spiritually beautiful representatives of human nature, and a spirit of great friendship always surrounded her, even during that period of her life when worldly scruples might have suggested a certain indifference to the sufferings of her heart. Besides her wonderful talent Duse is a personality—a character. She has soul-intellect. All is original, all of an exceptional degree, all of the rarest quality. Ardent, nerve-weary, like a highly-strung chord weak in the face of passion, she is strong in the burst of regeneration, joyful in inception, manly in strife and with cold clearness in indignation. She had a passionate longing for all that does not exist on this earth; she goes through life like a thirsty traveller in the desert. A long neck, an upturned chin, weary eyes—thus she passes along—and you feel afraid to call to her; she inspires caution.

And so this frail vessel of her being, which in life she bears in trembling hands, she carries on to the stage, and with what courage, with what prodigality of herself, with what lavishness towards others! " Duse only acts herself ! " some say; " Duse acts with her whole soul," others say;

"Duse acts with her nerves," and so on. In a word Duse's acting is "within." Yes, I have the courage not only to say it, but to welcome it; in the present case I greet the "within." Yes, she shows us her soul; she acts herself; but we have seen what a woman she is, what a beautiful soul. Duse's soul has no cause to hide itself, we are happy to feel its contact. Yes, in this case, and, I may add, only in this case, I recognize the artistic competency of the "within." Not only because this "within" shows me a unique soul, but also because, owing to the exceptional nature of this talent, the "within" never deceives her, it will always prompt her to artistic truth. Our defenders of the "within" need not triumph, they have no occasion to rub their hands and say with satisfaction, "Ah! so you also acknowledge the principles of the 'within.'" It is not the principles that I admit; I only take note of an exceptional phenomenon. She is so gifted by nature that the truth comes to her by intuition; besides, the instrument nature has given her is so rich, of such infinite diversity! Is it possible you think, that because Duse plays on her harp from "within," that your single chord when touched by your "within" will sound like a harp? Great phenomena seldom occur; to generalize from them is imprudent, and to try to build up a system of education on them is sinful, inasmuch as education is the responsibility of one human conscience for another. Yes, Duse "acts herself," but she herself is so varied that it is never the same. And so instead of comforting oneself with the idea that "temperament suffices" it is much more instructive to observe the various processes by which temperament expresses itself.

It is strange that I cannot say where and when I saw Duse for the first time; I would even find it difficult to say in what part. With her the woman predominates so much that I think of the parts she acts as of the costumes which she changes. More than in a certain part, I see her in a certain mood expressive of this or that feeling. I do not remember her Magda, but I remember her contemptuous indignation. I do not remember her "Dame aux Camélias" but I see her sadness. The predominance of the woman over the part is the real power by which she impresses herself on the memory. In the two parts I have mentioned, though they are totally dissimilar, for Magda is protest, and Marguerite Gautier submission, Duse employs the same business, the repetition of a word. Her former lover, her seducer and the father of her child, comes to Magda. In a long monologue he explains why he can no longer continue to be her friend, why he must disown the child and so on. All these explanations are sprinkled with disgusting expressions—half excuses, half justifications. She listens and only from time to time utters one word—"*gia.*" In Italian this word means "Well; yes; certainly; to be sure." But with her it means something quite different each time: "Obviously; well; go on; what a blackguard you are," and so on. These "*gias*" sounded like the lashes of a whip in the air; and he, seeing with what ease she agrees with him, becomes all the bolder, and the bolder he becomes the more cutting become the strokes of her whip. In the third act of the *Dame aux Camélias* she goes to a gaming house. It was the first time since their rupture that she has met the man she loves and whom she has renounced owing to the insistence of his family. Armando Duval does not know this, and looks upon her as a venal traitress. Before the whole assembled company he pours upon her a deluge of hideous accusations and a shower of " the contemptible metal." She listens to him with horror, sinks powerless on a sofa, and only utters from time to time one word: " Armando! " What is there not to be found in that word? With bated breath, and lowered voice, always at a different pitch, and a different depth! It means " Is it you? Come to yourself! Have pity! Are you in your senses?" Unforgettable, undescribable, never to be repeated! As we find the disobedient, revolting suffering of Magda in the oft-repeated "*gia*," so we find in the repeated name of her lover all the submissive, amazed sadness of Marguerite Gautier.

Most of all, I remember her suffering. Her merriment was of course infectious, with her caresses she was able to whisk away all earthly trouble, there was no end to her flow of irony, but what I remember most was her suffering. She had a most interesting part in that interesting English play, *The Second Mrs. Tanqueray*. A widower, not of the first youth, marries a woman of a questionable past. She is very devoted to him, very sincere, so sincere that she cannot bear to have even the shadow of an omission between her and him; before accepting his offer, she gives him a letter, which she asks him to read when he is alone; in this letter she tells him the whole of her past life and describes to him the difficulties of their future family and social position. " When you will be alone, read this letter. When you have read it, re-read it; and when you have re-read it, re-re-read it." It is impossible to reproduce the charm of this "leggerai, ri-leggerai and ri-rileggerai." What is it that makes this so astonishing? Why, this letter was the greatest burden of her life, and in this little joke she plays with this burden, as with a feather; the burden she leaves for herself; the feather is for him. I draw special attention to this scene as it forms the groundwork on which the subsequent suffering is drawn: after sunshine there is rain, and real heavy rain. In the third act there is an explanation with her husband. Nothing has come of their conjugal life; their social position is false, her husband's grown up daughter does not understand her step-mother,

I R

her husband is troubled, she is losing her strength; and here at last in this creature, tormented by small jealousies, small vanities, in general with all sorts of worldly rubbish that prevents her from living, suddenly a woman awakes—a real woman without any class or social bias. She paints a picture of her life for her husband, the past life, that was built on the care for her exterior, that transient, deceitful beauty, the present where beauty no longer exists, and there is nothing in its place—emptiness; a void. These are the general outlines. I do not remember the details, but that is not the point; she paints a picture of personal emptiness, but gradually a general picture is obtained of her own insignificance and of those like her, a certain perpetual irremediableness in woman's destiny, and all this depth of suffering arises from the bottom of some worldly trifles; out of a box that smells of gloves, laces, patchouli, the sorrow of the world arises. While she speaks her eyes suddenly become moist; they fill with tears; she continues to speak; the tears overflow and fall from her eyes,; two streams flow down her cheeks and fall like large drops of rain on her velvet dress. She sits on an arm-chair facing the audience and the light of the footlights is reflected in the two streams of tears. This is the highest picture of suffering that I have ever seen; comparable to this I only know in art the eyes of Titian's Magdalene, that overflow with tears. I wish here to draw an interesting comparison. I saw the same play given in Boston. Here the part was taken by Mrs. Patrick Campbell, the actress for whom it was written. I must say the English actress was charming and yet quite different. She was less beautiful, she acted an older woman, which made her position more tragic; from the very beginning she had not the slightest idealism, she acted a thoroughly shallow woman. All this I have called gloves and patchouli. All this was represented by

MRS. PATRICK CAMPBELL AS "PAULA TANQUERAY"

her as tragically small, even comically tragic. In the great scene of the third act there was not the same depth of that feeling of common humanity which Duse had, but for that it was a picture of such poorness of soul, such a worldly beggary, that its very smallness was touching, owing to the tragic position in which she placed this insignificant creature. It was very interesting. Duse portrayed the depth of suffering ; Mrs. Campbell showed deeply suffering shallowness. Whose was the greater art ? I must confess, the Englishwoman's. But I repeat Duse's was the most exalted picture of earthly suffering.

Notwithstanding the preponderance of suffering, what pictures she gave of happiness, such cloudless, childlike happiness. And it is here that she displayed her technique ; this is the side of her that is not sufficiently noticed by those who judge her. If we " recognize " her in suffering there is nothing of the real Duse we know in life in the pictures of childlike happiness she gives us ; here we can never say that she is repeating herself. Her childlike Juliet, the light carelessness of her Nora, the playful artfulness of her " Landlady," all this is not Duse represented on the stage; it is Duse representing something she has created, something that is not inherent in her nature. She had great power of work, and she planned out her rôles very carefully. The principal lines of her rôles were firmly fixed by her ; she possessed in the highest degree the technique of building up one act on the other. I never saw her in any of the great Shakespearean parts, but I have been told that as Juliet she was like a girl of fourteen in the first act and finished like a grown up, broken woman. She always remained within bounds ; never, not even in the greatest moments of passion, had she a shadow of hysteria—she who in life was so nervous, so ill-balanced, so hesitating.

I knew her personally, but have seen her seldom ; her

nearest friends often did not see her for months. She had social peculiarities, she sometimes disappeared, or shut herself up and would see nobody. In Florence she passed days on the terrace on the roof of her house, and scarcely ever descended to the earth. I saw her in Rome for the last time. She wanted to become acquainted with the questions of theatrical education that interested me. We talked for a long time together. I remember one word she said that impressed me greatly. When I said that I was blamed for paying too much attention to trifles she exclaimed, " Trifles! The theatre is like a rope, it is made of little threads twisted together. There are no trifles in the theatre." She loved all questions concerning her art, and approached them from every side. At that time her mind was occupied with the project of founding a colony for actors in the neighbourhood of Rome, where actors could live, work, play, walk about; where they could forget the struggle for existence and give themselves entirely up to art and rest. To give them the riches of the inner life—that is what she wanted, and it appeared to me, at that moment, the sick, suffering creature suffered most of all in not being able to share with others that in which she was so rich. Her soul shone out in each word, and even her silence was pregnant with soul, she listened with her soul. Her suffering eyes glistened, and how often her hand was raised to her temple to put back a black lock, that " disobedient lock " which d'Annunzio so often mentions in his novel *Il fuoco*. That lock of hair we also know very well on the stage; it is there that her social nervousness sometimes obtrudes itself in the part she is acting; her hand is raised to her temple too often, sometimes all the fingers are thrust into her black hair, and the hand arranges too often the dress that slips off her shoulder. These are slight signs of great mental worry.

In the second year of the War I received in Petersburg a request made in her name to recommend to her some part in a Russian play. This request was followed by a somewhat vague description of a part that appeared to her interesting. It seemed to me to be the prologue of May's historical play, *Pskovitianka*. At that time she was meditating a tour through all the countries of the Allies to act in each country a play of that nation for the benefit of the wounded. I wrote to her that, in my opinion, what she ought to act in Russia was Pushkin's *Don Juan*. By so doing she would not only pay a tribute to Russia's greatest poet, but in the rôle of Donna Anna she would not depart from the general European course of her repertory. I advised her, if she wanted to give something quite unique, to play both the parts. I see her plainly in both of them. Tall, black, weeping, with arms hanging straight down, holding a white handkerchief against her black dress; and red-haired, bright, sparkling, throwing herself into the arms of her lover. Why have we never seen this— Donna Anna and Laura both acted by Duse.

I am sorry to leave Duse. And how difficult it was to begin! The great old man Balzac said of literary work, "On le quitte avec regret, on s'y remet avec désespoir."[1] Each time I write a new name in my narrative, and begin a new portrait, I experience this despair; I think I shall never be able to surmount the difficulties, that I have nothing to say. And when I have said what I could, I am sorry that I have finished, that I must leave off.

When people talk of Duse the artiste it is inevitable that they add, "Yes, and what a charming woman she is in real life." When they talk of Sarah Bernhardt as a woman they inevitably add, "But what a wonderful actress she is on the stage." Yes, she is wonderful, because this

[1] "You leave it with regret, you recommence with despair."

is art itself, pure art, without any alloy. If I were asked what I consider the highest example of histrionic technique, I would answer without any hesitation—Sarah Bernhardt. Hers is the fullest, the most exact picture of scenic art that I have ever seen. And do you know when I felt it most? When I saw her for the last time in Paris during the summer of 1913. I do not remember what the play was. It was in costume of the Italian Renaissance period; she acted a man's part—a young poet. She was quite old; she could only stand leaning against the back of a chair, or supporting herself with a stick, her false teeth occupied too much space in her mouth and affected her diction; her voice had the cracked tones of old age. All this was entirely cold—call it as you like—warmth, temperament, soul, did not exist; this mechanical apparatus was empty. It was a technical skeleton; every "what" had evaporated, only "how" remained. I must confess this was the most amazing "lesson" I had ever had. She seemed to say, "Look, this is how, these are the means, these are the technical effects I employed when I was Sarah Bernhardt!" It was instructive; as never before, the technical web that underlay the whole of her brilliant past made itself felt; it was as if she opened out her cards after the game was over. Imagine a turbulent brook; you have always admired its noise, its foam, its splashes, but you did not know how this was produced; you only knew it was produced by the position and the form of the stones that were impediments to the water; you were unable to study their distribution under the water. But now the stream is dried up; all is on the surface, all is open to examination. Here you had all that the whole world had admired during forty-five years; here were all the wonderful resources of Sarah Bernhardt: the celebrated diction, the celebrated whisper, the celebrated guttural

cries, her celebrated "golden voice"—"le voix d'or."
Here I remembered the impression that voice made on me
in *La Dame aux Camélias* when she sinks upon her lover's
breast, not with her face downward but turned up as if
fainting, and says, "Je t'aime, je t'aime, je t'aime," and
she repeats the words numberless times, always fainter
and fainter as if sinking into the beatitude of unconscious-
ness. There I also remembered the tragic whisper that
in so many of her rôles produced a feeling of terror in her
audience. I remembered her hoarse shout, when in *Tosca*
she has stabbed Scarpia, and bending over his body repeats
one word, "Meurs!" and this word that sounds like the
roar of a leopard seems to pierce the corpse like repeated
stabs of the dagger; with this word she dispatches him
completely. And lastly the "golden summits," the fable
of the two doves which she reads in the second act of
Adrienne Leconvreur.

All this great diversity was her personal possession, her
speciality, and will never be repeated to the same extent.
Such a distance from joy to sorrow, from happiness to
horror, from caresses to violence, I have never seen before
or since. Such "polarity" in the art of the theatre our
generation has never been shown by any other artiste.
If in Juliet Duse showed us the two poles of the same
creature—from a little girl to a broken woman—Sarah
Bernhardt gave us, in *Tosca* for instance, really two worlds.
She enters the church where her beloved is painting images.
Who has not seen her portrait in the costume of the
Directory in a large exaggerated pink hat. Overburdened
with a large bunch of flowers she stands with a slightly
bent head, and admires the work of the man she loves;
everything pleases her about the work, but why has one
of the saints that are painted in the picture black eyes?
This reminds her of a woman who had looked at her

beloved. What nonsense, a mere trifle; he laughs at her, jokes about it, she forgets it and laughs; the whole scene is one of cloudless joy. And only when she is leaving she stops before the picture again, and after a short moment of concentration, she says " Fais lui des yeux bleus." [1] What was really so charming in the way she said it, was that you felt that underlying them were the words " all the same." This unuttered word was the seed of the whole future tragedy—" all the same," all this happiness proved to be a phantom; and in the last act when deprived of everything, exhausted by torture and mockery before the corpse of her lover, who has been shot, she throws into the face of those who have shot him, she spits into their faces, " Canaille ! " and jumps from the walls of the bastion into the abyss below, only not to die from their shots. From that " Fais lui des yeux bleus " to that " Canaille " there is the distance of two worlds.

As in Duse's repertory of suffering we find, standing alone, her sly, sprightly " Landlady of the Inn," so also in the tragic repertory of Sarah Bernhardt, in the midst of rôles with poison and daggers, we find the worldly little " Froufrou," the type of a giddy woman of society, encouraging men to pay court to her, playing with fire and never foreseeing what the consequences of it will be. The consequence is a wonderful scene between two sisters, a quarrel in which the little giddy creature unexpectedly opens out the very depths of her denuded soul. I remember in this scene—why all must remember it who have seen her —the trembling angry hands of little Froufrou in which a lace handkerchief is torn to shreds.

Her explosions of passion were the highest degree of art. She never made the impression at the culminating point of being over-strained, as if she could go no farther; on the

[1] " Make her blue eyes."

contrary she left the impression of having the power for more. A characteristic trait of the French is the understanding of how to husband their resources. They do not produce their effects by reaching the last limit of their strength, but in the beginning they lessen, weaken, lower their powers below the normal degree; what they call "reculer pour mieux sauter." None, even among the French, attained such a high degree of art in this as the great Sarah has done. How well she knew how to crouch in order to spring, to collect her strength, for throwing herself on her victim; how well she knew how to aim, to crawl up, in order to burst forth. The same can be said of her facial expression; what perfect knowledge she had of how to rise from a scarcely perceptible engendering of an idea to the point when it reaches its highest sway. It is also in *Tosca*, when exhausted, enfeebled, obliged to succumb to old Scarpia, to buy freedom for her lover at the price of her own honour, she is standing half stupefied near the table on which the old man had left his unfinished supper. He had gone to the writing table to write the permission to go. She is standing near the dinner-table with her right hand resting on the table cloth. Suddenly those eyes that are looking in bewilderment around become fixed—they have seen something: on the table, almost touching her hand, there lies a kitchen knife. How her expression changes, how that look seems to grow inwardly; how that look that was blunt seems to grow sharp, sharper than the knife; how, from having noticed, it changes to seeing, from seeing to understanding, from understanding to deciding, and lastly from deciding to a decision! And how all this fades away when she seizes the knife and hides it behind her back. Calmly she waits for Scarpia to approach her with the paper. . . . With the spring of a tigress she brandishes the knife. . . . He falls down stabbed. . . . It is here that she growls over him her celebrated "Meurs!" and then the Christian dread of the crime she has committed is aroused in her. She takes a crucifix from the wall and lays it on the breast of the corpse that is lying on the floor; she takes two lighted candles from the chest of drawers and carries them across the stage in her long hanging arms, looking like a priestess in some solemn procession, and having placed the candlesticks at each side of the dead man's head, and without taking her eyes off him, she slowly goes to the door, sets it ajar and, like a sheet of paper, she slips through the chink.

I have described this wonderful scene, but my object was to draw attention to the manner in which the expression of her eyes was developed; how here, in order to attain the highest point of horror, the eyes are first brought to a condition of indifference. This dynamism is the most important feature of dramatic art; it is the pledge of its resemblance with life; without it the art is dead. Because every movement in nature is of a developing character, always requiring its preparation; and the stronger the movement is so also must the preparation be proportionally strong. We can say in a word that the deeper the wound, the stronger the blow must be. The same can be applied to the effects of the voice—the whisper in which you feel the preparation of the subsequent screams; hissing that ripens into future growls.

Is it clear what I mean by the *technique* of the art? I mean all that thorough knowledge that lies beneath the temperament; that fixed, unvaried groundwork on which capricious inspiration works. The French actor Samson said, "Tout en livrant votre cœur, gardez votre esprit."[1] The eternal dispute is—technique or feeling—intellect or soul? But why always *or*; why not both, this *and* that.

[1] "Give away your heart, but keep your wits."

I think it is only a senseless spectator who thinks that on the stage all is feeling; I think that only an actor without talent thinks that he can act solely by feeling. A sensible spectator suffers at the absence of intellect, at the absence of consciousness in acting; and a talented actor finds the greatest degree of delight in the union of the most burning enthusiasm with cold, restrained reason. A friend of Shalyapin's, after the death scene in *Boris Godunov* rushed into his dressing room. " Is it possible that even to-day you will tell me that you did not live the part, that you did not feel that you were Boris ! " " I ? I was wondering all the time if the folds of my dressing-gown were all right. I was angry with one of the choristers for coming too far forward." Thus people who are far from the realities of the art of the theatre ascribe to actors the feelings of " living " the part they act, while actors only laugh at it. I was told by a gentleman, who, in his younger years, had been intimate with the celebrated Rachel: One night he stood in the wings palpitating with ecstasy as he watched her inspired acting. Suddenly, at the moment of the greatest intenseness, when the whole audience sat spellbound and she herself seemed to be raised to another sphere, out of that very other sphere a small ball of crushed paper was thrown into his face. The more exceptional the actor's talent, the greater his mental clearness will be; the more he affects his audience, the less he himself is affected; his personal condition will not pass over the footlights; to experience does not mean to cause others to experience; no skill is necessary to experience, whereas to make others experience requires mastership. No amount of feeling will inspire an actor with all the beauty and the whole diapason of the *intonation* which is at his command if he has not *cultivated* his voice technically; and no feelings will give the *pauses*, that admirable effect that is so little employed with us ; feelings will never produce it, becaust the pause, as a means of suspension, is a produce of the *intellect*. Alas ! all this is so little known with us, it is not even suspected. Whole generations have been instructed " to feel and then all will turn out well!" Will it though ? " Of course, only feel." How simple. Who does not feel ? Who will say that he does not know how to feel ? Who then is not an actor ? Everybody can be an actor. I believe at the present moment there are tens of thousands in Moscow alone who can be considered as studying the art of acting. But when I look at this influx, I believe more than ever before that art is only for the chosen ; in spite of all the preaching about " collective creative power " I am convinced more than ever before that out of a thousand minuses you cannot produce one plus ; I believe more than ever before in the strength of personality; I believe that the value does not consist of the number of people but in the quality of the man. What is art, if not the study of these qualities, and the power to reproduce their diversities.

Human diversities were better reproduced by Sarah Bernhardt than by Duse. A characteristic trait of the latter was that she went beyond the bounds of the type she was representing—she led you to the arena of general humanity ; she acted woman in general. Sarah Bernhardt acted a special woman : the epoch, nationality, province, class. She kept firmly, tenaciously to the text, not only to the words but to the type.

I shall say no more of Sarah Bernhardt. She is too well known ; there are too many portraits of her, and they have flown all over the world. In life, that is not on the stage, I saw her only once. She was affected, she was all artificial. Who does not know her ? A red tuft of hair in front, a red tuft of hair behind, unnaturally red lips,

SARAH BERNHARDT

a powdered face, everything made up, like a mask; a wonderfully supple figure, dressed as nobody else; in everything she was original, she herself was Sarah, and everything on her, or around her told of Sarah. She not only created rôles, she created herself, her style, her silhouette, her type, that had not existed before, and which was multiplied in numberless imitations. There is not a single theatrical name that has been so much hawked about and advertised as hers; scents, soap, gloves, powder—" Sarah Bernhardt." Not always is proud fame satisfied with solitude, which becomes her so well under her wreath of laurels, often her fidgety little sister " Popularity," and her half-respectable hanger-on " Puff," bustle and fuss around her.

After speaking about Sarah Bernhardt I promised to say a few words about Réjane. I leave the one with a light heart, and I approach the other with a joyful heart. This contradicts what I said when I passed on from Duse to Sarah. Don't cavil; inconsistency is one of the charms of life; it is one of the forms of variety. But it does not mean that I am commencing this new portrait without anxiety. Réjane is difficult to describe, more difficult than the previous two; nevertheless I want to place her beside them, I would like to place her above them. It is difficult to describe Réjane, first because she herself is less known, and her repertory is also less known. I place her *between* those two great actresses because she has so much both of the one and the other; she has much of Duse's soul and much of Sarah's technique. I place her *higher* than them for her art in fusing them together. The impression she leaves of wholeness, roundness, completeness in herself, places her higher than anything I have seen on the dramatic stage.

If Duse acted woman in general, if Sarah Bernhardt

acted diverse women, Réjane acted the Parisian woman. She concentrated her powers on them, and the authors, the producers of parts, provided her with them. Beginning with the semi-historical *Mme. Sans-Gêne,* continuing with the worldly, frivolous *Ma Cousine* and the touching, deeply sensitive cocotte *Zaza,* to the bitter tears of Germinie Lacerteu—they are all Parisians. It is not surprising that Henri Becque wrote for her that amazing play *La Parisienne.* The curtain rises, Réjane comes quickly in at the centre door, in a hat and cloak, she is followed by an indignant man. " Where are you coming from ? Why are you hiding ? Where have you been ? " and so on. In the angry interchange of questions and answers suddenly there is a cold break. " Silence " ; at that moment footsteps are heard—" Mon mari." The husband enters ; it is only thus that we learn that the first one is not her husband, but another. The whole play is nothing but a woman's expedients. I remember another scene. A young man she was leading by the nose falls upon her with reproaches ; to appreciate it one must have seen with what a naïve, perplexed expression she receives him ; his reproaches gradually grow weaker ; as he retreats she does not exactly turn the attack upon him but seems gently to jog him on ; he can hardly defend himself ; his reproaches change into excuses and she from the accused becomes the forgiver. He falls at her feet in tears and hides his head in the folds of her dress ; she strokes his hair. François Coppér has a small poem in which the two last lines give a picture of a similar scene :

"Et, vil esclave heureux de reprendre ses fers,
J'ai demandé pardon des maux que j'ai soufferts."[1]

She had always brilliancy and always humour. But under all this lightness, sometimes the chord of suffering

[1] " An abject slave rejoiced to wear his chains,
I asked for pardon, for the suffered pains."

would quiver and sound! Sliding down the dangerous incline of impropriety, approaching the very brink of the abyss of moral ruin, how well she knew how to restrain herself suddenly and stop in the bright rays of the sanctities of general humanity! How the motherly feelings were roused in the cocotte! How filial affection awoke in the prostitute!

Always laughing and jesting, there were moments when she seemed to lead you into a temple; the smiling mouth closed, a finger seemed to be raised to the lips, only a breath passed over the audience, laughter died away, the soul unfolded itself, and people felt their human closeness and identity when facing the highest values of the soul. And who was it who gave all this? A little insignificant woman. Not pretty, with a turned-up nose, with a flat, rather high forehead, with rather prominent hazel eyes—but what power she had over her audience! She was a combination of feeling, technique, and intellect; such a delicate, supple intellect, that there was not a single moment in her acting that was not an intellectual pleasure for the audience. Even when she was representing something stupid, and I can say that here more than anywhere else she showed her intellect; all the time that you were laughing at this stupidity, you admired her cleverness. For instance, in *Mme. Sans-Gêne*, when she appears dressed in a riding-habit that had been brought to her, she gets entangled in the long skirt, and trips; you never once laughed at the awkwardness of the person she represented, but all the time you laughed at her own ready wit; all your connexions with the person represented were tempered by your admiration of her art. In her acting the " what " became quite a secondary matter, all the interest was concentrated in the " how," and even this " how " became the real matter of art. In each of her creations you felt *her* as the one who set in motion the mechanism concealed within the marionettes. It is very difficult to render the delicacy of this duality—which really was, in her, unity. In her feeling and technique were so closely united that they could never be separated. She died not so long ago, but she could have lived to extreme old age, and would never have produced that feeling of a departed aroma, as Sarah Bernhardt did; her nature was too much of one piece to suffer such a decomposition. The aroma of her personality cannot be transmitted; I talk of her, naturally, as she was on the stage. It is impossible to explain her slyness, the sharpness of the intonations of her queries, the charm of her smile. A smile is expressive of her whole personality; her name itself is a smile; the playbills containing her name pasted on the Parisian advertising columns brightened the whole street with a smile. The name of Réjane sounded joyful, it exhaled health.

If she remains less in the memory of posterity than many others, the reason is to be found in her repertory; she acted for her contemporaries in plays about their times and written for her; she never touched the great repertory that deals with general humanity, she passed by the great rôles of the classical theatre, that theatre which speaks from the depths of ages and does not fear time. The art of the theatre is so unseizable, so transient! What remains of an actor when he is dead? His image flickers in the memory of those who had seen him; and then? The image of him who has acted the great universal image is easier remembered by posterity than the image of her who took with her to the grave that which she acted.

I only met her once—I wanted to say off the stage, but it really was on the stage. She gave two performances in the Petersburg Alexandra Theatre during the first year of my directorship. I went to one of them; she acted *Zaza*. Before the commencement of the play I went on the stage to welcome her. She was already lying on a settee from which she does not rise during the whole of the first act. Stretching out her hand to me she apologized for not rising, in the words of her part: " Je suis si lasse—je ni me lèverais pas même pour un prince." [1] The whole act she remains lying, still it is so lively, so diversified, that it is only when her maid announces that the hairdresser has come, when she stretches and says, " Décidément il faut que je me lève " [2] and, rising reluctantly, goes to her toilet table, and the curtain falls, only then you realize that the whole of that act she had been lying on the settee. It is one of the most charming inventions of the French stage.

Such was this unforgettable actress. This was real art —authentic laurels. She tore off the very tip of the hard shining leaf. Not to any tombstone do the dark green leaves adhere more caressingly than to the one on which is engraved the laughing name of Réjane.

I have purposely joined these three great names together in one chapter. By comparing them I think it clearly appears what qualities are necessary for a great actress, the presence of *personality* and *mastery of the art.*

[1] " I am so weary—I will not rise even to welcome a prince."
[2] " I suppose I must get up."

MUSIC IN MY CHILDHOOD AND YOUTH

INTEREST in music was early aroused in me. Musical traditions dwelt in our family. My maternal grandfather, Prince Gregory Wolkonsky, belonged to those circles of the Petersburg fashionable world who were the only supporters of music in Russia in the first half of the century. If Madame de Staël could say, "En Russie quelques gentilshommes s'occupent de littérature," the same might be said of music.

My grandfather was a distinguished singer, owing to his wonderful bass voice he had received the nickname of "Le petit Lablache" (Lablache was at that time the celebrated bass of the Italian opera). My grandfather's father, Prince Peter Wolkonsky, was Minister of the Court of Nicholas I. My grandmother was sitting one night in the Minister's box with her father-in-law, when she suddenly saw her husband on the stage among the choristers.

In connexion with this I remember my mother used to tell us that when they lived in Rome Pope Pius IX was very amiable to her father and that his was the only house where the papal choir ever sang; the celebrated castrato, Mustapha, also sang at his house, and the famous tenor, Rubini, was quite intimate there. My grandmother said that once when he was singing in Petersburg she was listening to him from the Minister's box and was so enraptured that she took a flower from her bodice and threw it to him on the stage. Her father-in-law was very much displeased: "To-day it is a flower—and to-morrow

PRINCESS MARIE WOLKONSKY (*née* BENKENDORF)

somebody will be dissatisfied and will throw a potato." It was thus that even laurels were subject to the censor in those days. Rubini's voice must have been something quite extraordinary. Having taken up her residence in Rome my grandmother had not heard him for many years. One evening they were sitting in their drawing-room, when suddenly in the next room some accords were struck on the piano and a male voice took several notes. Her work fell from my grandmother's hands, and she exclaimed "Rubini." Indeed, it was he who had just arrived, and without taking off his travelling coat had sat down to the piano. I had in Pavlovka an engraving of him with a dedication to my grandfather in his own handwriting.

My maternal grandmother, Princess Marie Wolkonsky, née Countess Benkendorf, was a pupil of Henselt's. I had a little book bound in white satin, in which Henselt had written and dedicated to her his "Romance in si bémol mineur." There is also an étude of Anton Rubinstein's dedicated to her; it is an early, almost childish work, and very insignificant; I think it is called "Undine." My grandmother played beautifully, but she had no strength in her hands and her chest was weak. It is through her I became acquainted with Chopin, Henselt, and some things of Bach's. She played not only the *great* old masters but the *forgotten* old masters: Thalberg, Field, Kalkbrenner, Heller and Hiller. In beautiful Fall, near Reval, on the shores of the sea, she used to sit down to the piano of an evening. To the accompaniment of her slender fingers, how many flaming sunsets burnt and sank into the bosom of the sea; how many twilights grew dim in the lofty drawing-room where there was a scent of flowers and carved wood.

My father possessed a very fine tenor voice and had studied much in his youth, quite exceptionally much for an amateur. He sang with all the Italian tricks of a real Italian singer. My sister sang charmingly too; she had a fine, sonorous, warm soprano voice. In this way, I acquired early in my childhood a certain knowledge of pianoforte and vocal music and the routine of an accompanist, which afterwards enabled me to approach more closely the art of many celebrated singers, both male and female. I will say a few words about those people who have played a part in my musical education.

I was six years old when I was brought up to a good-looking old lady in my mother's drawing-room; she wore a grey dress and a grey pelerin, trimmed with a fringe made of little balls. She was called Madame Kukolnik. She was the first music teacher whom my brother and I had. She was not exacting, and spoiled us with sweets. After that we had a certain Mademoiselle Roller, a strange sort of girl; I remember she wore forget-me-nots in her hat and round her neck. Of these lessons I only remember that she said, "You are again playing by heart." These two ladies did not get me on very far. Bernard's collection, "L'Enfant-Pianiste," on the title page of which there is a cupid swinging on the letter "L," was the only height I was able to attain. Soon it was found that I had no aptitude for music, but somehow I began to play duets with my mother, and then it was found that I was not at all dull, but, on the contrary, that I understood and loved music. I soon began to read music very well, but I did not understand to learn pieces. When I was about seventeen there began to appear what I may call "the velleities of the composer." It was decided at home that this must not be neglected, and Karl Wurm was engaged to give me lessons. Oh, how important the first teacher is! and what a bad one Wurm was! He did not at all understand to show me how to learn; he did not know how to interest me in technique. He did not even show me the principle of changing the accentuation, while learning a piece. And what a repertory! Wollenhauph, Spindler, Gurlith, Behr. I did not learn anything, I did not acquire anything, neither judgment nor confidence, with the exception of the conviction that I could never become a pianist. I gave up studying and became the most hopeless type of musical dilettante. It was only many years later, one autumn, when I was staying in the country, that I decided to seriously study a piece, it was Rachmaninov's " Elegie." I began to learn it, and suddenly I understood *how* one ought to learn, and all the *delight* of surmounting technical difficulties. After this, when I returned to Petersburg, I had several conversations at the piano with our excellent musician, pianist, composer, and charming man, Felix Blumenfeld. It is to him I owe that thorough knowledge that I applied to my subsequent studies. I obtained results—I played Chopin's " Études," but I, that is to say, my fingers, were past forty. I just succeeded in perfecting myself sufficiently far to be convinced that I might have become, what I never shall be, a good pianist. And now in the summer of A.D. 1921, having been cast out of the room in which there is a piano, I have not played on one for nearly five years. I am told that I, as a " professor," have a right to a piano and also to two rooms, but I cannot count that as a right after which one has to hunt. At the present time, the only unquestionable *right* that I possess in Soviet Russia is to my own thoughts.

With regard to the theory of music this is what occurred. When about eighteen I began to study under Professor Sachetti, a learned musician, a mine of knowledge, but not a source, his own thought was smothered under a weight of quotation. A charming man, but no pedagogue. His lessons gave me no more than what I had attained by myself. If nothing came out of my compositions I am myself in fault. I hated counterpoint, and without it nothing serious can be attained in music. At one time I sent some of my compositions, chiefly songs, to be looked through by Peter Tchaikovsky, with whom I was not personally acquainted. I received from him an interesting answer, giving his opinion, which was attentive, minute, and severe. The letter ended in this way : " If you have the time, study counterpoint and devote yourself to music, you have the qualities of a serious composer, you have harmonious imaginativeness and even a melodious inventiveness, though in a rudimentary state." Tchaikovsky's interesting letter is lost, with everything else that belonged to me. But I did not take this course, perhaps because my criticism was stronger than my capacity. I did not approve of myself ; or perhaps it was because I felt that it was not in music that I would find myself, but somewhere else where my musical " ego " would form an integral part. But this is enough about myself ; let us talk about those I heard.

At the dawn of my musical youth I met Stanislav Exner. He was a charming man and an enchanting pianist. He was a pupil of Reincke's. Through him I got to know the whole of Chopin, all Schumann, much of Beethoven and much of Bach. He had an enormous repertory, and a splendid memory, and the beauty of his touch was so original that it was possible to recognize his playing anywhere, in the way my grandmother recognized Rubini's voice. He was a real romantic, and in this respect a true disciple of his teacher, he poeticized everything that he touched. I shall never forget his rendering of Schumann's symphonic études or of Bach's celebrated *A-mol fugue* in Liszt's arrangement with the octaves in the bass. How differently the same thing can be played ; I do not mean the degree of perfection, but I mean the difference of colouring in the same degree of perfection. I heard that same A-mol fugue of Bach's played by Brassin; this was a geometrical construction; with Exner it was a poetic breath; but both the one and the other were splendid renderings.

Afterwards Exner became the director of the Saratov music school; under his direction this institution was renamed a Conservatoire. The house was built with the assistance of my brother Peter; his portrait hung in the hall. Exner's cultural influence was felt in the whole Volga district. I stayed with him twice, and he visited me in Pavlovka. During the War he went to the western front and served in the hospital detachment under my brother's direction. In the winter of 1918 somebody brought me a letter from him dated Saratov; he had returned to his Conservatoire and was a modest teacher in the institution he had created. Afterwards I began to dislike the pianoforte, especially in concerts; I thought it dull and I found it sounded woodeny, especially after the sounds of a string and wind orchestra. I of course make an exception for Anton Rubinstein, whom I often had the good fortune to hear not only in concerts but in drawing-rooms.

For many years the drawing-room of Madame Julie Abaza was the musical centre of Petersburg. Julie Abaza was a personality who will not be repeated—everything very original is never repeated. By origin she was German —her family name was Stube—she came to Russia as reader to the Grand Duchess Helena. The magnificent Michael Palace, the residence of the Grand Duchess, and which afterwards was converted into the Museum Alexander III, became the centre of all that was spiritually alive. One of her contemporaries says of the Grand Duchess that "She had something elevating about her." Poets, musicians, all that were active during the time of the emancipation of the peasants, passed through the apartments of the Michael Palace, all breathed the invigorating air that surrounded this remarkable woman. I remember the Grand Duchess Helena. I saw her once, when I was twelve years old. My mother had taken me with her to the Uffizzi Gallery in Florence. In the very heart of this wonderful gallery, in the round hall of the " Tribuna," we saw the Grand Duchess, with her maid of honour the celebrated Edith von Raden. I do not know about what the ladies talked, I only remember that the old lady patted my cheek with her delicate hand. It was there, in Florence, that she gave my mother her portrait. This portrait, the work of the photographer Shembosha, always hung in my mother's bedroom at Pavlovka, and whenever I looked at it I remembered the octagon hall of the Tribuna, Raphael's " Madonna " with the goldfinch, his " Julius II," Titian's " Venus," and Julio Romano's " John the Baptist," and I felt the unbroken silence that reigns under the glass dome, and I seemed conscious of the caressing touch of a hand coming from a distance.

Julie Stube brought to the Michael Palace her wonderful beauty, and her wonderful voice. At that time Anton Rubinstein and the Grand Duchess were meditating the establishment of the Conservatoire and the Russian Musical Society. Julie Stube soon acquired the reputation of a musical authority. Afterwards she married Abaza, who was at one time Minister of Finance. His house became the centre of the musical world. When I became acquainted with Madame Abaza she was already an old woman. She was tall, with a heavy but soft gait, in a white wig and white cap which blended together in a somewhat extensive construction. Her black dress was also extensive, and from time to time, while listening to music, she opened an extensive fan behind which her whole face disappeared; behind the fan something hasty and noisy took place, and a minute later the fan lay again folded together on her knee. She was convinced that in the whole world there was only one person who knew that she took snuff and that that person was herself. Alas! one day the Grand Duchess Helena's daughter, the Grand Duchess Catherine, presented her with a snuff-box. She did not give up her habit—perhaps she increased the size of her fan.

Anton Rubinstein was an intimate in Madame Abaza's salon. I have heard that in her youth she had been enamoured, not only with his music. In any case their friendship was quite touching. He played in her house often and with pleasure. With a wave of her lorgnette, she caused silence to reign to the very farthest corners of the large hall, and of the adjoining rooms. Woe to him who coughed or sneezed—it was a disgrace that could never be washed out. There was only one man, who could not get accustomed to this, who would stumble into the room with a tray at the most solemn passage of Chopin's nocturne, then Madame Abaza'a voice would be heard " Efim, Efim, how many times I have told you: No tea when there's music."

The acme of perfection was Rubinstein. His mastery over the keyboard was quite special, and I would have recognised his touch years after. I never heard Liszt but I cannot imagine that he was better. What concerts his were in the Hall of the Nobility! What a space there was with him, between caresses and blows, from whispers to thunder; how well he knew how to modulate his gradations, and what astonishment he caused by the endlessness of these gradations. It appeared that he had attained the extreme limit of the possible—but no, higher and higher rose his power. His audience opened their eyes in amazement, they stretched their necks; a sort of incredulity took possession of them, the whole audience in the hall seemed to grow, to rise from their seats, their eyes were fixed on the movements of his hands and concealed by outward attention a storm brooded that burst into thunders of applause when he became silent. He had a wonderful head, quite a Beethoven-like forehead, with a strongly marked relief; piercing eyes, and their piercingness was increased by his drooping eyelids; he seemed to be gazing from under a curtain; his mouth was large, his lips closely pressed together by the lower jaw, his long hair was thrown back and wilfully bristled up over the left ear, and locks often fell over his forehead in the heat of musical enthusiasm.

Rubinstein was very much prized by the people who knew him best; they prized his straightforwardness, his roughness and abruptness; I did not know him personally, I never approached him at evening parties. I was very young at the time and my timidity did not venture beyond my veneration. But at one of her parties Madame Abaza demanded that I should sit down at the piano after Rubinstein—just imagine after Rubinstein!—and play him some of my compositions. I consider these some of the most terrible moments I have had to live through. Rubinstein gave no opinion; but ordered me to bring him some of my compositions on the following day. He read through my MSS. at his writing-table; made a few remarks, spoke more about art in general, of the service of art and of its difficulties. I felt that something foreign was speaking in him, that he was paying no attention to me or to what I had brought him. Afterwards I heard he had said about me: " He has capacities, but nothing will come of them: he is a Prince." He made no mistake in his prognostications, but I think he made a mistake in the cause. After I had worked a little I did not apply to him, but I sent my productions to Tchaikovsky, whose opinion I have mentioned above.

I never heard Anton Rubinstein's brother Nicholas. Many placed him higher than Anton, and Anton himself used to say " What am I ? Now there's my brother, that's quite a different thing." I never heard him but will relate two curious anecdotes concerning him.

He was a great friend of Prince Michael Obolensky's and his wife's. Obolensky was vice-governor of Tver, and Rubinstein always visited him in passing. The postmaster in Tver was a passionate lover of music and played on the violoncello. He often complained to Princess Obolensky that his work did not permit him to absent himself and go to Moscow—" If I could only hear Rubinstein once in my life ! " One evening the Princess sent to invite him to come in for a cup of tea. He arrived and they introduced him to Nicholas Rubinstein. Rubinstein promised to play. They conversed together.

" I hear you play on the violoncello ? "

" Yes, a little——"

" Then send for your instrument. Let us play together."

The postmaster became terribly excited. He was petrified, he blushed, he stammered. His instrument was sent for. It was brought. The postmaster began to tune it. Rubinstein gave him the *La*. Suddenly all who were in the room sprang up and rushed to the postmaster ; he fell from his chair in a fit. He died that night. This is how Rubinstein's *La* killed the postmaster of Tver.

The second case which is known but to few refers to Nicholas Rubinstein's death. He died abroad ; his body was brought to Moscow. In the same train there was the coffin of some Baroness of Riga. At the frontier the two coffins got mixed, but it was only noticed when they arrived in Moscow. All Moscow was at the station—deputations, wreaths, etc. None of those who knew about it would decide to divulge the secret of the mistake. So the baroness was buried in Moscow with great honours under the gravestone of Nicholas Rubinstein at the same time that his remains are quietly lying in Riga beneath the monument of some Baroness.

It was also in Madame Abaza's drawing-room that I heard many times one of the most extraordinary singers that it has ever been my fate to hear.

I remember the first time I heard the Alexandra Panaeva. It was in the year of the Turkish war, 1877, at a concert for the benefit of the Red Cross given in Prince Beloselsky's beautiful house near the Anichkov bridge. There appeared on the platform not a woman, but a vision : tall, slender, dark, with blue eyes, a small waist and a charming bust. She held herself straight, confident, quite wrapped up in her art, she looked out boldly into the hall, but the audience did not exist for her, she was like Tatiana.

> "Bold glances she cast not around,
> Pretensions to success were none,
> No mincing airs had any found,
> Nor imitative tricks to please ;
> Gentle and simple she stood there,
> Amid them all, at perfect ease."

In the first division she sang the soprano part out of Rossini's *Stabat Mater*, in the second Mignon's air from Thomas' opera. Besides irreproachable technique, she had two qualities which were inherent in her, and for which she cannot be forgotten : a sort of veil in which she seemed to wrap up her pianissimo, and quite exceptional fire. This reminds me of a story she told of a concert she had given in Perm, when the audience surrounded her exclaiming " What a voice ! " One gentleman said " Yes, a voice, a fine voice ! It's not the voice though that is important, you have ' sacrifice,' that's what is of value." Yes, she had " sacrifice " that is " feu sacré."—the holy fire ; she seemed to shoot flames at you when she sang. And all, each note, each word, every letter that she pronounced, each pause and the fire itself obeyed her will; all was in the fire of triumphant consciousness. Panaeva is indissolubly connected with Tchaikovsky. He wrote for her. She was the first to sing his things from his manuscript. In the admirable portrait of her painted by Makovsky—one of the few good works produced by that very commonplace painter—she is represented with notes in her hand, and on their cover is the name of Tchaikovsky. Nobody could sing his songs as she did. " Why," " A Terrible Moment," " Both Painful and Sweet," " Not a Word, O my friend "—in these songs nobody else could produce such a blending of the musical sounds, with the meaning of the words. She was a pupil of the celebrated singer Paulina Viardot, who was Turgénev's friend. I saw the old lady in Paris in 1889. With what excitement she listened to the details I gave her of the successes of her favourite pupil! Yes it was a success. Her course through life was surrounded by adoration, flowers lay at her feet and when she sang—

> "Sun come out! I'll come out too,
> Sun look out! I'll look at you.
> At his glance the flowers dry,
> When I look all hearts will die."

these words sounded like a real, a true challenge of the luminary of day.

Alas! no happiness is lasting. She was the daughter of a very rich man, who did not wish that she should go on the stage. Years passed, and the time went on in a wearisome struggle. At last her father lost all his fortune and he was obliged to consent. I do not remember in what opera she made her debut, I was not in Petersburg at the time, but all saw that it was too late—it was not the same Panaeva. Her public career finished before it was hardly begun. No sunset had ever been so sad, because it had never been so sudden. She married a man much younger than herself. He was in some office and she gave singing lessons. They had a son and a daughter; her son was killed in the War in the first battle against the Germans. Yes, no sunset had ever been so sad, no withering was so sorrowful, and I think fate had never used its rights so mercilessly to cast down the creature it had raised up as in this case. But such is the power of *art*—when we say " Panaeva," we do not see before us a broken woman, a faded flower, a disconsolate mother, but we see the brilliant apparition, the rare artiste, a never-to-be-repeated phenomenon. And when I saw her for the last time in the streets at a distance, in a long black veil—such is the strength of *life*—I forgot the vision of former days, I lost the traces of former delight, and I bowed before one of those who are so numerous on the earth.

Panaeva is one of the four singers that I single out from the number of excellent singers I have heard, as the most precious units. As second I may name Alice Barbi. She had also fire, but an inner fire that was suppressed. Alice Barbi was concentrated, meditative on the concert hall platform. She sang in Italian and in German, she had an enormous repertory, but the real spiritual air of her musical soul was found in the old Italian masters : Monteverde, Caldara, Durante, Porpora, Marcello, and others. In this wonderful old music, with its sinuosities in which caresses and passion flow side by side, like ivy and flowers wind round the severe lines of old architecture, was the channel through which Alice Barbi was able to display the fire of her hot Italian blood and the severity of classical form of the Latin races. The first time she appeared in Petersburg was together with the pianist Cesi. It is strange he played very much, his programme was large and diversified, but if I were asked what Cesi had played I would answer—Scarlatti; he was so identified with that ancient Italian music which is all concentrated in the name of this old Neapolitan. Afterwards, Alice Barbi gave her own concerts; she added to the old Italian music much of Schubert and Brahms. She had not the brilliancy that shone in Panaeva, but she had much inner light which transfigured her; she had a wonderful gift of reincarnation; she was always changing, not only in her method of singing and pronunciation, but in her whole person, in her face, and her mood seemed to change according to what she was singing.

The third of my favourite four is Felia Litvinne. Brunehilde, Isolde! She is one of the greatest singers that has ever existed. The roundness, power and smoothness of this voice can be compared with none other. Her mastery over it and her sureness were such that it always appeared to me that if everybody, who was occupied with any sort of business—ministers, directors of factories, artisans—was each in his own sphere as sure as she was in hers, the world would be an earthly paradise. She deprived you of all uneasiness; in art this is what absence of danger is in life. I was never so charmed with her mastery as one night when she was singing Serov's *Judith*. I knew that she was ill, that she had a temperature of 100 degrees. I saw very well how difficult it was for her to take the high " *do* " in the last act, but she took it; I was waiting for it, I felt it approaching, but even here I felt no doubt, or uneasiness. It was wonderful with what a feeling of certainty she inspired you.

Litvinne was specially a singer for Wagner's music. She was of huge dimensions, excessively fat, but she knew very well how to conceal her stoutness; she did not fall into the error of most fat women and lace tightly, she draped herself. Her movements were smooth and majestic, she raised her long hand magnificently on her outstretched arm and drooping wrist; it was a splendid effect in the choruses, when they rose to the final crescendo, and with this increase in the volume of sound her wrist gradually stretched out, the fingers stiffened and assumed the form of a cupola. This trick of hers especially remains in the memory in the death scene of Isolde; to the end her voice never seemed to fail. With regard to this part I remember a story she told me. My predecessor Vsevolzhsky could not bear Wagner. Once Litvinne was entreating him to produce *Tristan* and he always turned it down.

" Mais, pensez donc, M. le Directeur, cette mort magnifique." [1]

" Oui, mais quelle vie ennuyeuse ! " [2]

He was very witty and sarcastic. The singer Medea Figner was singing the part of Mimi in *La Bohème*. She was very stout and Mimi, as all know, dies of consumption; somebody praised the way Medea executed the part. " Oui," answered Vsevolzhsky, " mais elle n'a pas le phtysique de l'emploi." [3]

Once Felia Litvinne put me into a very awkward position; she asked to be allowed to sing the part of Margareta; I opened my eyes.

" Yes, I know, you are troubled by my corpulent figure."

" I am even afraid."

She spread before me a whole series of reasons.

" I assure you Margareta need not be a slim little girl. I spoke to Gounod on the subject and he told me he represents her to himself as "une Flamande plantureux," a plump Fleming.

[1] "But, Mr. Director, think of that splendid death."

[2] "Yes, but what a tiresome life."

[3] "Yes, but she has not the phthisis of the part."

This irruption of Rubens into what I had always imagined as Albrecht Dürer frightened me; I had recourse to my last argument.

"But you sing Margareta in French, I can't permit such a Babel."

"I undertake to learn the part in Russian."

" But the opera is to be given next week."

" Three days are enough for me."

There were no other reasons for not agreeing. She sang the part, and I must say that I never have heard the last trio sound as it did when she sang in it. I must also note her quite exceptional pronunciation; I have never heard such clearness in the consonants.

I knew Felia Litvinne very well, I was often at her house, both in Petersburg and Paris; I have often accompanied her when she sang Schumann, Schubert, and Glück. She sang Glück charmingly; in Paris I saw her twice in *Alceste*. I shall never forget her gesture in the last act when she returns home and stretches out her arms to her children, when she did it the ends of her muslin veil spread out beautifully. . . . How interesting and how important in the theatrical art are the participation of inanimate accessories in spiritual manifestations. What affliction there is in the falling down of the folds of a veil, and what joy, how much agitation, there is in one that is raised.

The last time that I saw Litvinne was in Paris; I lunched at her house with the pianist Dumeny and Saint-Saëns. Litvinne sang the air of " Dalila " accompanied by the composer, and Dumeny played Bach's violin adagio, arranged by Saint-Saëns.

Now I must speak of the fourth. This is the most difficult; she is so original and I only heard her once. This fourth is the wife of the celebrated tenor Jean de Reszke; she is a Frenchwoman and her maiden name was

L<small>R</small>

Mlle. de Mailly; she was of the very highest circles of French society. She never sings anywhere but at home. I was once invited to an evening party at their house. She is very beautiful, tall and fair, with hair that is prettily raised over the temples. She stood up near the piano with her back turned to the accompanist facing us. There were a few accords and then I heard:

"Stell auf den Tisch die duftenden Reseden,"

the well-known song by Lassen with the beautiful refrain at the end of each verse: " Wie einst im Mai." The first line of the poem, the first phrase of the song, opened a new world for me, and I felt that I had before me a phenomenon of quite special artistic rarity. Look at the phonetic sounds in this first line; look at the consonants; I do not reckon such flowing sounds as " N " and " R," but without counting them among the twenty consonants there are five " D's " and three " T's." Have you ever thought of the mechanism of these two sounds, of how they are pronounced, of the phonetic charm which is produced by their correct pronunciation, and, lastly, of the psychological meaning that is given to a word by their proper pronunciation? " D " and " T " are produced by pressing the tongue to the palate, but the sound is produced not at the moment of pressure but of withdrawal; that is why a real good " T " is always produced after a slight delay. Test it on yourself; see how it will sound if you say " True love can be trusted." This is what I felt in Mme. de Reszke's singing.

The first words made me feel the perfection of the finish of which she was capable, and after the first notes the depth of the feeling that agitated her. It is strange that I cannot remember what she sang after this first piece; I remember that she sang in German, in French, and in Italian, but I am unable to say what the songs were. In my whole life I had never had a similar experience. I listened unconsciously, that is of course the reason why I have forgotten what she sang. It was such spiritual caresses that one might have forgotten all in the world, not only the names of songs. When she finished you were afraid to move, and thus destroy the atmosphere she had created. She sang much, and equally well in all languages, and at last she sang without accompaniment some Breton shepherd songs in the Breton dialect. What can I say more about her? I thought I would be unable to say anything, the feelings she had aroused in me were so intangible. I am glad I only heard her once; a second time would not have been the same, it would have been deprived of all the astonishment caused by novelty. Everything on the earth can be repeated, the first time is never repeated, it will already be the second. I remember when she had quite finished I went into another room because it was unseemly to remain with other people. Yes, I have forgotten what she sang, but I shall never forget her, in a white lace dress leaning against the piano tired, and singing as from a distance those Breton shepherd songs—passionless from a general point of view of our personal standard, but how deeply and passionately these sounds told of the ages old virginity of the meadows, fields, and the sea that does not know the contact of the towns. I see her in her white lace dress more rare even than the rare lilac orchid that was fading on her bosom.

These are the four singers who have produced the greatest impression on me. And I have heard many—innumerable, even those I have accompanied are countless. Once fate cast me on the platform of the Hall of the Nobility in St. Petersburg. At that time Sibyl Sanderson was singing in the Marie Theatre. I was to accompany her at a party given by the Grand Duchess Vladimir, and we were going through our programme in her rooms in the Hotel de France. Suddenly a deputation of students was announced ; they entered and requested her to sing at their concert that was to take place the same evening. She could not agree without the director's permission ; she asked me to help her in this matter. I drove off to find Vsevolzhsky and returned with his permission. The students were about to depart. " Et est-ce qu'il y a quelqu'un pour m'accompagner ? "[1] A student thought she wanted someone to take her to the hall and asked at what time he should come for her. It was explained to him that it was not a question of an escort but of an accompanist. The students had not arranged for one. There was a moment of perplexity and then I offered my services. Thus it happened that in the evening, on the platform of the Hall of the Nobility, I accompanied the waltz out of *Romeo and Juliet* before a crowded hall. I found in the hall that very remarkable violoncellist Bzull, who was well known to me, and who at the time was just beginning to become famous, but he died too soon. With him we executed as a trio Massenet's " Elegy."

And now I will relate what appears to me like a fairy tale or a waking dream. During the Japanese war, in order to collect money for the Red Cross, the Grand Duchess Vladimir thought of asking old Madame Patti to come to Russia to give a concert. She came. She was received with honour, and she and her young husband, the Swedish Count, lived in the Grand Duchess's palace. I was not able to go to the concert that was given in the Hall of the Nobility. I heard, that in its way, it was a sort of delirium ; twenty-five, or it may be thirty years had elapsed between this concert and her last appearance in Petersburg ; one

[1] " Is there anybody to accompany me ? "

can imagine what she must have felt when she appeared on the platform, and how she was received. I had not witnessed this, but I knew that I should have an opportunity of hearing her. The Grand Duchess gave a dinner-party in her honour. The Patti I saw at this party was quite another person to the one I had known in the distant days of my youth. I was about seventeen, when she, at the acme of her fame, sang in the Petersburg Italian Opera. When she appeared then in *Dinorah* and the *Barber of Seville* she was an ardent brunette, passionate, sly, and gay. Delving in the depths of my childhood I find another memory. We were taken to the ballet. It was the " Fisherman and the Naiad," and Vasem was dancing. I was for the first time in a theatre. Our governess whispered to me : " Patti is in the next box." I examined her properly and remember her well. I also remember she looked at Vasem's dancing and said to those in her box, " When I get home I shall certainly try to do the same thing." Now I saw before me a little old lady of sixty-two with red hair, very much made up and hung all over with precious stones like an icon. After dinner we went to the concert hall; she promised to sing. And it is here that my fairy tale comes in : I was asked to accompany her. Is it not a fairy tale—to have accompanied Patti ?

She sang four songs. Gounod's romance : " Le Ciel a Visité la Terre," Schubert's Serenade, " Home sweet Home," and Mme. Rothschild's romance, " Si vous n'avez rien à me dire." What can I say of the execution ? First, that I never felt even the shadow of uneasiness or fear, of that fear which ageing, not to say old, artistes inspire us with. The exactness, clearness, certainty, were irreproachable. First of all I admired the wisdom of the woman who did only what, and nothing more than, she could do. She who had formerly shone with all the brilliancy, with all the fire and sparks of colorature, sang her four smooth and soft pieces, she who in the cavatine in the *Barber of Seville* " Una vovo poco fa " in the whirlwind of her colorature fountain took the *Fa* above the line, here never went farther than the *Fa* on the fifth line. The result of this wisdom was that we never for a moment felt the pity old singers inspire, not once did we frown, not once did we smile at mitigating circumstances. What we heard, within its own limits, was enchanting. The caressing pureness and the softness of the notes, the amazing exactitude of the pronunciation. Here there was also something laughable and at the same time touching in her simplicity. I went up to her young husband.

" How wonderfully she sings."

" Yes, is it not wonderful how well my wife's voice has been preserved—at her age too. . . ."

It was not only the voice that astonished, nor her technical mastery over it. In the last song she gave so much dramatic force, such as in those past years we were not wont to hear from the former Patti ; the words

"Si vous n'avez rien à m'apprendre,
Pourquoi me regarder ainsi ? "

she pronounced with so much bitterness of wounded feeling, that this pretty, empty romance changed into a spiritual tragedy. And to all this you must add, that the whole time at each note, to each of your impressions you had to add the consciousness that it was the same Patti who had rattled over the whole world ; whose fame had commenced here, with us, in Russia, and that she had now, at her setting, brought to us here the last brilliancy of her radiance. You will understand the impression and the feelings of this unforgettable evening. With regard to myself I said it was like a fairy tale. Was it not a fairy tale to accompany Adelina Patti ? I call it my thousand and second night.

IMPRESSIONS OF THE OPERA

THE first opera I ever saw was Napravnik's *Nizhegorodtsy: The Citizens of Nizhni Novgorod*. I was taken to the Marie Theatre; this was in the beginning of the seventies.

At that time the Russian opera was neglected. There was enthusiasm for the Italians. The decided step that Alexander III took afterwards—the suppression of the Italian opera—was necessary to raise the Russian opera to that broad path of development on which it attained such a high standard towards the end of the last century. As long as the Italians were in Petersburg, the Russian opera could not develop. First, it was impossible to vie with such names. Stars of the first magnitude: Mario, Rubini, Calzolari, Pasta, Patti, Masini, and Cotogni shone with such brilliancy that they eclipsed all others. But the chief reason lay not so much in the quality of the Italian singers as in the influence they exercised over the public. The generations of our grandfathers and fathers were educated to the worship of single singers. People went to the theatre to hear a single aria. It was the enthusiasm for solos in its most pernicious aspect. When you add to this the character of the music that grew up from the music of Bellini, Verdi, and Meyerbeer, it is natural to understand the weakness of the educational musical influences. The sweetness of the cantilenas, the simplicity of the harmony and the ordinariness of the rhythmic pictures did not conduce to the development of musical judgment. And really what surprised most in that generation is how very unmusical those lovers of music were. They were in the full sense of the words " amateurs," " dilettante," but not musicians.

Under the influence of this enthusiasm for the personal element in opera there arose a sort of musical psychopathy. The gallery shouted, and after the performance rushed to the stage-door. The artistes, greedy for applause, adopted all sorts of tricks and mannerisms of very questionable taste. That most wonderful tenor Masini, whose voice is unforgettable if you have once heard him, emitted some of his notes in such a manner that one felt inclined to box his ears for such want of respect for music, and such an intrusion of his own personality. He was what might be called a " duffer " who had no respect for the general effect, and was only interested in his own personal success. In *Rigoletto* he sang his last air " La donna e molile " superbly. He came on to the stage holding a letter in his hand; he tore it up, and as he sang the notes of the song he threw the pieces into the air. After the third verse he was greeted by a thunder of applause from the whole hall and frantic cries of *bis*! What did he do? He thrust his hand into his pocket, drew out from it another letter, tore it up again, and threw the pieces into the air as before.

With such business and in such an atmosphere was the opera education of that generation. But the greatest mischief was caused by people being torn away from their own musical soil. For them all this Italianism was the height of art, above which they could see nothing. Besides, they could not feel Russian music at all. At that time Rimsky-Korsakov, Borodin, Musorgsky were coming to the fore, and the people could not understand this music. The strangest thing was, not that they did not understand this music, but that it seemed foreign to them; it did not appeal to their nature. What surprised me most was that these people did not feel the Russian element in this music.

Why, Rimsky-Korsakov is the very Russian earth singing to them. And they were deaf to it, some sort of a *Linda de Chamoinix* was nearer to them than *Snegurochka*. It was not only the want of understanding, Rimsky-Korsakov called forth laughter and derision ; I will say nothing of Musorgsky. I was at the first performance of *Boris Godunov* ; the opera failed completely amid hisses and laughter. It was not even saved by such a Boris as Melnikov.

At that time the condition of the opera in Russia (or more correctly speaking of the opera in Petersburg and Moscow) is well described in a little book which is probably unknown to any of this generation : *La musique en Russie*, by C. A. Cui. I think it was published in the 'eighties in Brussels, and it has long been a bibliographical rarity. With the customary sarcasm of that composer's pen he draws the destructive falsehood of the social-musical enthusiasms of that time, and of the humiliating position in which the Russian opera was placed. However, it must be confessed that the standard of the Russian singers was very low. In the long period that elapsed between the time of Glinka and that of Tchaikovsky who can we name ? At that time, when the Italian stage was producing constellations of undiminished brilliancy, only a few names can be mentioned, on the Russian operatic stage ; such as Petrov, the creator of Sussanin ; Lavrovskaia, one of the greatest contraltos, and Melnikov, a rare singer and a rare artiste. All the rest was sad. In the performance of *Nizhegorodtsy* I have mentioned a certain Platonova sang ; she howled. The tenor, Nikolsky, had a magnificent voice, but was fat, awkward, and just like a carter. A little later there was another tenor, Vassiliev, who was like a nasal church chanter. The celebrated bass Stravinsky was singing his last notes at that time ; he had no tone left, nothing but empty flashes like a grinding organ with a hole in it. But the chief defect of the Russian singers was that they were no masters of their art; they had not the elegance which hides the struggles with difficulties; they had not the lightness that Leonardo da Vinci demands of every artist when he says "*Che il lavoro sia immascherata.*"[1] They were heavy, awkward, and so were the Russian operatic performances. It was dull in the Marie Theatre and people did not go there. The work of the renaissance of the Russian opera was a difficult task. It was necessary to improve it, and it was necessary to teach the people to go to a place it had not visited.

By order of Alexander III the Italian opera was abolished and the Great Theatre was given over to the Russian opera; the public had no option. There are certainly not many examples in the history of art where an entirely extraneous and mechanical measure has had such inner influences. Placed in the front rank, deprived of rivals, the Russian opera developed till in a few years it attained a degree of independent value. Alexander III himself did not feel very much the new Russian music. Of the way he regarded Rimsky-Korsakov I have mentioned in another place. Neither Rimsky-Korsakov, Borodin, nor Musorgsky enjoyed any favour in the Imperial family. I remember while I was director of the Imperial Theatres speaking about the first performance of *Sadko*, which was shortly to take place, and the Grand Duke Alexis exclaimed, " Is it possible you can stand that sort of thing ? Is that music ? An eternal dzinn-bum-bum ! " And that is how most of the operatic melomaniacs looked upon it. Russian music was distant, strange, it was necessary to grow up to it. Then there appeared a bridge from the old to the new. Tchaikovsky appeared.

Even he did not conquer at once. He passed first along

[1] " Labour must be masked."

the road of symphonic and chamber music. In Petersburg there always was a great difference in the standard of the " symphonic concert " and " opera " audiences. The first were by nature musicians, for the second music was only a pleasant, light addition to theatrical impressions. They were sincerely touched by some sort of air like Gilda's, and could not feel at all the andante out of the fifth symphony. These people Tchaikovsky conquered with his songs. Fate sent him a beautiful, enchanting interpretress for them. In the full brilliancy of her voice and the bloom of her beauty Alexandra Panaeva opened out quite new and unfathomed depths of the Russian song. *In the Midst of the Noisy Ball; Why? A Terrible Moment; Not a word, O my friend; Both painful and sweet;* is it possible to count them all up ; all with which she agitated, all that she enwrapped in the mist of her pianissimo, that she warmed with the fire of her inspiration. The Petersburg salons were obedient. But he did not conquer the theatre so soon. His first operas were heavy : *Oprejchnik, Mazeppa, The Maid of Orleans* had no success. Tchaikovsky arose and became famous after *Evgeny Onegin*. This small opera, which, according to the ideas of the composer, I think was never intended for a large stage, had, during the time I was director of the theatres, attained its hundredth performance. It was so much liked by the public that one may say it covered the whole of Tchaikovsky, with the exception of *The Queen of Spades* and his ballets, which, according to the ideas of our opera lovers, have only a reflected value. For the great mass of operagoers Tchaikovsky will always remain the composer of *Onegin*.

The whole of Tchaikovsky's works will, of course, fade away into the past ; they will not outlive the century ; he will fade and he will fade quickly ; but quite apart from his value and with the change it will experience with years, Tchaikovsky marks a turning point. Not so much the turning point in the music (this had been accomplished earlier by others, and much more sharply), but the turning point in taste. His educational value was great, he was followed more willingly than those others, who were calling them farther, and who at last, through him, came to their own. The first contact with his music was not without pain. Around delicate, soft and sweet Tchaikovsky many hard battles were fought. One can imagine how the unmusical section of society looked upon him, when such a musician as the singer Melnikov said to me about *Onegin* " Well, and what are we to do with Tchaikovsky ! I love his music ; but how can he treat the singers in the way he does ; he forces the singers to pass from one key to another in their modulations ! " He probably meant what musicians call " enharmonism," but how old all this dissatisfaction with novelties appears in our days. My predecessor as director of the theatres, Vsevolozhsky, who had been brought up on Italian cantilena, said that Tchaikovsky's was not music. However, gradually he too gave in, and what may be called the Tchaikovsky epoch : *Evgeny Onegin, The Queen of Spades, The Swan Lake, The Sleeping Beauty, Nut-cracker* are all closely connected with the name of Vsevolozhsky.

This is now about thirty years ago, but I can well remember that time. I remember the novelty and the freshness which these two operas brought us. I remember their musical value, I remember the impression of the incarnation of the past that they gave. This is their special charm. This charm is found more in *Evgeny Onegin* than in *The Queen of Spades*. For the first time we saw the musical incarnation of the near past, but of a time that was already departed—the times of *Onegin*—in a musical setting. Of course Pushkin's poem had a great part in the success, but Tchaikovsky found the musical form ; this past sang to us, and sounded so naturally that it came nearer to us than Griboiadov's *Gore ot Uma* (The Misfortune of being Clever). It was pervaded with lyricism, which is not found in that celebrated comedy, and it is quite deprived of the reasoning of which there is so much in it. The Russian character that is to be found in *Onegin* is not the elemental Russian that we find in Rimsky-Korsakov and in Barodin. It was the Russian man set in a frame with his ordinary surroundings. Tchaikovsky appeared not as the singer of Russia, but as the singer of Russian life, in its nearest past. He gave us a musical incarnation of Russian country life. For this reason I can understand why the Bolsheviks hate him. They are right from their point of view. I do not wish to say by this that their point of view is right. I don't understand at all how one can hate an artistic representation of any period of the past. However hateful the past may be, its reproduction must be valued if it is good. The most uncultured way of looking at art is this inability of detaching the subject from the form and the want of comprehension, that the form is itself the subject of a work of art. But when bayonets are thrust through a work of Lampi's only because it represents an emperor, it is not surprising that a musical composer should be valued not for how he wrote, but for the subjects he described. For the very reason for which he is hateful to the destroyers of art, he is valued by those who value in art the vessel that preserves the relics of the fading past. Here I am speaking not of Tchaikovsky's musical value as such, I am speaking of his cultural-educational value. For the opera public of which I am writing, Tchaikovsky is entirely incarnated in this side of his creations. Those who adore him know so little of him as a whole, as the communists who are discrowning him. Both the one and the other only know the delicate author of the songs, the singer of personal lyrics, the elegant creator of the *Sleeping Beauty*, the witty toy-maker of the *Nut-cracker*. But neither the one nor the other, neither the worshippers nor the detractors know, or are capable of valuing the deep suffering of the author of the 6th Symphony; and equally foreign to them is the heroic flight of *Francesca di Rimini*, and the tragic sob of *Romeo and Juliet*.[1]

The consolidation of Tchaikovsky in the Marie Theatre coincided with a general improvement in the standard of execution of works there. This was doubtless greatly owing to the tenor Fiegner, who at that time had become very famous. He had formerly been a naval officer, a man with the outward forms of education; he brought to the stage a certain stateliness, a certain decorousness of movement; he brought that which till then had been wanting— elegance. His wife, an Italian singer, Medea Mey, soon learned the Russian language and introduced into the Tchaikovsky repertoire all the finish of Italian art, but also all the mannerisms of Italian routine. The Fiegner couple became the favourites of the public.

Parallel with the brilliant, but light and sparkling successes of Fiegner in the parts of Lensky, Hermann, and some other foreign operas the serious work was proceeded with the staging of the operas of Rimsky-Korsakov and Wagner. Here good work was done by our fine tenor, Ershev, which no lover of our native art can forget. He possessed a remarkably fine voice, of extraordinary strength, but unfortunately it was sometimes somewhat guttural. He had real musical and dramatic instincts, great youth

---

[1] English readers will find much of interest concerning Tchaikovsky and his works in the books about him by Mrs. Newmarch, especially in her translation of the beautiful biography of Tchaikovsky by his brother.

and a sort of childlike simplicity. He introduced into the life of the Russian opera such types as Sadko, Grishka Kuterma, Tristan, Sigmund, and Siegfried. There was something vigorous in his musical nature, something that raised and captivated, notwithstanding his unfortunate defect of a guttural voice. There was never any attempt at *réclame* attached to his name, and some of the very best recollections of pure art are bound up with it. From a scenic point of view he had one very unpleasant defect; he sometimes was as if bound, as if constrained. This was the result of some bad habit, that probably no manager had noticed, and against which he had not been warned in those years when it could still have been cured, and which, like all bad habits, increased with age. In moments when the part required complete weakness he was as stiff as he could be. In *Kitezh*, when in the part of Grishka he is tied to a tree, when he ought to have appeared quite broken he produced the impression of strain. He did not know how to be drooping. However, one of the most difficult tasks of the scenic art is to be unconstrained. At the same time it was just in this part of Grishka Kuterma that Ershev displayed the highest degree of rhythm, that is the accordance of the movements to the music that I have ever seen on the opera stage. Such a working out of the movements in accordance with the musical drawing we shall certainly never see again in this part. In the drunken scene each of his movements that seemed accidental (as the natural movements of a drunken man would be) were all thought out, directed and settled beforehand. Yes, a monument ought to be erected for Ershev in memory of the services he rendered the Russian opera.

Unfortunately a good example seldom has effect. People, although they admire, do not see the cause, do not understand the means, by which the effect that delights them is produced. Thus Ershev's rhythmic movements passed before the eyes and ears of his comrades, and even the managers, unobserved. The rhythmic principle was unknown to them. How often I have drawn the attention of the stage managers to the disorderly way in which processions pass over the stage; they go anyhow, some faster, some slower, some hurry on, while others lag behind and crowd together. I always was met by the same reply that proved the want of understanding or intentional antagonism to the rhythmic principles.

"Why do you allow them to go in such disorder? Why don't you make them go in time to the music?"

"How can one do that! They will look like soldiers!"

"What sort of soldiers will they be, if you make them go slower or faster according to the music?"

"Oh, no, that would be ugly. It would be laughable."

In the rare cases when the man understood my intention, he asserted there was an impediment, against which it was useless to argue.

"Yes, of course, this disorder in the movements is very sad, but what are we to do, when each time we are given different figurants you teach them and for the next performance others are sent."

And so I was never able to obtain a rhythmically staged scene, not even a rythmic march.

Of how little our managers feel the beauty of crowds on the stage, and how much can be attained by educating them musically I will give the following example. It was long after I had ceased to be director, but many of those attached to the theatre showed me consideration and applied to me, when I was in the theatre, for advice on this or that point. In this way one day I was talking with the manager of the opera about Siegfried's funeral. To the wonderful music of Wagner's march, there was displayed an impossible picture of clownishness. The choristers walked without any idea of concentration; with expressionless faces, without any order in the procession, without any show of grief in those who walked in it. I mentioned this and the manager said he would make the choristers buck up. I took advantage of this opportunity and suggested that he should make them carry their lances reversed, with their points downwards—as useless weapons—in sign of grief. The next time the opera was given I went to see what had been done. O horror! First, there was not the slightest spirit; there was the same disorderly strolling along, shaking from side to side. But what had they done with their lances? They had really reversed them with their points downwards and marched on using them for their support like walking sticks and sticking the sharp ends into the ground! . . .

I might end my reminiscences and impressions of the opera here, but one cannot speak of the Russian opera without making mention of Edward Napravnik. During forty years and perhaps even longer, he was the leader of our fine orchestra, and the chief constructive power of our opera. With all his pedantry, with all his inexorable dryness, he was an inspirer, he was a constructor. With some traits of smallness in his character he had a strong sense of duty, strict with others, he showed by his example exactitude in the execution of his duties. He had no pose, he conducted his orchestra with his head slightly bent on one side. His hand moved like a metronome without volition, but under this seeming indifference there was an iron will. It made you dull to look at him, but it was pleasant to listen to him. He was always greeted with loud applause when he took his place on the conductor's chair, and this applause was a token not only of approbation but of gratitude.

MR

Next to him I must mention his assistant, Felix Blumenfeld. He was a conductor of the romantic school, easily carried away and fiery. But, with all that, always in the full possession of his judgment. In no art as much as in that of the conductor is it so necessary to have the blending of spiritual fire with cold judgment. I shall never forget how in the third act of *The Valkyrie* he stopped the second violins, who had begun too soon. He was obeyed by the orchestra not as if he were a live metronome, but with the enthusiasm of comrades for the success of a common work. Under his leadership the orchestra was always palpitating with joy. He was not only a conductor, but also an excellent pianist, and a splendid teacher. Many owe much to Blumenfeld. I wonder where he is now.

Of course there are many I might still mention, but I cannot speak of all. I see I have not even mentioned Chalyapine. All know him, much has been written about him, and will still be written. His is universal fame. Without having any historical object in view I wanted only to mention those people with whom I had come into personal contact, or who in one way or another had made their mark in the changes in the Russian opera. From this point of view Chalyapine has also been of service, so to speak, of a local nature.

The question of pronunciation in singing has always been a sore point with us, and it still is, for who are the singers who take any notice of this side of their art? The teachers of singing are occupied with the voice, and the singers themselves only think of their voices. Pronunciation is neglected. They are not occupied with the word, but with the vowels of the word, as the vowel sounds are the conductors of the voice. The consonant sounds, which not only do not conduct sound, but even obstruct it, are not liked by singers, I may even say they are hated by them. At the same time the consonant sounds are the elements of strength, they are the element of reason in speech, in contradistinction to the vowels which are the elements of feeling. Why, it is only the presence of the consonants that change the *sound* that is sung into the *speech* that is sung. The want of clearness, and exactness in their pronunciation, was wearisome in our singers. When I became director of the Imperial theatres I sent a circular to the managers of the operas requesting them to pay more attention to the singers' pronunciation, to correct their mistakes, and at the same time I gave them a list of bad habits. My circular was received with ridicule. With the exception of old Suvorin, editor of the *Novoe-Vremia*, all the other newspapers laughed at a director who taught the artists. The well-known dramatic author, Potanenko, wrote an article in which he said it was ridiculous for the director of the theatres to give his attention to such trifles. It was obvious that nobody felt, nobody understood this question; it was evident that it was too soon to touch upon it. But then Chalyapine appeared, and what the director of the theatres was unable to instil, their colleague of genius succeeded in teaching them. The singers suddenly regained their sight (if it is permissible to use such an expression with regard to hearing). They suddenly understood that Chalyapine's whole strength lay in the part that *the word* played in his singing and what an important place consonants have in sound. The part that the word plays in singing, the part reason plays in the manifestation of feeling—these are the points to which Chalyapine drew the attention of the Russian singers. I think that *now* such sweet sounding gurgles, as those with which the singers formerly pleased themselves and charmed others, will be impossible. On these points it may be said that Chalyapine has founded a school.

This is what I wanted to say about my observations and impressions of the opera. I thought it my duty to say my parting word after this departing musical past. But few will understand; among these few not all will want to write, and of those who will write not all will think as I do. And, lastly, I would say, that the opera of the Marie Theatre displays in its development a large amount of work—honourable work—for the benefit and for the glory of Russian art, and the art of the world owes it gratitude, for having been the first to give flesh and blood to the works of Borodin and Rimsky-Korsakov. This glory no other opera can share with it.

WANDERINGS

ITALY

HAVE you ever crossed the Italian frontier? If you have, you will know the excitement you experience when approaching the coveted boundary; the depth of feeling will be familiar to you, the recollections, the expectations with which your whole being is filled to overflowing; you will have felt the delight that is kindled by every trifle—by the first Italian inscription, by the first sounds of the Italian tongue, by the Italian custom-house officials, who, by irritating your impatience, only increase the excitement of your expectation. And, at last—you are in Italy.

A dirty buffet, long-necked fiascoes of wine, green gorgonzola, yellow strachino, bad coffee in thick earthenware cups, hard twisted bread, long bad cigars with a straw in the middle. Yes, and all this causes a hymn to be sung by your soul.

The very names of the frontiers, are they not a trumpet that calls to you? Pontebba, Chiasso, Bellinzona! They stand like the gates to light and heat on the cold Alpine summits. They call to it; and flying over bridges that are boldly cast over abysses, creeping through dark burrows and tunnels, the train winds about, clatters, shakes, puffs, and rumbles. Through the mists and clouds the fir trees shoot up like arrows; above the rattle of the train the sound of waterfalls and the noise of streams can be heard; it is the struggle of water and stone. And all the water is going back and flowing towards you; we are going up the mountains, and the rivers flow down to the place from whence we came. All is cold, gloomy, and rugged around us.

But now we pass through the momentary night of the long tunnel. Suddenly, in the darkness, the outlines of the walls can be seen—we are nearing the exit. It becomes lighter and lighter; the rumbling is less often; the walls open out, we have rushed into the light. All around is soft, warm, and inviting. The streams accompany us now and run races with us. The engine without steam, with open valves, and with fixed brakes, glides, with the train, into the plains. The rocky semicircle spreads out wider and wider under the caressing rays of the sun. The vegetation that was capricious in the heights, becomes submissive as it engirdles the lower slopes. Around us the hardy oak is bent and gnarled, he does not like the southern side. The tall laurel proudly welcomes us; he is at home here, on these inclines. The loving ivy crawls up and clings to his stems, around his roots light crocuses and dark purple violets pierce through the soil, and from his branches there hang trails of wild roses; the whole southern flora besprinkles, waves, blossoms, and emits its sweet odours.

The silvery sea is spread out far below us, the smoke-coloured olive groves, the black spear-like cypresses rise above them, and like lines of sentinels descend from the slopes, vigilantly guarding the slumberous valley. And farther, still lower, we find a mixed nature, fields intersected by a network of thread-like canals, rows of fruit trees intercross and are decorated with garlands of vines which have spread from tree to tree—the work of many generations of men. White, blindingly dusty roads meet, separate, and are lost in the distance. There a dusty little ass is drawing along a dust-covered boy in a cloud of dust. There a grey ox stuck in the mud of the canal lifts up his proud horns and slavery, ruminating muzzle. The dry, pendent leaves of the maize fields rustle in the wind. Here is an arched bridge over a river; on either side of the stream near the bridge, squatting on the sun-baked stones, are a number of brightly clad women, soaping, washing and rinsing their linen. For a moment the sound of their shrill chatter reaches our ears. The train hurries on, but every day, year after year, century after century, at that very place, and at that very hour women have been on those very banks chattering in shrill voices as they washed their linen; the wind has borne away their gossip as the river has carried off their dirty soap-suds.

The train whirls on—it is gay. Puffs of smoke, torn away, spread out, descend into the maize fields, pay court to the fruit trees, and are lost in the light heat of the blinding day. . . . There's a whistle. The whistle of a train is joyful when the place it is approaching is joyful. It is now long since a cupola was visible in the valley, the belfry has long enticed us. There it is at last—the first Italian town.

The first time I went to Italy was in the autumn of 1872. I was twelve years old then, and we passed the winter in Florence. My mother, who had lived in Italy till she was sixteen, knew Italian art better than most people. Under her guidance I was taught from those early years to feel all the alluring beauty of the Italian past. But it is not only by her past that Italy charms, but also because this past blends with present reality. The charm of Italy lies in the undying youth of her past. Even then I felt it so strongly and so painfully. When we left Florence there was no place for me in the carriage that was conveying us to the station and I was told to go on the coach-box. I was glad that in this way I was alone, that none of those who were sitting in the carriage could see me, because I was shedding bitter tears.

Afterwards Italy became a spiritual necessity for me,

and I visited both the large and small towns. I especially loved the small towns—Orvieto, Perugio, Assisi, Arezzo, Sienna, San-Gimignano, Parma, Piacenza, Mantua, Bergamo, Ravenna, Rimini, Faenza, Folingo, Urbino, and how many more! I have not mentioned the south, I have not mentioned Sicily. Each little town with its own physiognomy, with its own special history, with its own people that have no counterpart elsewhere. And at the same time they have all the same special stamp—stony antiquity, century-old unchangeable strict outline, unalterable repetition of civic ceremonial, and commercial customs. And over all this unalterableness is poured the ever-changing working and idle crowd. Here is the noise and talk of the morning market; under the shade of red, green, and blue umbrellas are the bright spots of carrots, oranges, pumpkins, tomatoes, chafing-dishes with crackling chestnuts, bunches of grapes, the rattle of carts, the braying of mules and donkeys, the blinding sun, the smell of garlic, frying oil, and flowers. That evening idleness, that idle loitering, those military bands in the squares, those overflowing cafés with tables on the footpath and on the pavement, indolence and youth under the porticoes of the old palaces, under the morose eyes of the bronze horsemen, the marble lions, the sound of the splashing of old world fountains; and above all this carelessness it is only the ancient clock on the town hall, Palazzo Communale, that sends forth its warning that above this hour too the wings of death are spread as it was formerly and as it will ever be. Alongside of this warning of death is the constant daily presence of the deep rich past, which lives near, behind, in front, around you, and looks at you with the undying eyes of beauty. . . . Yes, Italy has become a spiritual necessity for me. It has become my second country now, perhaps my only country.

Of all the Italian towns Florence is still my favourite. Even when I had no time to stay there, I took care to stop in passing, if only for a few hours. I sometimes arrived in the morning and left it with the last train at night. Oh the delight of those stoppages! With what avidity you live those hours, especially when you are on your way out of Italy.

I deposit my luggage at the station, and leave on foot. One feels light and happy when walking, if the day is fine, on the clean, smooth Florentine pavement. I go round the old Santa Maria Novella with its frescoes by Ghirlandaio; I go along the noisy Via Cherretani; drivers' whips crack around. I turn to the right into the little Rondinelli and its continuation, Via Tornabuoni. It is a drawing-room and not a street. The fine morning has brought out all that is smart for a walk, or for shopping—Italian, English, and Russian ladies. What unexpected meetings, what questions. "Where do you come from? How long are you staying?" What pauses before the shop windows. Here is the little pavilion of the photographer Alinari, here is the music shop of the celebrated Milan publisher Ricordi, and here the jeweller Marchesini. Groups of smart ladies come away from the other side of the road, burdened with bunches of carnations, mimosa, roses, narcissi, and almond flowers. They have bought them on the steps of the Palazzo Strozzi. The whole length of its gloomy granite front is decorated with garlands of flowers and ferns, and along its foundations the flower-market is held, and in the midst of damp sweet-scented flowers are heard the voices of the Tuscan peasant flower-sellers and of the Anglo-Saxon purchasers. They separate, and some stop before the windows of the photographer Brogi. Here you have the whole of Italy in reproductions and in books; what a recreation it is to read even the titles of the English books in beautiful white Italian bindings. Next door is the confectioner Giacosa, who is not less remarkable than all the others. Let us go in, how gay, how tasty. A large plate-glass window, like the side of a huge aquarium, looks out on to the Palazzo Strozzi. The granite façade and frowning heavy doors, the celebrated bristling bronze corner-lanterns. . . . Let us go—each his own way.

I go to lunch. Close by, just round the corner, in a lane, there is a small cellar. Here cabbies, workmen, cattle-drivers, and porters have their dinner, but the food is more tasty here than in any restaurant; here the food is prepared in your presence on a large stove; here you get *fritta misto* and *gnocchi* on parmesan. The national dishes fried in olive oil are very toothsome; the frying-pans hiss and the stimulating odour rises to the vaulted ceiling that is covered with cinematograph placards.

After my lunch I again go out into that same Tornabuoni. During the heat of midday the streets are empty and quiet. I go into a lane, and in the shade of the cool, gloomy walls of the palaces I pass on to the beautiful Piazza della Signoria. The smooth stone walls of the Palazzo Vecchio lift up their teeth and, rising from the edge of the cornice, the tower soars into the blue sky. To the right the Loggia dei Lanzi raises its three arches; under this portico is the green bronze Persius of Benvenuto Cellini, and a whole population of marble warriors and heroes. The Rape of the Sabines, by Giovanni da Bologna, and the beautiful group of Hector and two women by Fedi, a sculptor of the nineteenth century, who was found worthy to have a place in this sanctuary: the soft folds of the marble falls like some thin material. To the left is a fountain with an ugly marble Neptune, the work of Ammanato, that unsuccessful rival of Michelangelo. The people have a couplet about that Neptune:

> "Ammanato, o Ammanato,
> Quanto marmor tu hai guastato!"[1]

How delightful is the street humour of Italy! It is never dejected, its creative power never flags. At each side of the chief entrance of the Cathedral of Florence there are two statues of the two patrons of the town, St. Reparata and St. Zenobius. Reparata is holding a palm leaf in her left hand, and the right hand is stretched out with the palm uppermost; her face expresses grief. Zenobius has a bishop's crosier in his left hand, and with his right he is giving the blessing, but, like an old man's, his hand is not raised very high and the hand has the palm turned downwards; he is also looking down. When the façade was opened, I think it was in 1885, that same evening an anecdote went the round of Florence. St. Reparata says: "Ho perduto un soldo."[2] and St. Zenobius answers: "Is non lo veggo."[3] The Piazza della Signoria is silent and quiet at that midday hour. Ragged workmen are lying fast asleep on the stone steps, and the marble has become smooth and like porcelain from the idle touch of generations of humanity. Proudly, watchfully, the bronze equestrian statue of Cosmo de Medici rises above the sleeping man lying at his feet. It is not a public place but a museum; a museum in which cabs stand and street hawkers sell vegetables. . . .

I pass by the Palazzo Vecchio and enter the Uffizi museum. I mount a high, a very high staircase; there are marbles on every side, and I pass through the halls of

---

[1] "Ammanato, oh Ammanato,
How much marble you have spoilt."
[2] "I have lost a penny." [3] "I don't see it."

the picture gallery. From Cimabue and Giotto to Caravaggio and Carracci, from the timid naïve Tuscan primitives to the unrestrained luxury of the Bolognese masters, the greatest ages of human art are displayed before you. All this I know, it is all near and dear to me; there is no other gallery in the world where you feel such a " hospitable welcome." The delicate Perugino, the enigmatic Botticelli, the powerful Fra Bartolommeo, the heavenly Fra Angelico, the sumptuous Titian, the luminous Veronese—all meet you as old friends. I leave the gallery and pass through a long, long passage, over the houses, over the bridge I go to the other side of the town. From the windows I see the muddy waters of the Arno. The Old Bridge, " Ponte Vecchio," with its two rows of little shops, swarms with the condensed life that pours across it from the streets. I go on and on through the long, long passage and at last reach the other side; I enter the museum in the Pitti Palace. Here we do not find the same historical character that is in the Uffizi, not that progressive development; here we are in the thick of the sixteenth and seventeenth centuries; in the reigns of Raphael, Andrea del Sarto, Fra Bartolommeo.

I leave the gallery and go round the palace into the Bóboli Garden. What scented quiet of the clipped laurel walls! In the midst of the dark green foliage marble gods and goddesses bask in the sun of this brilliant day, dreaming dreams of the past. Lions' mouths emit streams of water that fall into porphyry basins, which pass them on to others. The only movement in this immobility, the only sound in this soundlessness, is water. Gushing from the womb of the earth to the sunlight, the water is checked by man, and only comes out through a marble chink, but having accomplished the task imposed upon it by man it flows into the bosom of other waters. The white marble is covered with moss and lichens ; in the fissures of the sultry surface lizards crawl about, a dove is perched on the outstretched arm of the gladiator. I pass by the celebrated Neptune fountain ; in its basin lazy gold and blue fish glide about, they are as round as large carp. . . . Here at last is the terrace, surrounded by an open-work stone railing. It is sultry, but spacious. The breath of the vegetation causes intoxicating dizziness—the tart scent of the laurel and sweet olia fragrance. Huge, green, bronze frogs, with protuberant eyes, sit in the carpet-beds in the midst of fiery begonias.

The indescribable charm of Italian gardens! It bears you to something non-existent, to a world of lines and moving perspectives, it plunges you into a kind of resignation. Is it because, when we happen to be there, we seem cut off from the world, that Italian gardens cause such a feeling of blessed drowsiness ; and at the same time intense vital self-consciousness—strange, it is a sort of *non cogito, ergo sum.*

I drive in a calash along the winding Viale dei Colli, always higher and higher. Florence sinks lower and lower and spreads out more and more at my feet. From this height the muddy Arno looks like silver. The town is enveloped in golden dust. Surrounding the cathedral with Brunelleschi's enormous cupola the town lies looking like an obedient flock surrounding its shepherd, and Giotto's marble belfry stands like a watchman near the cupola— it looks as if made of ivory, with a red and black pattern on it ; this wonderful campanile which Napoleon said ought to be put under a glass case. . . . Now I have reached the very top. The road is level along the crest of the hills ; above me there is only the variegated façade of the church of San Miniato and the old walls of the fortress that was built under the direction of Michelangelo. We have driven on to the place that bears his name, the Piazzale Michelangelo. In the middle of it stands a dark bronze reproduction of his David. The square stretches out on all sides around it, on one side there is an iron railing and beyond it the abyss—air and golden dust. The evening bell sounds from San Miniato; it is answered by others; gentle, silvery chimes pour themselves over the Tuscan hills. . . . And below, the Arno winds about like a silver ribbon, and caresses the dark oaks of the Casine Park. The town seems to be burning in fiery dust. Beyond the town on the opposite chain of hills the Fiesole Monastery raises its belfry above the semicircle of its sun-scorched houses. . . .

" Dove commanda ? "[1] my driver asked.

" Via Alfieri 7."[2]

I have known my friend Carlo Placci for forty years. He is unfading. His interest never flags for art, science, discoveries, for the future, for the past; his humour never fades, it never dozes, and it is always unexpected. His capacity of living also never fades; he travels, reads, looks and sees, makes friends, learns and corresponds; and the resemblance of his profile to Savonarola's also never fades. He knows everything, he has seen everything; he has heard everything; the last book, the last opera, the last scandal—in a word, Placci is the " last word." He knows the whole of Europe, and the whole of Europe knows him. In whatever town he may arrive, by the next morning he has invitations for lunch, dinner, and supper for every day of his stay. But in his numberless acquaintances, and in his various connexions there remains one general tendency: he is sure to give the preference

[1] " Where do you wish to go now ? "
[2] " Alfieri Street 7."

ELEONORA DUSE

to "laurels"; as a poet strikes his lyre so the hand of heedless Placci plays with laurels. He has cultivated a whole grove of them around him, and the laurels like to crowd around him. Musicians, painters, authors, all who have come to Florence, are sure to be in his house. Via Alfieri 7 is a sort of junction where people pass and meet, who have never dreamed of doing so. Here, where his old mother presides at the hospitable board, I, just arrived from Russia, have dined with some English authoress who was passing through Florence on her way from India to London, or with some Frenchman on his way to excavations in Syria. I also met at his house the celebrated historian Pasquale Villari, the novelist Fogazzaro, the critic Nencioni, Mathilde Serao, the celebrated historian of Italian painting Berenson, the authoress Miss Paget, who wrote under the pseudonym of Vernon Lee. There I also met old Salvini. All that was long ago.

It was also in their house that I met Count Peter Buturlin, who died so young. His mother was a Spaniard, and he was born and brought up in Italy and knew Russian badly. A gift of poetry showed itself early in him. He wrote in English, and became very popular, but he was not satisfied with this. He was drawn to Russia. Here, by an extraordinary power of will, he forced himself to master the Russian language and Russian verse. He wrote a volume of sonnets—his only contribution to Russian poetry—and died soon after. They are beautiful verses; Italy breathes through the Russian speech, and a true chord of classical tradition sounds in all his lays.

One picture has imprinted itself in my memory; it is a Japanese picture. A young girl who is serving at court has been sent on a commission. She suddenly hears distant cries in the sky. She stops, looks up and forgets everything in the world.

> "Forgets the bonzes wait; the Empress is impatient";

she stands, immovable, staring into the sky at a flight of cranes. . . .

He read his verses to me, and how well he read. There is a beautiful English poem by him that was very popular. It begins with the words:

> "We wandered far into the fields, my love and I."

It goes on to relate how they gathered a whole armful of flowers. She carried it, but before they reached home all the flowers had faded in her hands.

> "'Tis sad to think we caused sweet things to die
> By wandering far into the fields, my love and I."

Placci knew how to call forth jokes, and he also possessed an exceptional gift of arousing thought. Possessing a great capacity for philosophical thinking, and a tendency towards the acceptance of the mystical side of phenomena, he knew at the same time how to take life and people with such joking lightness, with such buffoonery, that the philosophy crumbled away, and out of its fragments there arose a witty pun. This speciality of his character was well rendered by Hans von Bülow, the celebrated pianist and leader (who had been married to Liszt's daughter, but she had left him in order to marry Wagner). He called Placci—"Parsifalstaff." What charming wit there is in this fusion. Wagner's last opera—*Parsifal*, and Verdi's last opera—*Falstaff*. What poles of music, what poles of moods, and how well the one word expresses the peculiarities of this interesting character. Placci is wise, though he often talks nonsense; he possesses great creative powers, but he has frittered them away in little critical articles on art in which he does not display the totality of his powers.

In a word " Parsifalstaff." What Placci-Parsifal does is undone by Placci-Falstaff. He is a master in the art of interviewing; he loves to pump a man dry, to get all the information he can out of him. His thirst for knowledge makes the greatest charm of his companionship, next to his talent of expression. I owe much to him; much subtle criticism, much valuable advice, to say nothing of his flashes of wisdom, succinct definitions, delightful boldness of epithet—yes, I owe much to him and to his house.

I cannot think of Florence without thinking of this house. Placci's parents were Mexicans; they came to Florence for two months, and remained there the rest of their lives. I did not know his father, but his mother died only ten years ago. During thirty years I only knew her as an old woman. She scarcely ever talked, she only listened and enjoyed the noisy young life that surrounded her. Without words she was affable; no matter when you had met her for the last time—the day before or three years ago, no matter whence you came, from the next street or from Tibet, she always stretched out her hand to you and never failed to say " Comment vous portez-vous ? " And each time I thought " Non multa, sed multum." There have been few welcomes in life I have valued as much as this one. After dinner she sat down in the arm-chair in which she had sat for thirty years in the same place, and played patience; she was helped in this occupation by another old woman, Miss Gibson, who had brought up her daughters. While Carlo, Gennaro, and their sister Adelaide, a true companion and friend of her brothers, were entertaining their guests, their old mother sat over her patience enjoying the talk, laughter, singing, and playing. She liked her sons' friends, and the scent of laurels delighted her; only on one she had placed her interdict; she said to her son " Whoever you like; I am pleased to see all, but d'Annunzio I can't receive." This lady-killer found no mercy in the ethical codex of the old lady. "Only once, allow me to invite him, only once." The old lady consented. And the fascinating power of this wonderful being in his most commonplace human wrapper was so great that there was no further question of prohibition.

This was the atmosphere that surrounded me when I called upon them, sometimes only between two trains. It was quite special, unlike. . . . I remember I was once talking with my friend about this speciality and the dissimilarity of their house. "Tu devrais un jour décrire notre maison,"[1] he said, and now after twenty years I have done so.

I want to mention here, in passing, an impression I received last winter, that is in the winter of 1920 when still in Moscow. I was in one of the schools where I taught elocution and acting, when an Italian delegation appeared there. They had come to the Soviet capital in order to study the conditions of life in the Soviet paradise. What the conditions are under which instruction is given in our Soviet scholastic institutions only those can know who have learned or taught in them, or it were better to say, have tried to learn or to teach. Wrapped up in furs we sat and watched a lesson in eurhythmics according to Dalcroze's system. Among the delegates was a certain Kaffi, a son of the former costumier of the Imperial Theatres, who had been brought up in Russia, and was therefore quite able to compare what he saw with what he remembered. But it is not to this I want to allude now. I was explaining to him the meaning of the exercises that were being executed before us when he suddenly said "I know, I have read about them; with us in Italy a certain Carlo Placci has written about them." After all that has been written

---

[1] "Some day you ought to describe our house."

in the above lines, you will easily understand the impression that these words, spoken at that time, made on me. In the midst of desolate, cheerless trivialities, in the midst of the insulting hardness of all that surrounded us, in the midst of the oppressive darkness, entirely cut off as we were from the outer world, and the movements of the world, that name in the mouth of an Italian, who had just arrived, was for me like the olive leaf brought by the dove in its beak to the ark, it meant : there is still life there—it still continues there. Italy exists, and Florence exists. Shall I ever see them ? When ?

RECOLLECTIONS OF THE DUCHESS OF TECK

In the autumn of 1883 I crossed the Alps by the St. Gothard railway, in one of those splendid cars that are specially made to enable travellers to admire the views. Two small compartments open on to a covered balcony; the balcony is on the right side of the car, that being the finest view if you go from Switzerland into Italy. The train leaves Lucerne at about eight o'clock in the morning.

I was already sitting in my compartment when I saw an English family approaching the train. An unusually stout lady with an unusually fine face was walking in front. "Oh how steep," she said as she mounted the steps of the coach, while a good-looking stately man, a rosy-cheeked girl and a boy of about twelve years of age shoved her in from behind. They occupied the neighbouring compartment. As soon as the train began to rise into the mountains we met on the balcony. A common enthusiasm soon draws people together.

What a wonderful route. We wound round the Lac des Quatres Cantons, from which the train seems unable to separate itself—sometimes it goes into the mountains, then returns again to its smooth blue-green surface; but each time the smooth surface is farther beneath us and we are higher up the mountains; now we see the "Schiller-stone" looking into the water, there is William Tell's Chapel. The train mounts in circles like the flight of a swallow, always higher and higher. There beneath us we see the bridge we passed over ten minutes before, and above us is the bridge over which we shall go in ten minutes' time. The farther we go the higher we get and the towns and villages that are scattered in the hills are ever more distant— a geographical map is spread at our feet. The pretty white church of Flüelen; how invitingly it stands on a mound in the green valley, surrounded by mountains. Thrice we circle round it and see the old church from different sides and different altitudes, and each time it looks up inviting and mockingly.

English enthusiasm is always sincere, and is not afraid of its sincerity. My travelling companions and I soon were drawn together by a common admiration. They were affable, lively people. The English have a wonderful power of being quite sincere and simple even in the most reserved forms of intimacy. This strikes you forcibly when you compare them with Russians. We have people who embrace each other simply because they are " Russians abroad." Instantly everything is exposed, in half an hour each knows everything about the other; the bag is turned inside out. Some people think that affability is a question of topic; they can't understand that it is only a question of form. Our people do not understand that effusiveness is not the same thing as sincerity; that you can be very effusive and not be sincere, and you can be sincere and not at all effusive. With us effusiveness is taken for sincerity; and there is also a special railway effusiveness. A certain lady once related to all the occupants of a second-class railway coach how she had brought into the world her three children. What indecent frankness! The English are just the contrary; and it is quite refreshing. Well, in this way we passed the whole day together, we shared our impressions, in the most unconstrained intercourse, and at the same time I did not know with whom I was conversing, and I was not asked who I was. They were going to pass the winter in Florence, and I was going to pass the winter in Florence.

All that time the train was hurrying onwards. We came to the tunnels. We were obliged to go in to escape from the smoke and the soot. I was invited into their compartment; they had all sorts of tasty things; I did not remain in their debt—I had chocolate from Paris. Could I ever have supposed that the charming young girl whom I treated to chocolate would be the Queen of England? We soon arrived at the blue expanse of Lugano, and then to the blue-green waters of Como. About evening we reached Milan. We took leave of each other at the station. In the evening we met again under the dome of the Cathedral. That night I left for Florence—beautiful Florence.

On the first day after my arrival I learned that Queen Victoria's cousin, Princess Mary, Duchess of Teck, and family had arrived to pass the winter in Florence. I heard them described—they resembled my travelling companions. Two days later I was in the theatre; I looked up at the Royal Box, they were sitting in it, and they were even looking at me. At that moment an old gentleman, Duke de Dino, came up to me: " I have been commissioned to give you this letter." It is extraordinary how capricious memory chooses what it wishes to retain. I remember that on the paper there was the picture of a swallow. The letter was in a round childish handwriting: " We are very pleased to have found out your address, and hope you will come to see us; we live in the Pension Paoli. Your little travelling companion." I went to the box to thank for the invitation. This is how my acquaintance began with one of the most wonderful personalities I ever met in my whole life.

The Duchess of Teck was first cousin to Queen Victoria. George the IV had no children. Queen Victoria was the daughter of his second brother the Duke of Kent; Princess Mary was the daughter of his third brother the Duke of Cambridge. She married the morganatic son of one of the Princes of the Würtemberg House, who received the title of Duke of Teck.

It is difficult to define in what the exceptionality of this character consisted; we are so accustomed to see exceptionalities in what a man has added to his gifts from nature; we always ask what a man does? What interests him. A man's occupations are doubtless of great importance, but it is not only in his occupations that a man shows himself; in any case he does not show himself wholly there. A man often has recourse to an occupation to conceal himself. His occupation becomes a cloak under which the real man is hidden. As Nietzsche says, "it is only when a man is no longer able to show what he *can do*, that you see what *he is.*" The Duchess of Teck *was*—and that is enough for those who knew her. She was—that is she lived; she lived every moment of her life—fully, deeply; and to enter into the current of that life was an unspeakable advantage for any man. Whatever she spared you at any moment, were it her attention, her sympathy, did she share with you her enthusiasm or her indignation, in that moment she lived entirely and was wholly absorbed in what she said, and in him to whom she said it. How well she understood to attract a man, to fathom him and to do it in a manner that made the man grateful to her. The petals of the soul opened like a flower under the caresses of the sun. And how well she knew people. I am about to say something that is not up-to-date in the sense of an appreciation, but if ever a woman was born to reign she was that woman. She was a queen from her cradle. Her image remains ineffaceably imprinted in my memory.

She was of enormous proportions and at the same time wonderfully supple and active and her movements were harmonious and attractive. A proud and splendid head, a large energetic mouth, such as we see on the portraits of her grandfather, George III, large blue eyes, under thick dark eyebrows. Great in her impressionability, open in her sympathies, easily moved to enthusiasms and joys in all that can be called the real side of life, she was reserved, clever and charmingly facetious in her criticisms. It sometimes happened at a large dinner or evening party, she would bend towards me, or even only turn her head in my direction, and drop two or three words of wonderfully just criticism, but in a soft, forgiving wrapper; and immediately after her face would brighten and melt into smiles. Forgiveness was, I think, the strongest trait of her strong nature. She felt evil deeply, but even her indignation against a personal wrong faded away in smiles.

Such was the Duchess of Teck, as her friends knew her. She had many sincere friends, more among men than among women. I said there are people of whom you can say that they *have been*; it is unnecessary to say what they did. I find the same thought in Schiller, and how well put!

> "Adel ist auch in der sittlichen Welt. Gemeine Naturen
> Zahlen mit dem was sie tun, edle mit dem was sie sind."[1]

The Duchess of Teck belonged to the latter class.

Her family position was not quite an easy one. I do not know how it was she married; she herself told me that two future kings had paid her court: Victor Emmanuel of Piedmont, the future uniter of Italy, and Oscar of Sweden. She married Teck. He was a man of no great capacities, and of an unequal character. Hot-tempered and reckless, he singled his wife out as the victim of his ill-humour, and

---

[1] "Nobleness is also to be found in the moral world. Low natures pay with what they do; noble ones with what they are."

the presence of strangers or at large dinner parties did not hinder him from making her a scene. She covered everything with her smile and passed it off as if nothing had occurred. His semi-princely origin, the son of a Würtemberg Prince and a mother not of royal blood, weighed on his soul during his whole life, as something that could not be rectified. He considered himself the victim of his father's mistake. "Just imagine," he said one day, "if my father had not married my mother, I might have been King of Würtemberg." The royal descent of his wife only added bitterness to his incomprehensible, but sincere torment. All this was unhealthy. He died insane. I personally remember with pleasure his exquisite good breeding, the simplicity of his manners, and the charms of his hospitality.

For all that the Duchess was happy in her children. They—three sons and a daughter—all inherited more from their mother than their father. They are all representatives of fine healthy humanity. The second son, who chiefly resembled his mother, died about ten years ago. The eldest married the daughter of the Duke of Westminster, and was at one time the Military Agent in Vienna. The youngest, "my little travelling companion," married the daughter of the Duke of Albany, the youngest brother of the late King Edward VII. The daughter, Princess May, is now Queen of England, the Consort of George V.

I often saw them in their youth, both in Florence and in England, where I stayed with them in their beautiful country house, White Lodge, in the middle of Richmond Park, which had been lent them by Queen Victoria. I was always delighted by that truly English atmosphere of moral health. And what hospitality! They would willingly have altered the whole plan of their day to accommodate themselves to some excursion they wanted me to undertake. I remember once the Duchess wrote out a time-table of some trains for me, in her own celebrated and beautiful handwriting.

With the Duke of Teck I visited all the most remarkable London palaces. The wonderful house of the Duke of Buccleuch with its unique collection of miniatures; the palace of the Duke of Westminster, where I saw the celebrated portrait of the actress Mrs. Siddons, the work of Joshua Reynolds: an inspired woman and an inspired brush. I saw the fine picture gallery in the house of Lord Dudley; the son of the house showed us over the rooms, he understood little about pictures. His mother, the widowed Lady Dudley, was wonderfully beautiful; Herbert Bismarck, the son of the Chancellor, was long in love with her, and even proposed to her, but in vain.

I was at a ball in her house. Here I was presented by the Duchess of Teck to the Princess of Wales, the sister of the Empress Marie Feodorovna and subsequently Queen Alexandra. Conversation was not easy as a Rumanian band was playing all the time. The Duchess, who was sitting on a sofa with the Princess, made me a sign; I approached, bowed, kissed the hand that was stretched out to me, although Englishmen do not do so—with them kissing of hands is a sign of affectionate proximity, and not of official respect; they do not even kiss the Queen's hand. And so I saw, but owing to the Rumanian band did not hear, that the Duchess was telling the Princess something about me, emphasizing her words with the movement of her fan on the Princess' arm. The Princess looked affably at me, and more and more affably as the Duchess continued, but what she said I was unable to hear. The Rumanian band played louder, the Duchess's fan became more emphatic, the eyes of the Princess more affable, my bows became more grateful, but I can remember nothing else—and there was nothing else. At that moment the Prince of Wales, the future Edward VII, came up. I was also presented to him. I said I had already had the honour of being presented to him. He hastened to answer " Certainly, certainly, I remember." I saw very well that he did not remember, so I said it had been in Cannes at the Countess Mehrenberg's house. (Countess Mehrenberg, the wife of the Duke of Nassau, was the daughter of our celebrated poet Pushkin.) When I said it had been at Countess Mehrenberg's he remembered at once ; but it was interesting to hear *what* he remembered : " Oh yes, of course, I remember I was at the time in my travelling jacket ! " He really had entered the room apologizing for his costume ; during the conversation he had referred to it two or three times and departed still apologizing.

A few days later there was a garden party at the Prince of Wales's. This was usually the last function of the London season. There I saw Queen Victoria for the first and only time. She was small, stout, and dressed in an ordinary black dress that hung round her like a wide bell. She walked supporting herself with a stick. Her face was red, her eyes, that looked like glass, appeared astonished. I was the spectator of an interesting moment—when she greeted Gladstone. She changed her stick to her left hand and gave him the right. At that time he was in the opposition, not in office. I must suppose that the moment was of some special political importance ; in any case, a few days afterwards I saw the meeting of the Queen with Gladstone in all the illustrated papers.

There were always many musicians at the Teck's house, especially singers. There I accompanied a somewhat extraordinary man, a certain Dòeme. He had a fine baritone voice, and was very good looking. I mention him because he afterwards married the charming singer

Nordica. A very amusing occurrence is connected with her name in my memory. She was sitting at one of the performances at Bayreuth. Those who know the atmosphere of holy attention that reigns in that temple will understand what the audience felt, when suddenly, during a performance of *Parsifal*, the bark of a little dog was heard. In view of the whole audience poor Nordica was led out carrying a little lap dog in her arms. . . . She swore she would return to Bayreuth and force them to forget her shame. Indeed, two years later she sang Elsa in the very hall out of which she had been led, and, I heard, she had sung the part admirably.

I also met at the Teck's house the composer of popular songs—Paola Tosti, who was so well known in his day. A very mediocre musician, not serious, commonplace, he somehow managed to hit the taste of the day; he catered for the musical requirements of people for whom music was what, according to Derzhavin, poetry was for the Tsarevna Felitsa :

> "Poesy is lovely to thy ear,
> Pleasant, sweet and good to hear,
> Tasty as fresh lemonade,
> Drunk in summer in the shade."

He owed his success chiefly to England, that is to the drawing-rooms of the English fashionable society. His laurels were more prized on Olympus than on Parnassus. He had a wonderful talent; he had no voice, but he sang charmingly. Seeing this, every English lady without a voice thought she had only to take a few lessons from him to be able to sing as he did. He soon became popular as a professor of singing, and made a lot of money. This small, insignificant man made one of the most difficult conquests; he conquered London. Still, I may mention, that one day Tosti was accompanying Dòeme, who was singing various insignificant Italian and German songs, when he suddenly laid the "Meistersinger" before him. Tosti rose and gave his seat up to me.

The Duchess of Cambridge, the Duchess of Teck's mother, entertained an old woman's partiality for him. Twice a year Tosti came to London to see the old lady. Every day she would send him baskets of game and of fruit. By her will she left him five thousand pounds sterling.

The Duchess of Teck, or Princess Mary, as she was oftener called in England, was very popular. Several times I accompanied her to school festivals or some sort of "openings." How charming she was, how well she knew how to diffuse her own personality, and with a quite personal naturalness; without the slightest effort. Here she was Her Royal Highness and here the children stuck to her like bees round a hive.

How is it I suddenly remember a quite insignificant scene? We were driving—she and the children—near Florence, far beyond the Fiesole Monastery along the summit of the hills. We stopped the carriage and proceeded on foot; passed the cypresses, myrtles and laurels, in the light of a warm sunset—a sunset warm as those in the pictures of the old Sienese masters. It was difficult walking; we were tired. Suddenly we saw before us a tall Englishman with a long beard, standing, hat in hand, at the roadside.

"May I beg Your Royal Highness to accept a cup of tea, and rest in my house?"

"Thank you, with pleasure."

What a beautiful picture of the spiritual soundness of England, here in the Tuscan hills. An old brother and two sisters received their Princess. With what joy and respect she was welcomed. What kindness and cordiality she brought with her. I shall never forget the little round table on which she placed her teacup. On this table two red cherries and a green leaf were burnt in. "Oh, how pretty! How charming! Whose work is this?" One of the old sisters beamed with pride.

The Duchess of Teck died in 1898. She was buried in St. George's Chapel, Windsor.

A year later I was in London as delegate at the congress "for the prevention of the sale of women." Her sons, seeing my name in the papers, sought me out at once. Princess May invited me to lunch at her house. Her husband, the present King, had at that time, during the lifetime of Queen Victoria, the title of Duke of York. They resided in St. James' Palace. The present King George V was extraordinarily like his cousin Nicholas II. They were so much alike, that the story goes that on one occasion the Lord Mayor, thinking he was talking to the Russian Ctsarevich, asked the Duke of York if he would be present at the wedding of the Duke of York?

On that day, the sister of the late Duchess, the Grand Duchess of Mecklenburg Strelitz and her blind husband were also lunching with the Duke and Duchess of York. I sat between them. They were exceedingly amiable, although it was the first time they saw me, and, as it happened, also the last. The old lady began to pour out to me her trouble about her niece, Princess Jutta, whom I had seen in Petersburg, when she had been on a visit to her aunt, Princess Helena of Altenburg, who was going to get married to Prince Mirco, of Montenegro. I said that such a union might certainly seem in many ways not well assorted. We had been speaking in low voices, when suddenly she bent over me towards her husband and said aloud "Listen to what Prince Wolkonsky is saying." I was obliged to repeat quite audibly for all, that the difference of race, forefathers, education, ways of life, were such that it required much love to bridge over that abyss. I believe that the young people fulfilled all the requirements that were necessary to overcome these difficulties ; and are living very happily together. But at that moment I felt very awkward and wrote to Alexander of Teck that perhaps I had said something I ought not to have said, and begged him to make my excuses to his sister. He answered, there had been no harm done, but, on the contrary, it was all right, as the old man was very proud of his race. . . .

I wish to say a few words about some other foreign royal personages whom I have met.

I passed the autumn of 1889 in Gmunden, in the Austrian Salzkammergut. There, on the banks of the lake, was situated the house of the Duke of Cumberland, the son of the last King of Hanover. In the Austro-Prussian war of 1866, Hanover sided with Austria. When Prussia conquered, she annexed Hanover. The old and blind King was deposed. His son took up his abode in Gmunden. He was married to the Danish Princess Thyra, a sister of our Empress Marie and of Queen Alexandra of England. I visited them. She was charming, and although the mother of a numerous family she had retained something childlike, something celestial ; she made the impression of having invisible wings on her shoulders. In a huge hall, in which there were two pianos, there was also a large low divan, on which after dinner the father romped with his eight children, rolled them about, made them turn somersaults, and deafened all in the hall with frantic cries and shouts. In the midst of this hubbub, Princess Thyra and I played on two pianos. One day she played on her instrument Rubinstein's romance *Une soirée à St. Pétersbourg.*
OR

I improvised an accompaniment to it on the other piano which sounded very well. I afterwards arranged this accompaniment and dedicated it to her. It was published in Paris by the French music publishers Hammel. Many years afterwards, at a concert given in one of the Petersburg schools, one of the items on the programme was Rubinstein's romance arranged for two pianos by Prince S. M. Wolkonsky. The Empress Marie assisted at the concert, and when she looked at the programme she said " Oh, I know this, it was dedicated to my sister."

The Duke of Cumberland's mother, the widow of the last King of Hanover, also lived in Gmunden. She was a pretty and kind old lady and I dined several times at her house. The family of Count Prokesch Osten were always there. He was married to a former celebrated actress of the Vienna Burg Theatre, Frederica Gossmann, who, in domestic life, was known as Fifi. She had long since left the stage, but still appeared in charity performances. But although she was the mother of grown-up daughters she could not forget that formerly she had taken the parts of " ingénue " ; she tried to look young and was affected. This became a malady and I heard she died in a mad-house. Poor Fifi Prokesch was overshadowed by Frederica Gossmann.

Madame Mathilde Wesendonk, the celebrated lady who had played a part in Wagner's life, also lived in Gmunden in her beautiful villa on the banks of the lake. She was a very remarkable woman, both as a musician and as a thinker. She was not good-looking, but she had wonderful hands, and they had beautiful movements. She had an old husband who resembled Wotan and a son who was a distinguished geological scientist. I shall never forget Mathilde Wesendonk. She was wise and had something in her manner that was calmly sanctifying. Her favour was precious and she knew its value.

I often saw the old Grand Duchess Louisa of Baden. She was a daughter of the Emperor William I, and was thin, tall, impressionable, and had a morbid extravagance in her expressions. She was fond of relating stories, and her stories, if they were not a page out of history, were at least interesting notes on the margin of history. She was elegiac by disposition, and always had a tear in the corner of her eye. Sometimes I tried to alter this frame of mind, but I never succeeded. I remember we were once talking about remembrances, portraits, and archives. Wishing to shed on this elegy but one bright smile I wanted to tell her an amusing occurrence. Once in Berlin I went to see an American correspondent I knew. On the door, next to the door plate with his name, there was another with the inscription "Correspondent of the American Genealogical Society."

"What does that mean?" I asked my acquaintance.

"My fellow lodger is the Correspondent of the American Genealogical Society."

"I see that. But what does he do?"

"He makes researches in Europe for the forefathers of the present Americans."

"Does he make much by it?"

"You cannot imagine what some Americans are willing to pay only to know who their grandmother was."

"Are the researches successful?"

"They are always successful. For instance, he telegraphs to his client: 'In the Hamburg Public Library I do not find Elizabeth Jane in the year 1757, but in the Rotterdam Guildhall I have found Anna Jane in the year 1773.'" The answer came, "That's it, go on."

I began to relate this story to the Grand Duchess, but when I reached the point where my friend mentions the sacrifices an American is capable of making to find out who his grandmother was, she shook her head and exclaimed "Comme c'est touchant."[1] I naturally did not finish my story.

Once I was invited to inspect the portraits in the Baden Palace. The custodian of the palace was ordered to show me everything. While the Grand Duchess was giving us instructions about what to see, the meeting of a Benevolent Society was waiting for its august president in the next hall. And when I had finished my inspection the Benevolent Society had again to wait, because the august president wanted to hear my impressions.

Her uncle, the Grand Duke of Weimar, I saw in Baden. He considered it his duty to keep up the literary and musical traditions of the Weimar Court as they had been in the times of Goethe and Liszt, but he was not very successful in this. He was very much loved, but he enjoyed the reputation of being as good-natured as he was limited in mental capacity. Once when inspecting a gaol, he asked one of the prisoners for how long he had been condemned.

"To imprisonment for life."

"Well," the Grand Duke said to him with a smile, "I wish from my soul that this may be your last year."

He had a highly-educated daughter but she was very plain. As she was married to Prince John of Mecklenburg-Schwerin, the brother of the Grand Duchess Marie Pavlovna, she often came to Petersburg. At that time, in the 'eighties, one of the actors of the French company of the Michael Theatre was old Hytmans, a man with a red nose and large, round, glassy eyes. The Princess of Mecklenburg was given the nickname of "la Princesse Hytmans." There was a striking likeness. Did she know it? Probably

[1] "How touching."

not. But Hytmans, with a comical expression of despair on his face and his eyes turned up to the sky, would sometimes exclaim " Oh, cette fatale ressemblance ! "

Besides the Queen of England, I have met two other queens. I was once received by the Dowager Queen of Italy, Marguerita. I had been living in Rome for many years, but I went little into society and I had not been presented at Court. In 1912, I invited our vocal quartet Safonov, Chuprynnikov, and the brothers Kedrov to come to Rome. They sang with enormous success at a musical party I gave at my house. Princess Marie Baryatinsky, who was very intimate with the Queen, told her about the quartet. The Queen wished to hear them at her house, and invited me on that occasion too. Queen Marguerita was always renowned as a connoisseur of music, literature, and the fine arts in general. She was also renowned for her affability and her lively conversation. She received us most amiably, and listened to our singers with sincere delight. She also asked me to play ; at that time I worked a great deal and I was able to comply to her request without fear ; I played a Prelude by Glière and Rakhmaninov's *Baracole*.

In connexion with this visit I remember a wonderful morning. I had invited our singers, and also our well-known opera singer Mlle. Petrenko, who had come to Italy with Dyagilev's company, and who had also sung at my house, to lunch with me at the famous restaurant on the Palatinate Hills. There is a wonderful view from the glass pavilion, on the ruins of the Palatinate, on the Colosseum, and over the whole of the Eternal City. During lunch the quartet began to sing. How wonderfully it sounded in the glass pavilion ! All listened ; the sound of knives and forks died away, the waiters ceased changing the plates and serving dishes round. All remained silent as the sounds of the "Volga boat song" were wafted through the Italian air.

I met another Queen. In the last days of July 1914, almost at the eve of the War, I met the Queen of the Belgians, the wife of King Albert. I had come to visit my friends the Baryatinskys in Switzerland, in a little place called Valmont above Glion. Hearing that the Queen of the Belgians was staying in the same hotel I inquired who was with her. It proved to be my good friend Countess Chimay. I called upon her; she said that she would certainly arrange that I should meet the Queen. In the evening she let me know that I was invited to take tea with the Queen the next day. When I entered the Countess's room at the appointed time, she told me that the Queen had a very bad headache and could not receive me in her apartments, but that she would come out to us. She is pretty, delicate, and very shy; she has much thought in her eyes, and much feeling in her voice.

We sat on the balcony and talked about trifles. I little thought at the moment, that but a few weeks later events would happen which would not only seize her in their hurricane power, but that this delicate creature was destined to pass through the greatest trials, and by the firmness with which she bore them, not only gain the love of her people, but the admiration of the whole world. We talked on various subjects, among others about Dalcroze, who, with his pupils, had given a demonstration of his system in the Palace at Brussels, and the King's children had taken part in the lesson. We talked of this and other things—and an aeroplane buzzed over the lake.

All these years I have heard nothing about my friend Countess Chimay, but I know her as the possessor of an excellent character and a high understanding of duty and devotion. During the whole of the War I had before me the image of these two women, who were so nearly united by the bonds of close friendship. The one delicate but ready to bear any cross for the sake of her people; the other strong, protecting her for the sake of her children, for her people, for her fame. In imagination I saw them in the trenches, in the smoke, on the ashes of the hearths. I saw them bending over the wounded, and waving the colours over them. . . .

We sat on the balcony and drank tea. But I saw before me two remarkable characters. The Queen, by her right, the one to decide, to order, was like a child, ready to follow the orders of a higher power; the friend, who by duty ought to obey, was secretly the protectress, and the unperceived counsellor. In which was respect—in which gratitude? In both there was the one and the other. . . .

Like a piece of tightly-drawn silk the lake shimmered beneath us; under the awning it was hot on the balcony. The aeroplane buzzed above. . . .

These are my reminiscences of certain Royal personages whom I have met. I remember one of my old aunts, Princess Helene Kotchubey, my grandmother's sister. During the reign of Alexander III she was the lady governess to the Court; she loved everything connected with the Court, one can almost say she breathed titled air. Once when taking leave of my sister, with whom she had passed several months in Rome and in Germany, she said to her:

"Eh bien, ma chérie, tu a donc vu le Pape, la Reine Olga, et l'Impératrice Augusta. Eh bien, tu sais, pour un premier voyage, c'est déjà très joli."[1]

---

[1] "Well, my dear, you have seen the Pope, Queen Olga, and the Empress Augusta. For a first journey, that's not so bad, you know."

People look for different things when they travel! I did not look for them, but when chance offered me the opportunity during my wanderings, I studied with interest every " human document " that came in my path.

AMERICA

I was twice in America, the first time in 1893, when I went as Commissioner from the Ministry of Public Education to the Chicago Exhibition ; the second time in 1896 on the invitation of several American societies to give a course of lectures on Russian history and Russian literature. The first time I stayed in America from April to Christmas, the second time I was there for three months. It is difficult to write about America ; at least it is difficult for me to do so. There is but little picturesqueness in America ; it is not by picturesqueness that it impresses itself on the memory, as in outward forms. The towns differ but little from the average European type ; the difference does not consist in the form but in the size and the number. America is not a subject for the paint brush, but for the pen ; it cannot be described in colours but in numbers. Yes, America chiefly speaks in numbers. But the people who live there are free, profound, diversified. Are not the differences that appear in the great unity of human nature a valuable subject for observation, and is there not beauty in it too ? That delightful American thinker Emerson says : "Wherever there are outlets into celestial space, wherever is danger, and awe, and love—there is beauty." And wherever there is beauty, I must confess I am drawn towards it. I shall write about my two short visits to America what I can remember and as well as I can.

To enter the New York harbour on a fine bright morning is magnificent. It spreads out like a huge lake at the feet of the majestic statue of "Liberty," holding in an outstretched hand the lantern of a lighthouse high above its head. Beyond the harbour, the huge town lies piled up like a hill above it, in one place, a golden dome glistens brightly. My European eye expected to find a church there—it turned out to be the offices of the *World*. To the left of the town, the wide estuary of the river Hudson pours itself into the harbour; and to the right of the town, enveloped in a sea mist, lies the island and town of Brooklyn, and between it and New York, hanging over the sea like a thin cobweb, is the Brooklyn suspension bridge. The statue of "Liberty" was a gift of the French Republic to her Transatlantic sister. The second time I came to America I arrived in the evening, and then the torch in the hand of "Liberty" was burning, and round it, attracted by the light, hundreds of birds were circling; many of them strike against the lantern with such force that they get killed; a net has been hung up round the statue, into which they fall.

My second voyage was more exciting. The magnificent steamer *St. Paul,* of the new American line, which sailed from Southampton, accomplished the voyage in the comparatively short time of less than a week. But nothing is short when rivalry is involved. We were going along the American coast northwards when another liner came in sight; a beautiful fiery-eyed, puffing monster as it appeared in the night. A race began between them to see which would arrive first at the point where we had to turn to the left—to the West. They raced for a long time; I went to bed. When I woke the next morning, we had run aground; the steamer in its haste to turn had struck, fortunately sand and not rocks. It was foggy and rough. A building could be seen on the shore, a life-boat station. A rope was thrown across; then the people caught it and fixed it. Along this rope a basket was sent, and in the basket a telegram for New York. This telegram was a call for help, and New York sent boats to our assistance. Half a day was spent in the vain attempts to set us afloat again; only the water got muddy. At last, towards evening, we were told to take the least possible quantity of luggage, as we were to be taken off in the boats, and sent on in little steamers. I put my tooth brush into my pocket and took the portfolio with my lectures under my arm.

What a proud feeling it was to arrive in America on my own business; to set foot on this soil, not as a tourist, but as a worker, this is one of the most agreeable justifications of a man's existence. I took advantage of these prerogatives; I went to what was considered, at the time, the best hotel, " Waldorf," ordered a good supper with the splendid " blue-point oysters." Yes, America is the only country in the world where one is ashamed of having nothing to do. There was a very good caricature in an American magazine. A young foreigner says to an American lady " It's a defect in your country, that you have no leisured classes." " But we have them," she replied, " only we call them tramps." America is a wonderful country. How wonderfully she makes people work, how she develops the power to work, and the will to work. And this is done quite naturally without compulsion, without any placards or inscriptions on the walls—like in Soviet Russia—that " those who do not work need not eat." No, here it is in the air, it is at the roots of the life which all live. As children are taught to swim by throwing them into the water, here life teaches how to work; extricate yourself as well as you can. Not everyone knows how to, nor can everyone adapt himself at once to it, and I must say the first impression is terrible. You are astounded by the hurry of life: whistles, wheels, racket, hootings—constant hurry, absence of idleness, absence of rest, a constant movement onwards, a pitiless absence of retrospection. Have you ever in your childhood been in a factory, with whirling wheels, droning engines, hammers, pistons, straps, fire breathing furnaces, and suddenly you lost your parents ? Do you know that feeling of fear of being parentless ? That is the first impression. Afterwards you gradually get used to it. All around you people are running, and you begin to run ; you are obliged to run if you do not wish to be left behind.

America is rough. And it is a wonderful school. I owe much to America, but chiefly the capacity to work under all conditions. If I am now writing in a little room in a little lane in Moscow, with one window looking out on a dark yard, in a lodging that is inhabited to the last degree of denseness, where, in the next room from seven o'clock in the morning, four proletarian children cry and shout ; if, in the midst of all this and much more that one has to bear, I am able to work with a quiet and clear mind, I owe this to America, and her rough and pitiless school. Pitilessness is in the very air there, it is found in every trifle. If you ask your way in the street, or any other bit of information, you are answered in the most laconic manner, and this trifling information is afforded you with so much indifference that it sometimes gives you a feeling of dread—there is nothing human in it—an answering machine. Oh, the affability of the Latin races ! How far away it is ; you must forget it ; you must forget it, you must not expect more than the minimum of the indispensable. This has a terrible effect on a man who is not inured to it. Nowhere does a man reach to such an extreme of fatigue, of exhaustion, of great mental tension as in America (of course with the exception of Soviet Russia). And nowhere does the psychological condition of the questioner find a smaller degree of satisfaction in the reply he receives, than there. No matter however highly-tempered the questioner may be, the answer is always equally cold and to the point. Is it not a pitiless custom when you come to a restaurant footsore, worn out, hungry, with a parched mouth, and throw yourself into a chair imploring for something to eat and drink, and the nigger waiter silently lays before you the bill-of-fare, a small writing-pad, and a pencil and goes away. Yes, " extricate yourself as well as you can." This order permeates all answers and all inquiries.

When first I went to America I knew very little English —superficially. But the infection in the air there was so great that after two months I already read reports, and gave public lectures. At the Chicago Exhibition it was the custom that the Chief Commissary of each nationality should give a banquet to the American managers of the Exhibition. The time arrived for the Russian commissary to give his banquet, and I was asked by my chief to make a complimentary speech. This was my first appearance; afterwards I received many invitations. The Russian commissary was a certain Glukhovsky, a blunt, coarse and presumptuous man. He was a Chamberlain of the Court, and very proud of his title. If the secretary of the Exhibition sent him any official document to look through, he always threw it to one side, if it was not addressed with " Chamberlain " written after his name. He was red-faced and bloated, and his court dress seemed ready to burst. He was stupid, and that sometimes caused unexpected results. At that time there was a " Little Russian Choir " attached to the Russian restaurant. When the Russian section was to be opened our bishop, the reverend Nicolas, of San Francisco, came to assist at that solemnity. Glukhovsky was informed that the " Little Russian Choir " offered to sing at the " Te Deum," and they wished to know if they were to be in costume or not. " In costume, of course," Glukhovsky answered. The Russian section, as all others, was distributed in different buildings, that were scattered over the whole of the Exhibition grounds. Can you imagine that procession: the bishop, two priests and a deacon in their priestly vestments, all of us in uniform following them, and in front the " Little Russian Choir " in costume, with wreaths of poppies and oats, many-coloured ribbons, beads, loose trousers and fur caps.

I remember the day of the official opening of the Exhibition. One certainly could give the Americans a bad mark for the arrangements for this national solemnity. They did not show the slightest capacity in the organisation of the ceremony. It was a foggy April morning. The Exhibition was not ready on the day of the opening. Boards and lime were lying about and the roads round the buildings represented a reddish-yellow squash. After the official opening ceremony and the speeches, there was a gala luncheon. At this luncheon only the chief commissioners had places assigned to them; we others had to find places wherever we could. But such crowds of strangers had come from all directions that we were left outside. We had to look for a lunch somewhere else in the Exhibition; I went along the reddish-yellow squash in my white trousers and the full dress of a gentleman of the bed-chamber. We were disappointed. The restaurants were open, the waitresses were standing behind the counters, but it was impossible to get a dinner, the " checks " were not ready.

Here I may mention a curious occurrence. There was a young fellow in our commissariat, a sort of courier, he spoke several languages and executed all sorts of commissions, he might be called an errand boy. I don't remember his name, but as he was very small he went by the nickname of the " Chicken." While we, hungry and tired, in our full-dress uniforms were wading through the mud in search of a lunch the "Chicken" was calmly seated at a table just behind the one occupied by President Cleveland. I remember something more about this "Chicken." Many years afterwards, while looking through the illustrated supplement of a Petersburg newspaper, I came upon a short notice, which stated that one of the employees of the Russian Consulate in Chicago had died, and after his death it was discovered that he was a woman. His portrait was given—I recognised the "Chicken."

I saw President Cleveland once before the opening of the exhibition. On our way to Chicago, we, the Russian representatives, went from New York to Washington, to stay at the Russian Embassy there. Our ambassador at the time was Prince Cantacuzene; he told us that it would be proper for us to be presented to the President. At the appointed time we were in the White House. Cleveland received us in a round room in which there were chairs along the wall. Prince Cantacuzene presented us. The President remained standing and we too. One of our deputation was the sister of my sister-in-law, Princess Marie Shakhovskoy, who was in charge of our home industries department. The President was talkative and the conversation was somewhat protracted. Suddenly Marie Shakhovskoy left our group, and sat down on one of the chairs near the wall. She meant it as a "lesson" for the President.

As I said, after the Russian banquet, invitations to lecture poured in on me from all sides. It was evident that my début had produced a good effect. Already, immediately after the dinner, the vice-president of the Woman's Congress, Mrs. Henrotin, came up to me and asked me to give them a lecture on the state of female education in Russia. The subject was not an extensive one, especially in those times, and I had the necessary data with me. I prepared my report carefully and the lecture was a good one. After that I never ceased lecturing at congresses, in literary clubs, and by invitation in various educational institutions. These meetings were interesting, especially the religious congress.

While talking about the commencement of my career as lecturer, I must mention that exceedingly nice old man Professor Norton. I met him for the first time at a dinner party given by Mrs. MacVey in Chicago. Her house stands on the banks of Lake Michigan in the so-called North Side. The whole of Chicago is divided into South and North Sides. At one time only the South Side existed, but, after the terrible fire that destroyed the town in the seventies, and left only one house standing, the new town was divided; on the South Side there remained the shops, offices, and business establishments, while the masters, and all the rich people transferred their residences to the North. Charming quays with rows of trees were laid out and magnificent houses grew up. In this development of the town a large part was played by the celebrated Mrs. Potter Palmer, who, during the Exhibition, was the president of the woman's section. I must say a few words about her and about Mrs. MacVey before reverting to Professor Norton.

Mrs. Potter Palmer, a clever woman of business, realized at once what value the northern bank of the lake would acquire after the fire, and bought up a considerable area of land there. Selling this land afterwards in lots, in a few years she had increased her fortune so greatly that she became the richest woman in rich Chicago. Her house, like a granite castle, stands at the very entrance to the embankment—No. 1. She was a very pretty woman, from New Orleans, and possessed all the softness that characterizes the women from that town, she was also distinguished among her fellow countrywomen by a musical voice, so rare in those parts. With all her eminent business capacities and seriousness, she is, at the same time, a perfect example of that worldly frivolity that consumes the higher spheres of American society. In that land, where riches take the place of race, she had succeeded in adding to the greatest wealth, the most perfect social forms. She had become the queen of her town.

I frequented her house. The second time I visited America she even gave a dinner party " in my honour." I remember on that occasion a most unpleasant misunderstanding occurred. Long before my arrival in Chicago she had inquired on what day I was free; and the day was appointed for the party, but, as it often happens to me, I forgot when I was invited and arranged to give a lecture in the Chicago University on the same day. Of course it was necessary to give precedence to the lecture; I had to write a letter of apology and Mrs. Potter Palmer postponed her party to another day. To be honoured with a dinner is, in America, the very highest mark of hospitality and esteem that can be shown. It is impossible to describe the luxury. Crystal, silver, gold, the rarest flowers on a tablecloth of old Venetian lace; all this is so blinding that the food you eat becomes an accessory. The women are dazzling, radiant with health, dressed more magnificently than with taste; they are very voluble and loud of speech; the men are just the contrary—reserved, not very mobile, and little heard. But the whole gives you the impression of a sort of play; they are playing at " high society " as children play at " visiting." There is a large amount of " childishness " in the external behaviour of American women with all the good that the word expresses, that is childishness in their delight, childishness in their seriousness,

PR

childishness in their honesty. This side of the American women, which for many Europeans is not easily understood, and soon tires, adds, in my opinion, great charms to personal intercourse, it gives to it value and the absence of heaviness. But it renders sociality somewhat artificial; as I have already said—somewhat of a game. One day a lady sitting next to me at luncheon said:

"I think Miss Whitman entertains so nicely, and then, you know, she calls it *breakfast*, she does not call it *lunch*, and this is what makes you feel so comfortable; it reminds you of those lovely French déjeunays."

A strange combination is produced—simplicity of character and artificiality of form. Sometimes this is very tiresome. In the long run this artificiality of American society became very irksome to me.

Yes, it is difficult to reconcile one's self to the smallness of social distinctions in this land of immense distances, unnumbered inhabitants, infinite wealth. For a Russian who finds himself there, it is very difficult. In the land of liberty he does not feel free. I remember while I was staying in New York I was handed an invitation to a party in quite an unknown house—the mistress of the house was Russian, and was eager to see a countryman. I arrived and was received by a stately old woman. She was the grand-daughter of the last Georgian queen and she was married to an American doctor. She led me into a corner of the room . . . and poured out her recollections. I have never heard from a stranger such intimate disclosures, such personal, such private details. I can hardly remember them; I know that all this was told, not for me to remember it; some speeches are like rivers whose source is important, while with others it is the mouth. I heard, without listening; I only remember " Caucasus—Tsaritsa—institute." I remember a restless fan, I remember a diamond brooch in the form of an "A"—the initial worn by Maids of Honour; I remember distinctly the feeling of being in a cage. The black fan flapped like wings. It was the Caucasian mountains in the narrow New York drawing-room.

There are many strange things in the organization of American life, that is to say, in what is considered the "upper set." The respect for rank is nowhere so much developed as in this land of liberty. You will ask, how can that be respected which does not exist? Classes are formed, even where they do not exist. In New York there is the so-called "five hundred," they are the descendants of the first emigrants who left England in the *Mayflower*. Now so many people claim to be their offspring that it is certain the ship would have foundered if it had really borne all those whom their heirs say were on board. This is, of course, a sort of distinction, but distinction in America is quite outbalanced by the intervention of capital. This causes the most extraordinary change to take place, and all bow down before the power of gold. I once asked a lady:

"Do you know so-and-so?"

"I knew her formerly, but now she is too rich for me."

This is an example of modesty; now let me mention what a Chicago lady answered when I asked:

"In New York they have the celebrated 'five hundred.' How many of them have you in Chicago?"

"I think," she answered, after a pause, "that *we* are eighty."

I thought, if I go farther West, I am sure to come to some village where if I ask a girl I may meet "How many are you?" She will answer in the words of the well-known poem, "We are seven." I often said this in my public lectures with success. The Americans love to be told about themselves, and accept the most severe criticism when it is offered them in a wafer of humour.

In this land of liberty they love everything that has outward distinction. They have a number of clubs and societies, consequently there are numberless people who are able to put before their names president, vice-president, secretary, etc., etc.; the name of the occupation or calling sticks to the man as firmly as his own name, and adheres for ever, even when he has retired from service he remains senator, mayor, governor, judge. It is necessary, however, to add that this respect for rank is only an outer accessory of social intercourse; it does not affect in any way the business or official side of life. On the contrary, an extraordinary simplicity of relationship exists there. I remember I once went to the office of the Superintendent of Education in the Minnesota State. Three assistants were sitting in the same room. It was July and two of them were in shirt-sleeves. I was charmed by the simplicity of the mutual relations. It was impossible to notice which was the superior, which the subordinate by the manner they spoke to each other. I clearly felt that the American respect for rank was a kind of plaything, quite innocent in itself, and not a spiritual infection as it is in some European states.

In this land of freedom they love everything that distinguishes them outwardly. At public balls the " hostess of the ball " stands at the door to receive the guests, but she stands on a carpet, and she is assisted by other ladies, who have been invited to be members of the " receiving party," who stand next to her; they all are ranged on the carpet. As they enter, all the ladies curtsey to them, and they curtsey in return. Is this not play? It is a great honour to be one of the " receiving party." The next day they open the newspaper with beating hearts, to read their names in the second or third places—what satisfaction! The newspapers give great prominence to this side of social life, and encourage these snobbish proclivities. In Boston there is a small weekly paper, *Town Topics*. It goes to the last extreme of impudence in describing and commenting on the appearance of the ladies; nevertheless, all are eager to see this paper in order to look for their own name, and read with envy the names of others. I was once in a house where a number of this loathsome paper was lying on the table. My host pointed out to me with pride that for the first time he and his wife had been mentioned in *Town Topics*. This is a comic and despicable side of American life, and it is sad that it is encouraged by the Press.

In an educational sense the American newspapers play a somewhat unworthy part. They noisily accentuate the outward side of life; they invent loud-sounding headlines, and fill their columns with trifles. I remember that while I was in Chicago a little hippopotamus was born in the Zoological Gardens. One would have supposed that two lines in the column for various news would have sufficed. No, the newspapers gave a whole column about "The little hippo at the Zoo." Interviews are very much developed (who does not know it), but there is no real criticism. After my lectures, there were descriptions of my appearance but nothing about their subjects. Sometimes the programme of the lectures was given. Once on ascending the platform I forgot to turn down the hem of my trousers. So the next day I, or rather my trousers, were honoured with a whole column. It was only after the last lecture that the newspapers gave an appreciation of the course and of the lecturer. When I inquired of a well-informed person why this attention was reserved for the end, he answered "Because if this had been done sooner it would have served you as an advertisement, and in America advertisements must be paid for ; nothing is done gratis." A very unpleasant side of American journalism is the unsigned articles. This anonymity gives it something you are unable to appeal against, and naturally acts in an authoritative manner on the public.

Let us return to Mrs. MacVey, the lady who introduced me to that amiable Professor Norton. Her house, on the embankment of the North Side, was No. 3. She was charming, kind and hospitable. On my second visit to America she insisted on my staying at her house.

"But, Mrs. MacVey, I shall stay in Chicago three weeks."

"Three years if you like."

Her husband was a good example of a refined, cultured, well-educated American, which did not prevent him from attending to his business and money matters. Every American has his home and his office ; the office is for business, the home for rest. Business swallows him up entirely, it is the Alpha and Omega of American existence. I remember one lady told me that once Pullman, the inventor of the Pullman cars, had complained to her that he felt tired.

"Why don't you give up business, Mr. Pullman, and take up a hobby ? "

"But business is my hobby."

This is very characteristic. The whole organization of life has atrophied in them the feelings that are attached to rest, to respite. I always thought that in Russia a small shopkeeper of some provincial town, when sitting on the earth mound round his house, watching the cows returning home in the evening in a cloud of dust, enjoys more rest than Pullman when seated at his dinner-table. I once dined at Pullman's. On the dinner-table, between crystal and silver, roses and orchids were lying half hidden by feathery ferns. When we sat down Mrs. Pullman said to the butler in an undertone, " The lights." And suddenly beneath the fern leaves tiny electric lamps, that looked like glow-worms, burst into light.

In America, that is in some American houses, luxury suffocates you, not so much by its existence as because it is so emphatically underlined by its possessors. You sometimes have the impression that the price is still marked on each article ; as if it could never be forgotten. It really seems that the price has only just been washed off the plate from which you are eating. I remember a story told me by Mr. Nelidov, who had been our ambassador in Constantinople, Rome, and Paris. He once dined at the house of a rich American lady. The table was smothered in luxury. He was chiefly struck by the crockery ; there was a different service for each course ; at last for dessert such a magnificent service was placed on the table that he, who was a great lover and connoisseur of china, turned up a plate to see the mark of the factory. Noticing that it was one of the rarest Sèvres, he congratulated his hostess on being the possessor of such a wonderful service. She only shrugged her shoulders :

" If you only saw what we have for state occasions ! "

But to return to Mrs. MacVey. She had both worldly and intellectual interests. She was quite touchingly interested in my lectures ; she did not miss one, and she read them over again at home ; she chose acquaintances for me who might be of use in my visits to the universities. I can truly say she was like a mother to me in that distant land. Let me tell of a touching occurrence. When I was staying at her house, while giving the lectures at the Chicago University, she always drove me in her carriage to each one. Two days after lecturing for the last time, I left Chicago. The evening before, we went to a concert. As we were driving there, she suddenly exclaimed :

"Did you notice that?"

"What?"

"The horses wanted to turn to the right. They thought we were going to your lecture!"

By the touching way in which she noticed the constancy of the horses, I saw how much she prized all that concerned my lectures.

Dear, kind Mrs. MacVey. But she was also infected with the itch of worldliness.

"All these lectures are, of course, very interesting—history, literature, Turgénev, Tolstoy. But you really *ought* to tell us something about the Petersburg society."

"Is that so very interesting?"

"Certainly. Russia is so far away . . . we know so little. For instance, when is your season?"

"It begins in autumn and lasts until Lent. Sometimes there are a few balls after Easter. Those spring balls are very pretty."

"Now say that in your lecture, Prince Wolkonsky; use that very word—'spring balls.' You understand, Russia is so far away, we know so little, etc., etc."

However, dear, kind Mrs. MacVey was unable to convince me; besides her husband did not support her in her demand. So (I think it is the third time I mention it), it was in her house that I made the acquaintance of Professor Norton. Charles Eliot Norton, the flower of wisdom, culture, and charm of manners, was a professor of the Harvard University, near Boston, a specialist in literature and the history of art, and an ornament to the human race. He was already very old when I knew him, but I have never seen such a blending of age and youth as was found in this man, and in the same way as age and youth were blended, so also he united seriousness with humour. He sparkled with delicate criticism, his laughter was soft and refined and he never allowed it to burst out; he seemed to have it under his control. He was the last representative of that generation of New Englanders who still spoke with the pure English accent, without that horrible American twang, which increases in every new generation. He belonged to the group of such men as the philosopher Emerson, the poet Longfellow, and the author Lowell. He was their friend, and the spirit of idealism, which was almost extinguished in the next generation, still burnt within him. I remember two anecdotes he told me about Emerson.

In his old age that celebrated author lost his memory. During the civil war for the emancipation of the negroes it was arranged that Emerson should give a lecture in Boston for the benefit of the wounded. It was many years since the old man had appeared in public. The largest hall in Boston was filled to the last place. Emerson appeared on the platform: " Ladies and Gentlemen ! " Silence; all waited in expectation. The silence continued, it became oppressive. Emerson did not know what to say. Suddenly the whole audience burst into a storm of applause. Emerson bowed in silence with tears in his eyes. The applause did not cease until he left the platform. There was no lecture, but the collection was enormous.

Another of Norton's stories. He and Emerson were following Longfellow's coffin. Emerson pointed to the mournful hearse and shook his head as he said " I don't remember who he was, but I remember that he was a good man."

From the moment we met, Norton showed me such appreciation as I have seldom experienced since. My remembrances of him are among the most precious I possess. The appreciation of my work, the support of my opinions, the approval of such a man were more than a recompense for me, they were like finger-posts on my path. Whenever I think of him I remember a saying of Darwin's I once read: "The approval of an old man is useful to a young one—it helps him to go along the right path." By the way, Norton was a great friend of Darwin's. He said that Darwin was a martyr. In his early years he had suffered from weak lungs, and in order to cure them the doctors had advised him to make a voyage to Australia and Polynesia in a sailing vessel. His health improved, but for the rest of his life he suffered from sea-sickness on land.

I owe to Norton my career as a lecturer in America. He invited me to come and stay at Harvard after the close of the Exhibition. His house was called Shady Hill. He was a widower, and lived there with his three daughters. The eldest was very pretty and played on the violin; they had a portrait of her painted by the celebrated English artist Burne-Jones. The other two daughters were plain. As Norton was a student of Dante, and had published an English translation of the *Divina Commedia*, the students of the Harvard University had given them the nicknames of "Paradiso," "Purgatorio," and "Inferno." Among other works, Norton published a translation of the correspondence between Goethe and Carlyle. I had a copy of this volume that Norton had given me. I had a number of letters from him written in his own beautiful bold handwriting. Norton was a fine reader, especially of dialogues, you always felt the presence of three persons: the interlocutors and himself, and his relationship to the speakers. I have seldom seen any man greeted with such delight as he was when he entered a drawing-room. His whole person seemed to exhale something conciliatory; the most burning questions lost their venom on his lips. We were once talking about the possibility of a conflict between the æsthetic and the ethical principles, the ideas of beauty and of goodness. He said : " By being beautiful the rose already makes you good." His whole moral outlook appears to me like a calm sunset, sinking but not losing its radiance.

In that hospitable home I rested after the hurly-burly of Chicago. I gave several lectures in the University and in the students' societies, while Norton wrote about me to other universities. While in Harvard I met many interesting people, among others, William James, who afterwards became a celebrated psychologist, and the German Münsterberg, the well-known investigator of experimental psychology. I have the pleasantest reminiscences of my stay at the Harvard University. The students were hospitable and several times honoured me with invitations to their clubs ; the professors were more attentive than I deserved ; the President of the University—that is how the Proctor is called there—Eliot, offered me the chair of Russian literature. Norton surrounded me with attentions, he could not have done more if I had been his grandson.

During my first visit to America I had three lectures that I repeated in different places ; they were on the Education of Women in Russia ; on the World's Parliament of Religions in Chicago, and on my Impressions of America. Wherever I spoke I tried to dispel the foreign prejudices about Russia. There they knew little, I may even say nothing, about Russia. The stereotyped stories of snow, wolves, and secret police were repeated in the daily press and other publications. Everything that did not possess that type, had no success, and even aroused suspicions.

One American young lady confided to me naïvely that she did not like Russian novels and stories very much as they were not very typical; she much preferred American books about Russia, they were much more "Russian." In order to destroy these prejudices I had quite a special system. I understood that, to take a Russian, a patriotic standpoint would lead to nothing. Patriotism is a subjective feeling, it is praiseworthy, but its object is deprived of all contagion for foreigners. Who is not a patriot? Who does not love his country? But it does not follow that a stranger who does not love a foreign country is unjust. It is praiseworthy to love your own country, but it is not at all obligatory to love a foreign country. That is why I did not take the standpoint of subjective patriotism, but rather the standpoint of general humanity. I was not indignant at the foolish questions I was asked about Russia and the Russians, but I repeated them in my lectures and examined them from the point of view of human injustice. Occasionally I ridiculed them and compared them with some conditions of American life. When the report of my lecture in a Boston newspaper was headed "The Impressions of a Tartar about America," I purposely alluded in my next lecture to the Tartar yoke in Russia and how it was cast off, and I said that "to call me, who was a Russian, a Tartar would be the same as if you Boston ladies and gentlemen were called by the name of some tribe of Red Indians, only because, before you, they had inhabited this place. I did not say that in Russia there was no secret police (where is there none?), but I tried to inspire them with the beautiful side of Russian life, Russian art, the Russian soul as it is expressed in this art. I evoked in them a fellow-feeling, and then blamed them for its absence in their usual judgment of Russia, and the Russians. I showed up their narrow sectarianism, the absence of humanity in their national, political, class and other prejudices. Finally I entirely left my defensive position of wounded patriotism and took up the position of one proclaiming justice on the grounds of general human fraternity. Sometimes this had very unexpected results. Once, after the lecture a lady, who had evidently retained all the generally preconceived ideas of a " Russian," came up to me and asked :

" Are you a Nihilist ? "

" Why do you think I am one ? "

" Because I consider what you have said are American ideas and not Russian ones."

" Are Americans Nihilists then ? "

" No, but Americans preach fraternity and justice."

" Yes, but they do not have recourse to bombs. Why do you want to enrol me among the dynamitists ? "

Alas, the Russian riddle abroad! How painful it is, and how difficult to solve. If I had told the Americans the most improbable, or the most impossible tales about Russia, they would have believed them, but because I spoke of the most ordinary things they appeared extraordinary to them, in a Russian. The understanding of the furthest countries, those in another hemisphere, the most exotic lands, Tahiti or Fiji will be closer to the truth than the understanding of Russia in Europe. In this, Russia herself is, of course, greatly in fault. Once at an official dinner my neighbour at table, who had something to do with education, and with whom I had conversed for a long time, suddenly asked me " Are you a typical Russian ? " What could I answer? I said " There are many who think as I do." But could I tell him that we are not all obscuratists or belonging to the " Black Hundred " (by-the-bye, this name was not invented at that time, and how could it be translated?). But there was nothing that distressed me more than the *surprise* of foreigners.

I must mention another interesting occurrence. After one of my lectures two Russian students, emigrants, came up to me, they had both a Jewish type. "Well, you would certainly not have spoken in that way in Russia." The lecture had been on the education of women. Next day I heard that they had given a report of the lecture to their companions in the same manner, saying I must either be a sympathizer with the secret agitation, or I pretended to have liberal opinions for the sake of applause. At the next lecture I mentioned these reports, and said I wished to deny in this way the sympathies which were attributed to me as I did not agree with those ideas. But with regard to the supposition of my two fellow-countrymen, that I would not have spoken in such a way in Russia, I begged to be permitted to offer to the inspection of the audience a small book—it was a Russian translation of my report on the education of women, that had been made in Russia by order of the Minister of Public Instruction. I begged to be allowed to present this little pamphlet to the University library. This produced a very unexpected effect, which was shown by strong marks of approval; but my fellow-countrymen disappeared.

I repeat, the Russian riddle is great, dark, and difficult to solve, and I repeat the roots of this riddle are not only to be found in foreigners' want of information, but also in Russian realities. What troubled me most in the ignorance of the criticisms, was that it was not directed on what it ought to have been, and I was troubled by the one-sidedness of the foreign conception of Russia, and I was perhaps mostly troubled by their preconceived opinions. "When we think of America," I said to them, "do you know of what we think?—of Lincoln, of Emerson, of Longfellow, of Edison. Do you think that we have no names equal to these? Why is it when you think of Russia you *only* think of prisons, of secret police, of Siberia?"[1]

It was in this spirit that I spoke at my lectures, and I must say on this foundation I strengthened the bonds of sympathy and trust that existed between me and my audience, which grew stronger in proportion to the length of the course I gave.

Here I approach a question which confronted me in America. When I mentioned the two Russian students who had spoken to me after my lecture, I said that they were Jews, it was not from a feeling of Judæophobia, but only to be accurate in my account. I never was a Judæophobe, and even now, after the revolution, when my own eyes convinced me of the enormous part they have played in the tyranny which they have laid on our life, and lastly for their responsibility for the greater part of the cruelty that has been practised in Russia, I still cannot accuse them of the complete responsibility. I knew many Jews in Moscow who passionately denounced the injustice and the crimes that were perpetrated; I also knew some that were ruined like the rest of us. When I was confined in the Moscow Cheka (the Bolshevik prison) and we were allowed to walk about the yard, I remember that a quarter of the prisoners were Jews. Of two of my best—I may even say of my only real—pupils and followers in my courses of declamation, one was a Jew. However, I allude to this, not to speak of my connection with Jews, but to mention how I was treated by those Jews I met in America. My lectures had a kind of attractive (and

[1] I do not see that the same people who were so severe in judging the former régime have kept their standards in judging the present state of things in Russia. It is one of the riddles of our time: The excessive severity towards Imperial Russia and the criminal indulgence towards the Bolshevik atrocities.

calming) influence on them. I felt this wave of Jewish trust chiefly in Chicago. At that time there were a large number of Jewish emigrants from Moscow in that city. I was once taken to inspect a Jewish school. I remember the director pointed out a little girl who had only just entered the school, and who knew scarcely any English. I spoke to her in Russian. I shall never forget the excitement that shook that small and ugly little creature. Her head bent lower and lower and her fingers worried her pinafore. In answer to my question of how she liked her new country, she answered she could not get accustomed to it. " Was it nice there ? " The head bent still lower, the fingers worried her pinafore more rapidly, and her voice became dull, as she whispered, " Yes, it was nice there." The director patted her head; " Never mind, never mind, you'll soon get used to it," and turning to me he said " We shall make good American citizens of them." I know that here I am touching upon a great, a universal question; I do not do this in order to solve it, but only to say how I came into contact with it.

After passing three weeks in Harvard I went to San Francisco to embark there for a voyage round the world; and on my way there I looked in at the universities to which Norton had given me introductions. I also had letters of introduction from the U.S. Ambassador, Mr. Andrew White. A man of great culture, he had been the first president of the Cornell University in the New York State, and he had given me an introduction to the president at that time, the professor of philosophy, Schurmann. This was the first university I visited after leaving Harvard and bidding adieu to kind Norton. Cornell University is like a fairy tale. Near the little town of Ithaca, in the hills, high above the lake, stand granite palaces; one palace is the auditorium, the second the library, the third the gymnasium, the fourth the hostel, and so on. A tower rises above the library whose high pointed roof is covered with yellow tiles; the "straw hat" of the Cornell University is seen from afar.

I visited a good many universities. This is where I lectured: In the Columbian University in New York, the Cornell University in Ithaca, the Harvard University, Cambridge, the Ann Arbor University in Buffalo, the Art Institute in St. Louis, the Chicago University, the Californian in San Francisco, and the Leland Stanford University at Palo Alto in California. All these institutions produce a most striking effect. Space, the luxury of the building materials, every accommodation for scientific work, hygienic arrangements, everything makes them oases of quiet, light, repose and peace. It is only he who has experienced the turmoil of American life, the bells of the tramways and the telephones, the tapping of the typewriters, the whistles of the underground, on the ground and above ground trains, the roar of the streets, the shouts of the newsboys, the signals, the bursting into light and the dying away of the electric advertisements, only he who has experienced the importunity with which the American street life pursues your hearing and your sight—only he can appreciate the conditions of peaceful quiet which this land affords to the scientific workers. The American Universities are oases of thought; in the stormy sea of life, they are islands of repose. In this repose science ripens. Of course not all work equally hard in these fields of thought. The professors work more than the students; the students are too much allured by their clubs and their sport. But those among them who are preparing themselves for a life devoted to science are strenuous workers, and on strictly specialized lines. I asked a student of natural science what his speciality was. "For the last three months," he answered, " I have been studying the abdominal parasites of the white ant." Three places impressed themselves on my memory like oases. The first oasis was Cornell, which I have already mentioned. Another was the Wellesley Woman's College in the neighbourhood of Boston. It is situated in woods on the banks of a lake. This is one of the most joyful reminiscences of my life. I think that however much happiness may be in store for these girls in the future, the happiest time of their lives will be the months they passed in this wonderful Wellesley College. What a charming sight it is to see these young girls surrounded by nature and science. And everywhere—in the woods, on the lake, in the lofty corridors, you hear the Wellesley cheer in young ringing voices.

Every university in America has its own cheer, with it they greet and express their approval. Harvard utters three throat sounds on " A " and then shouts the family name of the person they wish to honour. Cornell calls on one note " Cornell-yell-yell, yell-yell-yell, yell-yell-yell " and the family name. Wellesley has a very pretty musical cheer ; I give it in notes :

You can imagine how pretty this sounds, called by young female voices under the vaults of the corridors, in the hilly woods, on the resonant calm lake. I must mention a pretty detail. On the broad staircase of the chief building there hangs a portrait. This is the founder who built the college with his own money. He desired that his name should never be written, that it should never be mentioned.

To be worthy of a cheer is considered a great honour. I remember an event that is very dear to my heart. When you leave Cornell you have to change trains at the next station. I was sitting in the waiting-room; when I went on to the platform I saw a group of young men standing on one side. When I passed them they cried Cornell-yell-yell, yell-yell-yell—Russia! This greeting at a little roadside station on the other hemisphere was very pleasing to me at the time.

The third wonderful place is the University of Leland Stanford at Palo Alto in California. Leland, the only son of the millionaire Stanford, died, and his father built the university in his memory. In California, two hours' journey from San Francisco, on the high cliffs of the seashore, surrounded by fantastic Californian vegetation, stand the university buildings, built of unhewn stone in the style of an old Spanish monastery, with columns, endless galleries and porticoes. It is strange to see modern people in these surroundings; to see bicycles in the courtyard of such a monastery. I told them that if I had been the founder of the university, I would have made it a condition that the professors and the students should wear the monastic cassocks of some order that did not exist.

From San Francisco I embarked on my voyage round the world. I shall tell in a later chapter of some of the impressions I received on that voyage.

I have already said I was twice in America. My second journey was undertaken in the following circumstances. In the spring of 1895 I was in Sicily when I received a letter from a certain Lowell, the director of the Lowell Institute in Boston, to invite me to give a course of lectures on Russian history and Russian literature. Before answering him I asked my father's assent. I received my father's reply when in Florence, on my way home. I remember as if it were yesterday; I was sitting at my friend Placci's and wrote to Lowell my consent. I remember Placci was reading a newspaper, when he put down the paper and said "That's your signature." He had heard by the sound of the pen that I had finished the letter. Thus I signed a contract to give in February, 1896, a course of eight lectures in the Lowell Institute of Boston. During the summer I wrote them in English, on our estate Pavlovka, and started for America in January. The first lecture was to be given on the 5th of February.

The Lowell Institute was founded in 1839. It is not an educational establishment. The founder, Lowell, did not wish that the Institute should have its own hall. It is only a society to arrange for public lectures and the lecturers are invited from all parts of the world, but the same lecturer is never invited more than once. The Lowell lectures are among the most popular in America, and anybody who has lectured there requires no further recommendation. The audience is a pleasant and clever one, though somewhat cold; the Boston audience is considered the most difficult to please in America. This reserve is all the more striking when compared with the volcanic demonstrations of the audiences composed of students. Before leaving Russia I had sent my programmes to all the universities I knew. When I arrived in America I found quite a number of invitations to lecture. I remained three months and travelled from town to town. There were two weeks in which I had two lectures in New York and two in Washington; the distance is the same as between Petersburg and Moscow; I travelled in the night and lectured in the day. How easy it is to travel in America. At night you have a Pullman sleeping-car, in the day—a long coach with plate-glass windows on each side and before the windows revolving arm-chairs, which you can turn so as to be able to converse either with your right or your left hand neighbour or the person sitting opposite you, or lastly, towards the window to look at the scenery you are passing through. There is a splendid lavatory; there a negro attendant cleans your clothes and boots. Before you arrive you are asked where you are staying, in which hotel or any other address, and you receive a receipt. You step out on to the platform with your umbrella and gloves in your hands, and go about your business. When you reach the hotel your hand luggage and any other you may have is waiting for you.

I published my lectures in English in Boston. When I returned to Russia I published them in Russian, and the same year they were translated into German by a certain Miss Hippias. In each of these languages they went through two editions. In 1896 after I had left Harvard a chair of the Slavonic languages was founded there. About the publication of my lectures I remember the following circumstance: I submitted them to the well-known Chicago publisher McClurg, whom I knew personally. He offered me very inadequate terms, and I told him I would think about it. A Boston publisher offered me much better terms and I settled with him. When I informed McClurg, this man whom I had often met and dined with in friend's houses, had the face to write to me that he was sorry, as his proposal had only been "a tentative one" so to speak—a trial balloon.

In the American character there is doubtless a certain outward dryness. Under the influence of that pitilessness of which I have already spoken a certain hardness of character is developed, which is, of course, good as a quality that resists external evil. But on the other hand this very dryness, which has become a habit, sometimes obstructs the outward manifestation of inner impulses, or causes them to appear timid and awkward; people are afraid of giving free vent to their feelings—to transgress the rules of manhood. But the armour that is necessary in life's battles, is ridiculous when it is not laid aside in times of security and peace. This is why, wherever feelings want to manifest themselves, a certain constraint is perceptible, and in the psychological relations of life there is a kind of flatness and the absence of distant and deep perspectives. I once dined in a house where the hosts were particularly attentive to me. I noticed that they wanted to please me in every way. After dinner they asked me to play on the piano; of course they begged for something Russian. Suddenly the hostess asked for the Russian Anthem. I knew they would do so, that request never failed. But this time the host, wanting to give me a special mark of sincere attention, said "Wait," and going up to the mantelpiece on tip-toe he took from it something, and again walking on tiptoe, he slyly came up to me and placed on the music-stand a small icon of the Virgin Mother, which he had brought from his voyage to Petersburg, saying "Now you will feel quite at home." In accordance with their wish I played the Russian Anthem and thus I actualized at the piano—" orthodoxy, autocracy, and nationalism."

I do not know how far I have been able to render—of course not American life—in these hasty lines it would be impossible to do that—but my impressions of American life. I myself have a clear perception of this picture: Large masses of workers, all, without exception—the poor and the rich. Above this mass, like foam cast up by the sea, the moneyed aristocracy—light playthings—with shallow interests. In the midst of this sea of life, agitated by material and political party troubles, in the midst of this hunt for profit, in the midst of this never weakening strain of work, business, finance—like islands protected from the world—are the universities. I repeat, I am not giving a picture of American life, I am drawing a picture of the part of American life that I saw and how what I saw impressed me. A wonderful country! I shiver at the very thought of living in America, and at the same time I am filled with admiration. I shiver because I have never felt in any other country (except in one of which this is not the place to speak), not in any other country have I felt such an insulting contact of the outer life with spiritual sanctities. Nowhere have I felt such an absence of the ideal, such a triumph of the material; nowhere have I found such deserts of thought, such a famine of art. By one unimportant example, I felt to what an abnormal form the perversion of æsthetic principles could descend. Small busts of Washington, Lincoln and other popular heroes were being sold in the streets. These busts were made of pulped paper—papier mâché—not of common paper, but of banknotes that had been withdrawn from circulation. The busts were not all of the same price; the price varied according to the value of the notes that had been employed in their manufacture. Is it possible to imagine anything more terrible in the way of bad taste and worse in the way of artistic inventiveness. All the busts were equally hideous, but the eyes of the purchasers were attracted with envious admiration to the ones that cost most. Yes, in this land of liberty you feel at moments that your breath is taken away. The late Professor Norton knew this feeling very well. About that time Bourget's *Sensations d'Italie* was published. Norton said to me, why don't you write " Choques d'Amérique." I remember when I read aloud to him the lecture of my course in which I speak about the " Westerners " and the " Slavophiles," of the relation of historical criticism to Peter's reforms, and, in general, of the course of Russian self-judgment, he exclaimed " I am astonished at the amount of reflective work that has been accomplished in Russia." His exclamation was typically American. A man can suffocate in that atmosphere if his feelings are not blunted. But the greatest majority do not notice it. There is a well-known story told of a citizen of Chicago, who finds himself in the next world, and walking about there he looks around and exclaims with satisfaction " How nice it is here, one feels quite at home in heaven." " You are mistaken," he was told. " You are not in heaven but in hell." I always thought that the greatest felicity would be to close my eyes in Chicago, and open them again in Venice. Nevertheless, the picture of this citizen of Chicago, who being in hell thought himself in heaven, is very typical of one trait of the American character—of his boundless optimism. The American is firmly persuaded that he lives in the best of worlds, and that the best of countries in the best of worlds is the United States of America. Self-criticism is not in his nature, and if it makes its appearance in literature, if there are satirical writers, they do not give the impression of having grown out of the American soil. Satire, criticism is pessimism. An American is, above everything, an optimist. Pessimism seems dull to him; the critic is a stranger for him. That is why such a distinguished man as Norton was never popular, though he had numerous and faithful friends. The critic is a grumbler; the American a whistler.

But notwithstanding all this, notwithstanding all the prosaic horror of the hammering, the ringing, the rattling, of those sign-boards that twirl about by day and wink at night, notwithstanding that Dickens said " The mission of America is to vulgarize the world " ; notwithstanding that after America I saw the many-coloured rainbow of the East, such fairy tales of humanity as India, Ceylon, and Cairo, when I reached home the most vivid pictures I retained were my American reminiscences : the whistles, the wheels, the droning, the hum, the hurry—the eternal hurry—the absence of idleness, the absence of rest, the movement forwards, the pitiless absence of looking back. The fairy tales grew dim before the flaming advertisements. Fairy tales are of the past ; advertisements of the future. America is the window of the future ; but it is terrible to look out of that window. The artist will shudder, the philosopher will shake his head.

In the midst of the turmoil of human existence that is spread over the whole earth a natural thought occurs to man—it is to save a portion of the earth from the encroachments of man, to protect, if only a part of nature, from the attacks of civilization. As in other countries museums are founded in which to preserve the remains of former civilizations, so in the United States they have thought of turning a portion of nature into a museum. In the so-called Yellow Hills beyond the great Salt Lake and the Mormon territory, an enormous tract of land has been enclosed and turned into the National Park. Rocks, hills, valleys, forests, and rivers have all been rendered inviolate by law. A wonderful tract of land has been chosen. There you find petrified forests, glazed rocks, geysers that throw up fountains of hot water which descend in waterfalls into the cold, turbulent river ; a sky-blue stream, whose bed is red with coral deposits, flows through a chalky-white plain. Fish are not caught in the rivers, neither are animals nor birds shot in the woods, and when a tree falls across the road, only that part of it is removed which obstructs the passage. You require six days to drive round this park. The trip is arranged very comfortably ; large open char-à-bancs convey the travellers ; you start in the morning from one hotel and arrive in the evening at another. Half way there is a stoppage for luncheon at a restaurant. . . . This was one of the most beautiful impressions I had. How fresh, how young old mother nature appears in the midst of the prematurely old young civilization.

Everything is eternally young. Younger and more eternal than anything else is human nature, that inner nature, that gives it life. Why do I suddenly remember such a trifle? Near one of the hotels in the National Park is a spring, near the spring a seat. I sat down on the seat ; looking round I saw a letter lying on the grass. I picked the letter up, and began to read it. What a sad page, what a sorrowful story of a wasted deceived love. A girl had written to her lover, that she does not know what he is doing, that he has forgotten her. This is neither new nor old. What suffering there was in this absence of reproach, what devotion, what a desire not to bind *him*, and what love for her own bonds. And then, through these dry tears, what touching details of daily life, in the hope of interesting him. Gossip of one thing and another— " You had ought to have been here to see Jenny graduate ! It was perfectly grand." What interest did he take in Jenny or the books she received or the gold watch her mother gave her? The letter had been thrown away and was lying on the grass, and the evening dew had already wetted the paper with its tears.

> " Es ist eine alte Geschichte,
> Doch bleibt sie ewig neu."[1]

[1] "It is an old, old story,
But still is ever new."

Why have I just remembered this? And why do I conclude my impressions of America, to describe which figures are necessary, with this picture of a broken heart, and its fragments cast away near this spring? ... Why?

ISLANDS

" There is an island in that distant ocean."
                                —LERMONTOV.

ISLANDS have always had a kind of mysterious attraction for me. They are separate worlds. Planets on earth. Surrounded, difficult of access, disconnected, they retain the individuality of their colouring as well as of their contours; the individuality of their people as well as the individuality of their flora. The island has a concentrated existence. The island observes, the island is attentive, the island waits. The island knows better than anything else on earth the meaning of approach, the meaning of receding; it knows the meaning of welcome—a huge mass growing up from a distant point; it knows the meaning of farewell, long and painful, when a whole world departs and disappears as a point on the distant horizon. The island has learned the painful insult of the words " passed by," the burning alternation of hope and despair; it has felt the hot cry of the signal call, and the cold silence of dull indifference. The island knows how to rejoice; it is not spoilt; nothing has grown tiresome for it, if it be not tired of itself. It is naïve, it is easily surprised, and the blueness of the surrounding waters is reflected in its eyes. It rejoices, but beneath its joy sorrow is hidden, as if life brings it more farewells than welcomes. Washed by the surrounding waters the island loves the sea more than the land, it is nourished by the sea, the dry land is its indulgence, the sea is its life, the land is its dream. But it is itself the dream of all that surrounds it ; none but it can so well feel that :

> " Like as the ocean enfolds this earthly globe,
> So life upon it is enclasped by dreams."

The life of an island is enclasped by dreams and it requires a lengthy, a tenacious contact with the mainland to remove from it this veil of dreams. Alas ! This veil is passing away. Those times are gone when the fearless European vessels breasted the waves of the distant oceans, penetrated beyond unknown horizons, and cast anchor near virgin shores. Now there is nothing unknown on the earth and there are no more virgin shores. Everywhere there are harbours, landing-stages, custom-houses, coal depots. . . .

But imagination is stronger than reality and islands have always had a mysterious attraction for me.

What excitement, what an influx of life there is in the eyes of all when land is suddenly seen from the deck. " Land ! " How can the same word, with the same signification, have so many meanings. What a difference there is when we on the dry-land say " Land " and when from the deck somebody shouts " Land ! "

The " Land " which I saw was the island of Madeira. In 1886 I passed two months there with my invalid brother Gregory. The little town of Funchal has spread out its houses and gardens on the slopes of the hills to the very seashore. The white houses peep out of the groves of palms, lemon, and laurel trees, without incommoding each other, all can look over the roofs on to the sea. An enormous striped white and black cathedral crowns the town with its cupola from the top of the hill. High above the town over the tops of the fir-trees the two white belfries of the church on the hill look down on the sea. When you arrive in Madeira, before you have had time to look round, you are asked, "Have you already been on the hill?" It is the pride of the inhabitants. There is another phrase which you hear repeated many times. If you ask your way to this or that place every direction will inevitably commence with the question, "Do you know the Cathedral?" The Cathedral is the point from which all roads start.

Oh! what a small town it is, and how neglected, how far away and what small interests it has. . . . Invalids—invalids everywhere and everything is for the invalids; they lie on the sunny verandas covered up with blankets and gaze over the sea at the horizon. The air is soft, moist and sultry like a hothouse. Now a ship is seen in the offing; in four hours the mail will be in. My brother is lying on a wickerwork-couch, and behind him a little monkey is crouching on the back of it. This monkey is quite tame but cunning and cruel. The other day it jumped across the whole veranda, skipping along, dragging after it a small green and yellow parrot whose neck it had wrung. . . . It is quiet. It is always quiet in Madeira; in the whole town there is only one wheeled vehicle, the char-à-banc belonging to the English clergyman. Everybody else drives about in sledges. Goods and people are conveyed in sledges drawn by oxen over the pavement which is made of very small stones. Blinds protect from the sun, and over the hot stones instead of snow, sledges squeak along; the drivers run in front and cast down tallowed entrails in front of the runners of the sledge, which glide more easily, and the squeaking abates.

A strange town—a fragment of Portugal cast into the ocean. Old, sonorous names, double and treble—marchionesses, countesses. The Portuguese language sounds pleasant to the ear; it is softer than Spanish. The type of the people is not handsome, and it ages early. They remember journeys to Lisbon, they think of Madrid and dream of Paris. Some of the women have married rich English wine merchants. Most of the men leave the island, the old families are all ruined, the houses and the vineyards have passed into the hands of the English. The finest villa that year was inhabited by Ushakov, the well-known Moscow merchant, with his wife and family. His wife had been very ill with lung troubles, and for her sake their numerous family had come to live there. Their hospitable house was the centre of gaiety for the dull islanders; there dinners, suppers, and dances were given, tableaux vivants were got up, and illuminations were arranged. The gaiety was at its height whenever a foreign warship put in. The young girls looked through telescopes hoping to see one, for if it was not an English one there would be a ball at Ushakov's (he did not receive the English). And then the officers came ashore; they left the stormy sea to enter the overflowing sea of Moscow hospitality. Then for two or three days there were wild jollifications, and then the vessel departed, followed by the eyes of the islanders till its smoke could be seen no more.

Thus the life of the world passed by, only touching the green island at a tangent, to take in coal and bananas and then proceed on its course. The little town is pensive and smells of fennel. "Funchal" means fennel in Portuguese. It counts up the arrivals and the departures, and takes note of those that die. It has no life in itself, the death of others brings its life, and the conversation often resembles a leaf in a book of memories; it is the text of an old album; all know that an old album is naught but a cemetery. No, Funchal has not its own life. There are sometimes jubilee days from Portuguese history; then they have fireworks, but they are lighted not as in the rest of the world at night, but in the daytime, not for the eye but for the ear; nothing can be seen, but there's a stick, noise, hissing, and explosions—the populace exults.

Only once I left the coastal region and climbed up above the town into the summits of the hills and saw from there the centre of the island on whose borders I was living. There is a spot up there, in the middle of the hills, which is called Rio Trio (the cold stream). What a sonorous name, and, in that high temperature, what a sweet sounding one. We mounted the steep rocks, with only the sea and the horizon below us. It was dry, and the vegetation which was coniferous was also dry; but at the foot of the pines there was soft green moss, and growing out of it, among other flowers, what do you think we found? A strong large-flowered fuchsia, with a red funnel and double violet petals, growing wild. In the hottest places, where on the borders of the road adhesive liana catches hold of the tenacious bushes, in the spots where the sun baked most ardently in the midst of sultry stones, I found wild heliotrope. It is dry up there, but along the hills, out of the highest clefts, long cornices stretch out on all sides; these are parapets behind which water flows, and then runs down the hillsides.

> "Spring, why art thou hastening to the valley?
> Is it to men? Try how it is with them."

And along these parapets, which hang over the abyss and stretch out for miles, boys run about in fearless carelessness.

What can impress itself more on the memory than contrasts? After the dry sultriness on the southern slopes of the hot rocks to come suddenly into the cool moisture of green valleys. We entered into the shade of laurel woods; we were met by a holy rustle beneath their mysterious crowns; their mighty stems, before they divide, bear upwards on their twisted branches the succulent verdure that clusters round their roots—they are covered all round with trembling green ferns; and delicate goat's-beard that descends to the lowest branches. Nowhere, not even in Ceylon, have I seen such luxuriant vegetation. We went to the highest point, from where the sea is seen all around; here there could be no doubt that we were on an island. I remembered how Pièrre Loti sat on the island of Tahiti with his little native girl at the top of the hill and looked down from an immense height on the surrounding horizon, when suddenly the little native girl asked, " How high up must one go to see your country ? "

We were standing at the edge of a precipice, out of this precipice a crag rose before us, on the summit of it there was a sort of platform. How tempting it was, but how terrible. It was impossible to jump on to it. But between it and the mainland on which we were standing and that tempting platform there rose out of the abyss a sort of sharp stone tusk; in its side, one might say in its cheek, there is an indenture, a small step, on which you can place one foot while you step over with the other on to the platform. It was terrible to execute this feat, but the movement required for the return was still more terrible. To go there was an act of voluntary choice, to come back was a necessity; in the one case the principle of " can " acted, in the other it was the principle of " must." I mention this circumstance, because it appears to me that this was the bravest act of my life, as far as bravery can be compatible with uselessness. The return journey to the town was much shorter, that is to say, quicker than the ascent. We accomplished the greater part of the way gliding over the stones of the road in a sledge. In a quarter of an hour after having left the pine wood, having slid down the steep hills, we found ourselves at the foot of the

Cathedral belfry. " From the Cathedral " everybody knows his way home.

My brother Gregory was very ill, and his temper was often trying for those around him. He was interested in social-political questions and he was a constitutionalist. He once went to Darmstadt to present to Nicholas II a note on political reforms for Russia. I remember in his rough copy of this note there was the following phrase: " Sire, do not prepare for your Consort the fate of Marie Antoinette." He said, " No, I must not be sentimental," and struck out this line. The note was handed in and the next day he received from the Emperor's aide-de-camp, Count Heyden, a letter, in which he was informed of this in the name of the Emperor. The letter ended with the words, " You can go away now." This was mentioned at the time in the German newspapers. My brother returned to Russia at the time of the opening of the Duma, but he did not join any party; he remained solitary. In him were harmonized, in a restless blending, an impetuous yearning towards innovation and the sweet attractions of olden times. He remained solitary. He too was an island. He died in 1910 in Mentone and was buried in the cemetery there.

On the 2nd of December, 1893, I left San Francisco in the White Star liner *Oceanic* for Japan. We sailed in a terrible storm that lasted five days. On the sixth we were greeted by a brilliant tropical calm. During two days we sailed on, and in the evening of the second we approached Hawaii, one of the Sandwich Islands that had first been discovered by Captain Cook. We assembled on the starboard side of the deck and greedily breathed in the scent of the vegetation from the land. We arrived at this distant corner of the earth when it was passing through difficult moments. A revolution had broken out there. The palace of the last monarch of the Sandwich Islands, Queen Liliuokalani, was occupied by the rebels and the windows were done up with sand-bags; the inhabitants were excited, but on the whole the revolution was mere play. The Queen was sent to a country house, foreigners seized the power and proclaimed a republic under the protection of the United States. There was nothing dreadful in this, the sea glittered, the sun baked, the palms waved their crowns; the long streets with their smoothly trodden down red lava roads stretched out beneath the palms, the houses and their verandas looked out gaily from among them, all smothered in flowering creepers, and it was only on the postage stamps that the effigy of Queen Liliuokalani, in a low dress, was crossed out by the word "Republic" printed in red letters. I do not know if it was because we only touched at this island for a few hours, and therefore could not have time to penetrate into the life interests of the inhabitants, but the insignificance of man's passions had never struck me with greater force than it did there, under the brilliant rays of the sun and surrounded by triumphal nature. We looked into one of the local schools for natives, where we were received very amiably by the American teacher, who offered us refreshments and told us about the political events that had just taken place. On the table there was lying the local English newspaper, and I was astonished to find in it reports of the papers I had read at the educational and religious congresses. Among the passengers was the bishop of the Zante island, the most reverend Bishop Latas, who was also returning home from America. His picturesque figure in a cassock, with the panagia on his breast, struck everybody. He was an amiable, talkative man, who greatly enjoyed the voyage, but the beauties of the Pacific ocean were poisoned for him by the uneasiness with which he awaited the reception that he would receive in Greece. For some reason he feared mostly the Greek minister Trikupis, as he seemed to expect a rebuke for having taken part in the Chicago congress. He often came up to me on deck to communicate his fears, but then a more optimistic mood would succeed, and he said, " Peut-être tout ça c'est des chateaux en Espagne." [1] He said this possibly wanting to say " dark thoughts." It was evident it was so. Afterwards I sent a telegram of greeting from Athens to him in Zante ; in his answer he thanked me, and said that his affairs had gone off satisfactorily and he added, "Ris souvent chateaux en Espagne Pacifique." [2] After a halt of six hours in Hawaii we proceeded on our voyage. The island receded and melted away. The strip of sand on the beach became more dim, the outlines of the palms grew more indistinct ; here and there canals full of water that traversed the feathery verdure of the sugar-canes glittered like bits of looking-glass, and you saw the blushing outlines of the purple hills ; all went away, became lost to view, and at last Hawaii sank into the radiance of the sea and the sky. We bent our course towards Japan.

Japan is also an island, but it is an archipelago ; it has not that solitude, that concentration, it has not that tragic visionariness, that hovers over solitary islands. An archipelago is a sort of choral dance. There is something wonderfully joyful in this succession of land and water, of this play of meandering waters and promontories : there is much life, much human intercourse in these calls from island to island ; there is much playful beauty in these bits of the sea that resemble lakes or rivers ; here is a continent that has crumbled into the sea, and has scattered

---

[1] "Perhaps all this is only castles in Spain."
[2] " Often laugh castles in Spain Pacific."

its fragments ; here the sea has torn away from the mainland a portion of its sea-board.

Japan did not please me. My visit was not at the right time, I was there in winter. Japan must be seen either in the autumn when the chrysanthemums are in bloom or in spring when the cherries are blossoming ; I saw Japan under snow. And the Japanese did not please me. They are always smiling at you, and giggling. This involuntarily raises suspicions of what they do behind your back. The Japanese women are dolls. They are gigglers ; if you show them a finger they will laugh. Of course in Tokio I saw what is shown to all foreigners : the fantastic Yoshiwara, the women's quarter. In the streets here all the houses are surrounded by verandas which are closed in with golden gratings ; in these cages, on cocoa-nut mats, smiling Japanese girls sit in bright-coloured kimonos and wonderful head-dresses. They sit there with their trains spread out around them, with broad sashes which are tied in large bows on their backs, warming their doll-like little hands over bronze pots filled with glowing embers. The women are turned into playthings. Outside these gratings there are crowds of men, looking at the girls, calling to them, making their choice. I even saw some children in this gazing mob. It is said (can it be true?) that many girls enter these houses in order to earn for themselves a dowry. All this seems incredible for our European understanding ; all this transports us into other culture, into another race.

Oh, how inexorable the question of race became ; it was like an impregnable stronghold looming before my eyes during my journey round the world. Look at Japanese art. What can be more lovely? It was in Japan that I saw the connexion between art and nature for the first time. When we were approaching Yokohama I already saw from the deck of the liner the outlines of pines growing on the capes and headlands—low, stunted, spreading, like those evidently caricatured forms which are found in Japanese art. When I saw a Japanese little dog, all shaggy with curls of hair on its brow, with a beard and whiskers, I understood the source of those porcelain griffins with which we adorn our mantelpieces and cupboards. And when I saw the doll-like Japanese girls with their elaborate head-dresses stuck through with long pins, sitting on the floor round the bronze brazier, I understood how much realism there was in the affected women we see in Japanese art. Notwithstanding all the beauty in Japanese art it is not the real food for my soul. It appeals to me and it delights me, but it is not the answer to my inner aspirations, and it does not elevate my soul to the heights for which it yearns. It was only in Japan that I understood the reason of this. I understood that I liked a Japanese object in so far as I could bring it into my house and accommodate it to my own furniture; I admired it without coming out of the European atmosphere. I therefore liked comparatively small objects. But here, in Japan, I saw large buildings, temples, gateways, palaces into which, when I entered, I was in another, a Japanese atmosphere, and this atmosphere was strange to me. This strangeness is racial difference. Not in education, but much deeper than in personal education is the root of this strangeness to be found; it lies in the deep wombs of human nature, in the mysterious heredity from former generations. *Race* is the thing that speaks loudest in man; it is the racial feelings that are the most powerful in man, and their source is found in the depths of his past. And that is why things of another race are foreign to him; he prizes them, he admires them, he likes them, but he can *live* only on that which comes from his own race. Those who understand this feel deeply how absurd the labour is to replace this natural creative power of human nature by that invention of man's imagination which is called class differences.

No, I did not like Japan. At that time I was in opposition to the general opinion ; it was then the fashion to be enraptured with Japan ; this fashion was especially introduced by the sailors of all nations. For them Japan was in some way a sort of Capua : geishas, tea-houses, in every town a yoshiwara, in Yokohama the most famous in the whole East—No. 9, chrysanthemums, cherry-blossom, mandarins that are peeled for you by beautiful fingers and fall before you in a special way like open stars. Of course in all this there is the charm of novelty, exotic tartness, but much is also owing to its cheapness. The first Japanese girl that I saw was at the Chicago Exhibition ; she was a waitress in a tea-house. She was enchanting, one never was tired of looking at her. I thought how pretty she is, how courteous she is, what a charming smile she has ; but when I saw in Japan that all were equally pretty, that all were equally courteous, that all had the same smile, and that they smiled on all in the same way, then after I had been there two weeks I wanted to run away, and I did run away, I ran away from that smile.

In Japan I made the acquaintance of a very remarkable man. He was our Bishop Nikolai. He had passed more than thirty years in Japan. He was a zealous missionary ; it was owing to his preaching that numerous Orthodox pastorates were established, and the Orthodox cathedral in Tokio was constructed. He was a man of great wisdom, profound erudition, and one of the men who knew the Japanese best. Among other works he had translated all the Japanese epics into Russian ; this would have been a treasure such as no other European literature possessed, but unfortunately his work fell a victim to one of those conflagrations which can only take place in Japan, where all the houses are built of wood and all the partitions are made of paper. Bishop Nikolai told us many interesting things about Japan; to listen to him was in one way pleasant, but in another unbearable. He was completely carried away by his subject, he stuttered and stammered in his excitement, he began sentences which he left unfinished, as he passed from subject to subject. I remember when I said what an unpleasant impression the eternal Japanese laughter left on me, he said it was the result of one of the fundamental principles of Japanese education; from early childhood it was instilled that it was only woman for whom it was proper to show what she feels, but that every man who has command over himself must hide his feelings. That is the origin of this smile; the smile in Japan was the veil of the soul. I also remember a story from a Japanese epic. Three of the national heroes are sung of in their legends. I do not remember the names of two of them, but the third, the favourite of the people, was Tukugava. This is how the national tradition portrays the difference of their characters and their connexion with people. What does each of them do when the nightingale ceases to sing? The first says, " Kill him! " The second says, " Make him sing! " But Tukugava says, " Wait till he sings again."

The most reverend Nikolai was an extraordinary man and a rare example of one who separated the principles of religion and nationality. At that time, when in Russia the chord of national religion was drawn to the last degree of tension, when it was said that only the Orthodox could be real Russians, and only a Russian could be a real Orthodox, Bishop Nikolai was able so to place his missionary work in Japan that, even during the war with Russia, the services were continued in the Tokio Cathedral, and there was not the slightest friction between the Japanese of different faiths.

Japan is a strange country. Always laughing, yet absorbed in thought; it is like a plaything, but serious, small but strong. We experienced its strength on our weakness. I learned the reason of both the one and the other when at the time of the Japanese war I read somewhere the words of a song that the Japanese mother sings to her child. The song asks " Why do the Russians suffer defeat ? " and the song answers " Because the Russian mothers have no love for their country." Japan is a strange country. When we think of it we see ironclads and heavy artillery; when we dream of it we see doll-women in toy houses, toy-men in doll gardens. And all this appears not to be life, but animated toys. The sides of the hills cut up into troughs; the silver sheen of the artificially retained water, the pliant rustle of the bamboos; the bare-footed gardeners tripping along the dry ridges between two flooded fields; at the top of an arched stone bridge, above a pool of sleeping water, a dreamy doll, in a yellow kimono with a lilac sash tied behind, and a hairdress with long pins stuck through it, is standing dreaming under the shade of a many-coloured umbrella; on the sleepy surface of the water in the midst of green split-up leaves the ruby-coloured water-lilies open out their nest-like blossoms; there is a stork in the sky, a crane near the water; the white snow-capped cone of the Vulcan Fujiyama; chrysanthemums, glycine, cherry blossoms, irises—had all this, taken from nature, gone over to the screens, the vases, and the bronzes, or had it gone off the bronzes, the vases, and the screens, and become animated in nature?

Yes, Japan is a strange country.

After toy-like and child-like Japan, China strikes you by its seriousness and its ancientness. I only touched at China. We were bound for Ceylon and called at Hong

Kong. While the ship was in port we had the opportunity of going up the Pearl river by night as far as Canton, to return the next night to our vessel which was to sail again at sunrise. Canton is said to be the most Chinese town that can be seen in China. I can remember but faintly the few hours I passed in China, but the impression left by them was something infernal. I passed the whole time in a palanquin. The couch on which I reclined was suspended from two very long bamboo canes, which rested on the shoulders of two Chinamen, who, with short, elastic steps, bore me along through an endless labyrinth of streets. At both sides of the streets there were not houses, but shops with open stalls in front of them ; there was a smell of meat, of vegetables, of fish, of roasting, of fumigatory pastilles ; on the stalls there was blood, entrails ; skinned dogs and monkeys were hanging on the walls. The air became more and more unbearable ; over head there was a trellis of bamboos that was thrown over the street from house to house, from which depended boards with inscriptions in Chinese characters ; this covers the whole length of the street like a ceiling, and it is only by twisting your neck that you are able to see a bit of the sky. It was stinking, stuffy, and weird. But it was the crowd that was the most weird. In this narrow but endlessly long space crowds of people swarmed all the time, unceasingly and in such numbers as I had never seen before. This endless stream of yellow-skinned women and men pours onwards ; this " yellow danger " streams forwards, and never ceases ; the street comes to an end, it turns into another, and still this stream of people never abates. And the whole of this crowd is talking as only an Asiatic crowd can talk—with the emphasis that a man uses when he wishes to convince another by shouting him down. The never-diminishing flow of this human avalanche, the absence of any respite in this overstraining sound, and the impossibility of fixing one's eyes on a single immovable object acted like fumes that made you giddy. At last I had to shut my eyes. The elastic bare-footed gait of my bearers had a lulling effect. Suddenly something happened I had never experienced before; waves of silence seemed to wash over me. I opened my eyes, and saw green meadows, trees, rice-fields, and behind me the high walls of the town and in it a high fantastic gateway. Birds chirped—a blessed quiet. But it was too late, my head had begun to ache; it was the most severe headache I have had in my whole life. I went to my cabin, and cried out with pain during the whole night. I shall never forget Canton. With the first gleam of dawn we left Hong Kong for the Pacific ocean. The Pacific ocean, which is usually stormy, was calm. The sails were set:

"Swell, swell, obedient sails!"

The smooth ocean shone. The silent prow of the vessel cut through the water and the air, while the heavy, noisy stern drove to right and left the foam that was raised by the screw and spread out wide behind it the traces of its course. White gulls flew round and round; they swooped down, caught something and rose again; and the smooth, round shining backs of the playful dolphins rose above the surface and sank beneath it again. We went on thus for five days. Each morning the English ladies said good morning when we met on the deck, and they added politely "Lovely morning." How fond the English are of greeting you with a barometric confirmation.

On the sixth day we again touched the land at Singapore, on the southern extremity of the Malay peninsula. It is the central point of meeting of all the world's great routes: from America to Africa, from Japan to Europe, from

Australia to America. All races, people of all colours, of all shades, of all languages, meet here. I went on shore. I had time to see the celebrated Botanical Gardens—palms, bananas, huge ferns, and gigantic bamboos. In this kingdom of dreams and fairy tales it was found necessary to have one inscription to remind visitors that "It is forbidden to pluck flowers or to break the bushes." And these words, in this town where all the races of the terrestrial globe pass and meet, were written only in one language—in Russian. Laden with oranges, bananas, and pineapples, I returned to the ship. An English lady was lying under the shade of the awning; she had not been on land, but was making notes of the voyage.

"Have you been in the town?"

"Yes."

"Have you seen the natives?"

"I have seen them."

"Can you tell me if they feed much on rice?"

"Oh yes, on all the door-steps families were sitting eating rice out of a pot."

The hand worked rapidly across the white paper; the pencil becomes bolder when the mind is enriched.

We weighed anchor. Our route was to Colombo, in Ceylon. Again we had a brilliantly smooth sea, and each morning "a lovely morning." At night our foamy tail left its fiery phosphorescent traces far behind it.

> "The dome of heaven glorious with starlight
> Mysteriously looks down from its great height,
> While we sail on, surrounded on all sides
> By glowing glitter of abysmal tides."

What unison in the countless stars! What unison in the answering throbbings of the heavenly firmament and the rippling ocean! What harmony in the horizontal progress of the tall vertical masts. What unity of reflections in my own soul. For the first time it occurred to my mind that the lines

> "The book of the stars was revealed unto him,
> And the speech of the ocean made clear,"

must be taken not as an enumeration of successive alternations but as two expressions for one unity; not first the stars and then the waves, but the stars and the waves as a simultaneous revelation of nature.

In Singapore, just as we were leaving, and at the moment I was speaking to the Englishwoman who was writing her impressions of the voyage, I saw a tall figure wrapped in white ascending the companion ladder, a dark face framed in black hair looked out of these white wrappers, and the eyes of our acquaintance from the Chicago Religious Congress, Dgarmapala, smiled upon me.

"From whence?" I asked.

"From Japan."

"Where are you going?"

"To Colombo."

"Why did you go to Japan?"

"On our Buddhist business."

"And now?"

"I am going with a Japanese deputation to Ceylon. The Japanese Buddhists are sending an old, a very ancient statue of Buddha to the Ceylon Buddhists. Would you like to see the ceremony when we arrive? I will tell you the day and the hour."

We arrived at Colombo on the evening of the tenth day. Dgarmapala was met by a deputation. When we took leave of each other he said, "To-morrow evening at six o'clock, here on the pier."

I do not remember ever having seen a sight like the one I

saw on the following day. The ancient statue was taken off the steamer the next evening and carried between lines of native women and men. It was carried along under palm trees, flowers were scattered before it, garments fluttered, light rainbow-coloured veils escaped from their fastenings and flapped in the air. The swarthy crowd stretched out like a long ribbon, and the many coloured turbans looked like the huge flowers of some fantastic peonies rising above the flimsy finery of female caprice. Thus they moved forwards, and behind the crowd the sea glittered between the palms. Sometimes at the invitation of Dgarmapala I sat down in his char-à-banc, which was drawn by a humpbacked ox. I remember in my geography book these oxen were called zebus. We arrived at a gateway; beyond was a green meadow on which rose various pavilions, only roofs supported by white columns without walls. They were Buddhist temples.

Before the centre temple there was an orange-yellow crowd. They were the priests; they all had chlamydes thrown over the left shoulder, their bare right arms were free. It was just like the chorus in an opera. They all had shaven heads. In front stood the high-priest. I was led forward and presented. I bowed. The high-priest looked to one side. I bowed in that direction. He looked to the other side, I bowed again, no notice was taken of me. One of those who accompanied me bent down to my ear and whispered " Do not be surprised, it is the law; the servant of God is the brother of all men; to bow to all the people in the world is impossible, but to bow only to one is unjust." While the preparations were being made for the service of prayer we went into the inner apartments of the high-priest. He conversed with me, of course, through an interpreter. He asked me if I knew in Petersburg Professor Minaev, a great Sanskrit scholar. I answered

I had been his pupil in the university. The high-priest was delighted and said he had known him too, that he had been in Ceylon, and had been their guest in that very room; his work was highly prized. He gave me a book he had written; it was in incomprehensible characters but ingeniously written. We returned to the temple. Then the speeches began, complimentary greetings and replies. I sat on the platform among the honoured guests; the high-priest also sat there. I did not understand a word that was said in the Bengali and Japanese languages, but I watched the extraordinary picture that was before me; the women wrapped up in muslins sitting on the floor, men standing around near the columns, lamps hanging from the roof, the starlit night that could be seen in the openings between the columns, and the tall palms visible against the night sky. Suddenly there was a whisper in English at my ear; the high-priest begged me to say a few words. I had to stand up. I told them the same thing with which I had greeted the Congress of Religion in Chicago. In Dostoeffsky's *The Brothers Karamazov* there is a story about an old woman and a carrot; it was this story I told them. Here it is as told in my own words:

"An old woman, a great sinner, was suffering the tortures of hell. One day she saw, high up in the blue sky, an angel fly past. She wailed. The angel stopped his flight and looked down. 'When you are before the face of the Almighty, tell Him there is an old woman who has suffered more than she can bear. Will the Lord not be merciful and relieve her suffering?' The angel flew away and made his report. 'Find out,' the Lord said, 'if she did a single good deed on earth.' The angel returned to the old woman. 'Yes,' she said, 'I once gave a little carrot to a beggar.' The angel reported this. 'Take a little carrot,' said the Lord, 'hold it out to her and let her grasp it, and then pull her out; if the little carrot is strong enough, she will be saved.' The angel did as he was bidden. The old woman caught hold of the carrot, the angel began to pull her out of hell; and the old woman rose out of the flames. Suddenly she noticed that another sinner had caught hold of her leg; however, the little carrot was able to support them. The angel pulled and they rose higher and higher. The old woman looked down, another sinner had caught hold, and then more and more, a whole chain of them were holding on to each other and hanging on to her leg. The old woman became afraid and she began to kick; they would not let go, and there were always more and more hanging on. Then she cried out with her whole might ' Let go! The carrot is mine!' She had hardly said this when the stem of the carrot broke, and they all fell back into the eternal flames."

It was not difficult to add to this story a little moral applicable to the present occasion, that the good on earth belongs to all; that spiritual value cannot be private property, as Goethe wrote to Carlyle, "Das wahrhaftig Schöne Zeichnet sich dadurch aus, dass es der ganzen Menscheit angehört." This "carrot story" had an enormous success in America. "The carrot is mine," was heard at meetings, and in private conversations, and in the field where football was being played. This same carrot story I told to the simple Indian listeners. I spoke in English and a native translated it into Bengali; I said a sentence, and waited for it to be translated and then went on. It was very interesting to watch the laughter of those few natives who understood me while I was relating the story in English, how their laughter whetted the attention of those who did not understand, and how, after the translation, they burst into laughter, in which laughter the first joined in again. When I finished, when the marks of approbation had subsided a most incredible thing occurred; the high-priest rose, came up to me, and, before all the assembled people, pressed my hand. One of my fellow-travellers whispered excitedly into my ear, " I have never seen him do such a thing before."

Thus ended my first day in Ceylon, and the whole of my remaining stay in the island was tinctured by these first impressions; what a fairy tale it was; what intangibility, how unseizable; there was nothing material; only visions, colours, immateriality. The general impression was—vegetation. Wherever you looked there were plants, leaves, stems, twigs, flowers of huge dimensions, to which the eye was unaccustomed, in such extraordinary bounteousness of vegetative power; and, for our European eyes, with what richness! Can you imagine the rarest hothouse plants thrown out into the street, or growing on the sides of ditches or along walls. You have doubtless seen in conservatories an inner, a second hothouse, it is very hot there, very damp, and it has a nice scent. The most extraordinary plants grow in this house, the most delicate ferns, wonderful leaves, dark green, with pink, white and red veins. It was these I saw there near the walls. These plants grow there like nettles and dark leaves grow in our land. When I admired all this I looked with pity on the natives; they do not realize that they are surrounded by the greatest treasures of nature; that is to say, they must certainly feel the beauty, but the rareness of their surroundings they evidently cannot feel. Strange thoughts come into the mind. If we in Europe built hothouses to cultivate these rare plants, the time may come when some lover of botany will build a " refrigerator " in which he will grow nettles and burdock. But besides their rareness, which forms the subjective principle is their objective value, and if it were possible to grow whortleberries in such a "refrigerator" in Ceylon, where they would be rare; still peaches and pineapples, that grew along the walls, taste much better, and their walls are more pretty than ours. Notwithstanding all its beauty, I must confess I do not like nature where there is no grass—no green grass on which you can lie down under a tree with a book. This nature is wonderful to the eye, but to enter into it, to mix with it, is somehow difficult. It appears to you like stage scenery, incredible scenery. The most incredible that I saw was along the railroad from Colombo to Kandy. Kandy is in the hills, it is not so stifling there, it is a summer resort. But what a road! The train winds about in the hills; these hills are like a conservatory: palms, ferns, bananas, philodendrons, paulownias, araucarias. And the noise of the train seems heretical in the midst of this tropical virginity. But the most wonderful thing among all these wonders is the tulip-tree. The enormous stem near the earth seems to have twisted several times round itself to form a pedestal, and then, like a smooth column, it stretches upwards beneath its spreading crown; on this crown are borne enormously large red blossoms like red flower beakers. When they are ripe, they fall singly, heavily to the ground; it was quite like a scene from *Parsifal*. What a superabundance of beauty, when such a red beaker is torn from its green heights to fall at your feet! When many have fallen what a carpet they form.

Ceylon is the kingdom of laziness, of drowsiness; no rapid motion is possible. Even the eyes, the most rapid of our organs, move only slowly there. I remember we made an excursion into the interior of the island to see some old ruins. Three of us, two English ladies and myself, were seated in an arba[1]; in it was also seated sideways, but nearer to the front of the arba, the dark-skinned native

---

[1] A bullock cart.

driver; he was almost lying, with his legs hanging over the side of the cart, and from time to time he whipped up the hunch-backed zebus with a long bamboo rod. How the sleepy laziness with which he did this annoyed me. What indifference whether the draught animals went any faster or not. And then, suddenly, I understood—the ox could go no faster, then why should the driver use more energy in whipping it? Yes, our Russian driver uses energy in whipping his horses, but why should this driver of sleepy oxen be energetic? I understood how the movements of man were influenced by the nature that surrounds him. Those who live near mountain streams have a brisk, quick, firm gait; those who live near our quiet rivers that flow between soft crumbly banks, have an indolent, slow gait. Our yamshchik (driver of a post vehicle) whoops as he drives his troïka, the driver of the sleepy oxen dozes. And we dozed, and all around us dozed; the tall feathery bamboos dozed, the heavy lianas drooped on the branches, and a thick, sleepy serpent crawled across the road in front of us, and on the other side of the road it was swallowed up by the sultry, sleepy earth. Oh, the green and sunny dales! How beautiful is the endless depth of your verdure and your sunshine! How sunny your green is, how green your sunshine! I read once on the title page of a magazine " The dales of æsthetics." How bad that sounds, all bristling and prickly. But if we transpose the words " The æsthetic dales "—how soft. We drove softly over the sweating forest earth. Heat! We were wet, and sipped warm soda-water. Ice is the most precious thing there; almost more valuable than precious stones, which are so plentiful in Ceylon. Moonstones are quite cheap; you pay ten times as much for them in Petersburg. And pearls; unfortunately it was not the season for pearl-fishing when I was in Ceylon. There is a tempting custom there. You buy a barrel of oysters—it may happen that all are empty (this is often the case), but there may be a pearl in each oyster (this never happens). It is a sort of game of hazard.

In Ceylon you simply have to drive away precious stones, that is, you drive away the native dealers in them. You lie in the veranda of the great Oriental Hotel in a deep arm-chair with long arms that resemble oars, the Englishmen place their legs on these oars in the most indecent poses. But custom, the great law-giver, has legitimized this. Well, while you are lying in this way and drinking cold lemonade through a straw, dark-skinned natives in white garments, their black hair coiled into a chignon and fixed with a comb like a woman's at the top of their heads, come up to you and spread out before your eyes rubies, sapphires, or moonstones.

" I don't want them."

" Only look at this one. What a stone."

" I don't want it."

" You need not buy it. Only look at it."

" I've seen it. Go away."

" Well, but just say what do you think it's worth."

" I don't know, its all one to me."

" No, only say what you think. You need not buy it. Well, what is its price ? "

" Ten rupees. Go away."

" Ten rupees ! What do you mean, Sahib ? For such a beauty, fifty would be too little."

" Go away."

" And you say ten."

" Go away."

" Ten rupees ! Ha, ha, ha. Well now, thirty."

" Go away ! ! ! "

From all parts of the veranda you hear " Go ! " And

suddenly somebody shouts " Dzhao ! ! " This, the native translation of " Go ! " has the same effect on the native as " Pish " has on a cat. The veranda becomes empty, and quiet reigns.

The inhabitants of Ceylon, as in the whole of India, are of mixed races. One race, like these vendors of precious stones, is dark, languid, supple, and wears chignons ; these are the Bengalese, a race that astonishes by its simple naïveté ; they are like big children. Then there is a very strange race, I don't remember how they are called. They are almost white, like our Caucasian race ; they are short, stumpy, and strong, and are not only without chignons, but have their heads shaven, and what surprises most is their resemblance to the purest Roman type ; they could stand as models for the busts of emperors and senators. They have quite an original way of draping their muslin garments ; they can always be distinguished in a crowd. But one of the strangest phenomena, in the domain of anthropology, are the so-called Tamils. They are the most splendid types of the Caucasian race in their build, and at the same time they are as black as the blackest negro. This is the finest type of the human race, cast in black bronze. They are only found in Ceylon and in the southern part of the Malabar peninsula. There is something wonderfully noble in their manner; it is to the last degree aristocratic. I often saw some vulgar European come up to one of these Tamils, a fruit vendor, and I have wondered at the anomalous way in which nature has apportioned the self-consciousness in people. Why, the European ought to feel himself lower than him, and he ought to feel himself higher than the European, but in reality it is quite the contrary. And neither the one nor the other would confess that he is dwelling in error. I remember one day one of these black Tamils was walking along the seashore. He had only a loin-cloth on his body and a red shawl on his head; it was windy, and the red shawl became unloosened and had only the resistance that the man's forehead offered to the wind. The women of this type are very little developed physically, it appears as if their growth had been stunted; they grow old very early, like all southern women, and they disfigure themselves in a strange manner—they make an incision in the lobe of the ear and hang heavy iron rings to it, in order to stretch it as much as possible downwards. This is begun in childhood; there are girls on whose ears as many as three or four rings are suspended; the ideal all try to attain is to stretch the ear so much that one ring suffices to touch the shoulder. The most beautiful women I saw in Delhi; their colour was like coffee with milk, they had black almond-shaped eyes like hinds, showing much white; they were serious, and mysteriously wrapped up in their white garments, and they wore silver studs in their nostrils that look like little flies.

When one thinks of the rest of India Ceylon recedes into a kind of vegetable haze, resembling a huge flower. Of course, the fact that I was no sportsman greatly contributed to this impression; for others Ceylon is a green thicket crackling under the heavy crushing tread of elephants. For me it it a flower, torn from the mainland; it is immovable and silent. In all the rest of continental India there is movement and chatter.

The most original town I saw in India was Jaipur, the capital of Rajpootana, half-way between Calcutta and Bombay. How charming this rose-coloured town is. It is the residence of the Maharajah, and the whole town seems a " royal diversion," a sort of theatrical performance in the open air. In crossing the square my driver stopped near the fountain that formed, so to speak, the centre of the stage, and, sitting in my calash, I looked at the performance. There they were leading about the royal horses; what saddles, what shabracks, and what horses! I remember one bay horse, smooth as satin, with a white mane and a white tail and one white foot, so highly prized by the Arabs. There I saw the royal panthers being led about; they are used for hunting four-footed game, as hawks are employed for hunting birds. There too, the royal dancing girls were taking a drive in two large carriages, twelve or fifteen in all—dark-skinned does with black eyes surrounded with white, dressed in gauze, with rings in their ears, silver patches in their noses, and jingling bangles on their swarthy arms. . . . And what a crowd; what a picturesque crowd! What aristocracy in this democratic crowd! Oh, how the Aryan race has degenerated in our Europe! What a feast for the eyes it was! people of every tint of sun-tanning; light-coloured tissues of every hue of the rainbow that is fading away under the burning rays of the sun.

Yes, Jaipur is perhaps the most fairy-like place I saw in the eastern fairy-lands. I remember a fig-grove in the outskirts; on the fig-trees blue peacocks were perched, and their golden-eyed tails hung down among the branches, and through this grove I rode on an elephant. To ride an elephant is unpleasant, it jolts along somewhat like a cart on four-cornered wheels.

When one talks of islands and of the ocean, it is difficult not to remember the desert—that ocean of sand. A crafty enchantress, tempting and drawing you towards herself, and at the same time a great soother. In that flat plain there is a sort of majestic horizontality, and in its terrible unity, rare verticality, like the origins of timid transgression. A camel (that ship of the desert) comes along; he treads softly with his soft feet on the soft sand. The swarthy driver, in a blue shirt, with a white skull-cap on his head, follows the camel; from time to time he drives the camel on with a guttural cry on the letter " A." What inexplicable meanings there are in this " Haa "—entreaty and submission, and sadness; it is as limitless as the limitless surrounding desert, and bottomless as the bottomless sources of the race of man.

I cannot picture to myself a desert other than the Arabian desert; it was also at one time different to what it is now, as everything else on earth. Between Tunis and Stax, in the midst of the desert, there are the ruins of a huge Roman circus with nothing around it : the desert, a coliseum, and cactuses. This proves that there was once a Roman desert. At present, on the shady side of this enormous circus, Arabian nomads have pitched their tents, a human nest—microbes in the crevices of a Roman skeleton. This reminds me of a peculiar species of lice that only exists on the wens that grow on whales when they have attained the age of a hundred years. A huge old whale is like a coliseum in the desert; it is old, frowning and proud in the midst of the gnarled cactuses, inflexible in the disunion between its Roman majesty and the poverty of these Arabian nomads. I still see the motion of their waving burnouses against the background of those immovable Roman stone outlines.

The camel treads lightly. It is comfortable to sit on soft cushions on his high hump; you are rocked gently. The driver utters his guttural, stimulating cry—is it a human complaint or the sigh of the desert ? There come a party of women with veiled faces, carrying water pitchers on their heads. Water, the most precious thing in that ocean of sand. A horseman wrapped up in his burnous is riding towards us. He is mounted on a splendid Arab horse, a light bay with a black mane, and tail and a white spot on its leg close to the hoof. The Arab has a cord twisted round his turban and a long thin rifle is slung across his back. Now an Arab in a white burnous is approaching ; he is balancing two bunches of red pepper on his head, they hang down on either side almost to the ground. The transparent pods burn like red wine transpierced by the rays of the declining sun. There, in the midst of the desert, kneeling on the ground near his reposing camel, looking towards the setting sun, the bedouin performs his evening devotions. And every day at this evening hour, like submissive corn that bends before the wind, the submissive turbans bow in prayer, and the East, bending its knees in prayer, looks towards Mecca.

Let us go in the track of the departing sun. We have had enough of the East, we are drawn homewards. The Mediterranean sea calls to us. Oh, cradle of our race, our spiritual country ! Between Asia, Europe, and Africa, that blue laughing sea ! It is called the Ægean, the Marmora, the Adriatic, or the Ionian, but it all is the Mediterranean. What can be more beautiful than the Archipelago that lies between Asia Minor and Greece ! They are like stones thrown by nature to enable man to cross on them the quaking abyss from the ancient world of contemplation into the seething world of thought and work. What a juxtaposition of worlds : the islands of Asia Minor, like sprinklings of Greece on Asia, and Turkey, like Asiatic splashes on the delicate Greek shores. And then there is Greece, not of course this one, but the former, the antique, the one that is called " ancient," and why should it be called so ? What can be younger than ancient Greece ? When a grandfather tells his grandchildren about his own youth he grows young again ; so do we when we think of ancient Greece ; we too grow young, Greece is the youth of humanity. Brilliant, harmonious, with tabour and cymbal, with moist eyes, beautiful and wise, crowned with laurels she stands there divinely terrestrial in the midst of the Mediterranean sea. Everything flows from her, all is engendered in her, all is found in her: the beautiful, the wise, all that has been, and all that is to be. She has always enshrined in herself the hope of the ages. When great disturbances have occurred, when the world shook under the axes of barbaric invasions, when the way was lost, and the lights were extinguished, when even her holy land was trodden under heretical heels, and the sacrilegious hand bent down her divine neck, then in the gloom of the barbarian invasions she passed on, over the sea, her ancient torch, to her sister Italy, and the beacon of the Renaissance was kindled there. Yes, the Mediterranean sea rocked our spiritual cradle. The waves of the Adriatic kiss the shores both of Greece and Italy.

The Dalmatian shore of the Balkan peninsula is a splash of Italy—the Italian speech, the Italian Church, Venetian buildings, and on all sides you find looking at you the Venetian lion of St. Mark. On both sides of the Adriatic Sea, from the Balkan shore to the Apennines and from the Apennine shore to the Balkans, the marble lion of St. Mark is always staring into the distance and holding in its paw the open book in which the first word is "Pax Tibi." While all the most blood-stained pages of the history of our long-suffering Europe had their origin there, all was conceived in that corner of the Adriatic Sea.

What softness rests on those shores when the "war of races" is not aroused. Corfu! What a delicate island in the shade of her rustling olives. They are huge old olives, hollow-stemmed, and young silvery leaves grow on them. On a hill above the high cliffs of the seashore the olive trees have spread the shade of their leaves, and below, beneath the cliffs, in the blue sea, there is an island with a white monastery on it. And all is framed in the shade of the rustling leaves. Here, too, on this island of Corfu, stands the tasteless villa of the Empress of Austria, the unfortunate Elisabeth, which was afterwards bought by William II. What proves greater want of taste to build or to buy?

Here is wonderful Cattaro, above a harbour deeply cut into the hills lying at the foot of gigantic mountains; from below one can see a white ribbon that winds about to the very top of the mountains; this is the road to Cetinje. I had just time from one steamer to another, so I started over the mountains. I saw in this way rocky, wild, and sterile Montenegro. I arrived in Cetinje at eight o'clock in the evening and started again at six in the morning. What enormous exertion only to say " I had been there."

Now we come to charming Ragusa. Old, old fortified walls, dotted all over with white and pink oleanders. The whole town is sprinkled all over with oleanders, and everywhere spear-like cypresses shoot boldly upwards, and above it is shaded by weary spreading platans. Here also we find an island and a monastery; on this island a special species of sweet-scented grass grows; it is cared for and cultivated by the monks. It is quiet on this island—sultry and sweet-scented; bees hum and lizards scud about. There is a bust of the American, Gordon Bennett. This millionaire, and founder of the *New York Herald*, who has encircled the terrestrial globe with the wires of his telegraphs, to catch the events happening in the world for the pages of his papers, found repose here; he was beneficent; towards the monastery, the monks raised a monument in his memory, and lizards play about its pedestal.

And here is stern Spalato—the palace of the Emperor Diocletian, it is half in ruins and in its skeleton a town has been built; the staircase leading to the imperial dwelling is a street, the entrance door—the gates of the town. History has requisitioned this palace as property of the people.

For more than two hundred years this Dalmatian shore has looked upon Italy, and it is only now, after the recent upheaval, that it has been joined to her, and when Venice looks across the water she no longer looks on a foreign shore, but into her own distant possessions.

Venice! That marble town that has grown up on those sandy islands. I remember my mother once asked one of the peasants, on our estate at Pavlovka, who had been a sailor, which of the towns he had seen in this voyage round the world had pleased him the most? "Venice," he answered, " because it is warm in winter there; instead of streets they have canals with marble palaces, and the people sing all night." What a pretty description, and how complete it is in its conciseness—climate, art, and man. This tiller of the Tambov government, chose from his reminiscences water, marble, night, and music—the same of which poets have sung, the same that musicians have placed as titles to their songs, the same that Pushkin saw when he wrote:

> " The aged Doge reclining in his gondola,
> Beside his youthful spouse."

Oh, the soundless moonlight on the marble palaces, the trembling moonlight on the sleepy lagoons! . . . Breath of the night. The shadow of a long gondola passes by; like a star the lamp twinkles at its prow, and like a fiery blade its vertical reflection cuts a path in the water along which it is to glide. Like a swan's neck the metal crest of the gondola rises above the prow. In the hollow, almost blended with the cushions of the seats, two shadows, weary of enchantment, lie embraced. Behind them on the high poop the thin shadow of the gondolier dips his sleepy oar into the sleepy water. And it appears as if it were not he who is propelling the gondola but the lamp at the prow, and the oar is only dipped for the sake of the splashes. The night breathes gently, it inspires when the water rises, it respires when the water falls. A bell rings in the distance; the bronze sound falls at night on the sea and melts away. To which of the islands? Chioggia, Murano, or Burano? All is quiet, and like drops falling on the silence come the sounds of distant singing.

The sun rises above Venice. It rises out of the sea, and quickly, hurriedly, the victorious rays chase away the morning mists that crawl upon the smooth surface of the water. There appears before them out of the coolness of night a row of sparkling palaces that are already bathed in the warm light. The cupola of St. Mark is lighted up by the sun, near the cupola the Greek horns that are raised on high glitter, the white and coloured marble, the gold balls beneath the crosses all sparkle on the open place, before the open sea. But in the narrow, hidden away canals, where between the high walls of the tall palaces the lazy night is still loitering, the sun-rays chase the shadows and drive them away. They run away from the cornices of the gloomy marble gateways, they run away from under the balconies, they hide behind the round columns, they crawl into the chinks, into the eyes and nostrils of the marble masks, and pause under the outlines of the vaults of the bridges. The smooth lagoons glitter in the sunlight, and the fishing boats have borne out to sea the incomprehensible marks on their red sails.

Venice has awakened, it rings with the talk of men, the splatter of mirth, the ringing of bells from the belfries, and the patter of feet. Yes, of feet; in Venice you do not always go about in gondolas, you can take long walks in Venice. How delightful these small streets are, bustling and noisy. How I love those small shops—fruit, jewels, vegetables, forged iron-ware—how pretty is the waving of the Venetian women's shawls, they are black but have been rendered soft by the salt sea air. The streets in Venice are loudly loquacious, there are no wheels there, there is no other noise than the noise made by the people. I love these little streets—bustling, talkative—I love these red, boiling arteries of *living* Venice. But how much more I love the green veins, the drowsy canals, of *somnolent* Venice! The gondola glides along between marble walls; there is neither chatter nor bustle here, the splash of the oar, the call of the unseen gondolier from behind the corner; a meeting and a slight concussion of the sides of the gondolas and again a drowsy rocking. Suddenly there is another call, and from round the corner, through the passage between two palaces, like a silent mass of vegetables, a barque floats out. . . . Around us there is only marble and water, the marble is reflected in the water, the water splashes the marble; the marble plunges into the water, the water woos the marble. And if suddenly a sun-ray pierces through the gap between two high buildings into this drowsy mysteriousness, how the reflection of the marble aroused by the sunlight plays on the surging water, and how the smooth marble reflects the colours of the rippling waves!

There are two Venices in Venice: the live, heart-throbbing red Venice of the little streets, and the lethargic, green Venice of the sleepy canals; and at each encounter of these two Venices there is the arch of a bridge: the red above the green; the green below the red. To what dreams did the imagination of man rise, to what celestial heights, to enable him to produce on earth the fairy-tale that is called Venice?

I am sitting before the Café Florian on the Piazza of St. Mark under the arcades. The sun is merciful under the large striped umbrellas, it is shade transpierced by light. Raspberries with ice, eaten out of cold glasses, are very refreshing. On the Piazza before the Cathedral, children and foreigners are feeding the pigeons; the grains of Indian corn are scattered about like golden rain and the pigeons hover in crowds in the air and on the flagstones; they crowd together, shoving each other away, flutter their wings, peck, fly away and return. Amidst all this feathered rumpus come the sounds of children's laughter. The great cathedral looks upon them through the vast openings of its five great doors, and its columns, mosaics, friezes, marble scrolls, golden cones, cupolas, crosses, and the balls on which they rest, glitter in the sunlight. A whole world of marble and gold is shining and burning there. And all this shone and burnt centuries before me. It has shone and looked in the same way on the smart Venice of smart Carpaccio, on the magnificent Venice of magnificent Veronese, on Goldoni's lively powdered Venice, and it looks in the same way on our contemporary crowd— grey, undefined, and crafty. How much we prize that which is unchangeable; "in the days when the earth totters," how we value that which cannot totter. And people who do not change, how precious they are. Precious as all that is rare; rare, as all that is precious. That is why Italy is so precious, because even in all the changes that she has experienced she is always the same as she has always been, because she is saturated with the past, every present moment in Italy is full of the past centuries. And each moment, no matter how different it is, is connected with the others; from the depths of the past there lives in each moment respect for the previous one. Through how many violent shocks this country has passed, but it has never been entered on the pages of its history that any monuments have been destroyed ; what has been destroyed was destroyed by barbarians from without, it has never had its own barbarians. The whole history of Italian culture is a record of respect and preservation, and when the belfry of St. Mark fell down Italy reconstructed it. Oh, the oppressive enigma of time ! Humanity is dangling at the present moment between the past and the future— a lost paradise, in the past, a promised paradise in the future, and we cry with the poet :

> " Sun consume the present,
> For the sake of the future
> But spare the past."

Love for the past is the first indication of the capacity for culture, as it is love of that which does not change. The past is ; by virtue of having been, it *is*, is and does not change. Schiller said :

> " Dreifach ist der Schritt der Zeit :
> Zögernd kommt die Zukunft hergezogen,
> Pfeilschnell is das Jetzt entflogen,
> Ewig still steht die Vergangenheit." [1]

In our contact with the past we find in this immovableness rest for our souls. The educational power of the past consists in its teaching of respect for that which does not change. This is the cause of the educational power of those countries which have a long past.

The most ancient of all that can be found in Italy is of course Sicily. An Island ? It is almost not an island ; it seems but a step across the sea from Reggio to Messina. Sicily is not so old in monuments as in old legends, in names. Here we find the spring that gushed out of the rock to

[1] " Three-fold is the flight of time,
Halting comes the future onwards,
Swift as dart the present flies,
Steadfast only bides the past."

quench Hercules' thirst; the town of Trapani received its name from a sickle lost by Cronus, Jupiter's father. Are there any legends on earth that go farther back than Cronus, the god of Time? I have never felt such close contact with antiquity as in the little town of Girgenti. Situated on the crest of a hill as if seated in a saddle, with vineyards sloping down from it to the dark blue sea below, and in the midst of the green vines stand the golden brown ruins of three Greek shrines. A few olive trees dim the brightness of the sea, and on the meadows cattle graze. And yet so close seemed the connexion with antiquity that it appeared to me that those were the very cows mentioned in the Iliad and the Odyssey. Even in Greece on the Acropolis, standing in front of the Parthenon, I did not feel such immediate contact; there I felt something of the atmosphere of a museum, here everything was in its proper place untouched and surrounded with what had surrounded it then. Girgenti is proud of its temples— *i tempi*: the hotel is called "Albergo dei Tempi," the wine of the place—*Vino dei Tempi*. Syracuse is also old, but it is not like charming Girgenti. In Syracuse everything is in museums, in glass cases. If ever you happen to be in that museum, in the hall where the coins of the times of the Syracusian tyrants are kept, look for those on which the consort of Hieron II is represented; she is wonderfully charming.

What is there not in Sicily? Greece and Rome, the Arabs and the Normans and everything is crowned by gigantic Etna.

"Ils sont beaux, quand il fait beau temps,
 Ces yeux presque Mahométans,
  De la Sicile." [1]

[1] "How fine they are, in fair weather,
 Those eyes almost Mohammedan,
  Of beautiful Sicily."

At the foot of Etna lies Catania, the birthplace of Bellini. A little to the north, nearer to Italy, Messina, a large and flourishing town that was destroyed by an earthquake in a few seconds.

I was in Rome that winter. I well remember the terrible stories. Pictures of the misery were shown in the cinematograph. At the time of the earthquake two Russian warships were passing Sicily; they at once cast anchor and sent a company on shore, and our sailors helped to unbury and to save the inhabitants. They displayed great courage and earned much sympathy from the Italians. Whenever the Russian naval uniform appeared on the screen it was greeted with applause in the cinematograph theatre. I remember having read in one of the papers the account given by a doctor's wife. They were seated at table when they felt a terrible shock. What happened to her husband and children she could not remember, but she sank into a dark abyss and lost consciousness. When she came to, she was lying in a sort of coffin; she felt there were walls all around her and no exit. How long she remained lying there she could not remember. Broken by hunger and cold and weakness, she again lost consciousness. In her dreams she heard knocks, they came nearer, but she was so weak she could not open an eye. Suddenly there came a stream of fresh air, and on her closed eyes a ray of bright sunshine. Something seized and lifted her up, and before she could understand what had happened she heard " paroli di conforto in una lingua sconosciuta."[1] They were the Russian sailors'. At that time the Russian sailor was a synonym of sensitiveness and valour. I do not know how it is now.

I must mention the last island of my narrative. I was on the island of Corsica, in Ajaccio, Napoleon's birthplace.

---

[1] Words of comfort in an incomprehensible language.

A small, insignificant town. The rocky island is unattractive. Its greatest charm does not lie in its real qualities, but in those that our imagination lends it—of course Napoleon. The whole meaning of Corsica is Napoleon. I only see one real charm in it. Its hills are covered with a sweet-scented grass, or more correctly speaking a low bush, they call it "cyste." It emits a delightfully resinous scent, that can be smelt on the sea when the vessel is approaching. Well, and this real detail has been consecrated to the name of Napoleon; there is no description of Corsica in which it is not mentioned that Napoleon loved to recognize his Corsica from afar by this scent. Strange! Why, thousands of people before him had breathed in this scent and had recognized Corsica from afar, but all this was different and unworthy of mention, the only thing of interest was that Napoleon breathed it in, and loved to do so; it is only his inspiration that has become legendary.

In Corsica you meet many women in black; they have a strange custom there, they only put on new mourning when the time for the old mourning is expired. There are families who never leave off mourning. The women wear a strange black covering for their heads, in one side of which a whalebone is inserted; they spread out like large shades, or like sails. . . . There is but little of interest in Ajaccio. Above the town is the large disproportioned villa of Prince Capodistrias; it was built of the stones of the destroyed *Tuileries Palace*. There is so little of interest in Ajaccio that I don't even remember if I saw the house in which Napoleon was born.

I cannot think of Napoleon without remembering what a large place islands have played in his destiny. The eaglet flew away from Corsica, the eagle covered half the world with the shadow of his wings, to alight in chains on St. Helena. And between these two islands there is a third—Elba. It was only wanting for him—to his fame—to experience captivity and flight; he was banished to Elba to give him this glory. But he only rose to fall.

"There's an island in that distant ocean."

And he fell on that island. When I think of the island of St. Helena I see before me the statue by the sculptor Vela in the Pitti Palace in Florence—" Gli ultimi giorni di Napoleone."[1] He is seated in a dressing-gown with unbuttoned collar, gazing with his deep-set eyes into the far distance. How much is expressed in that extinguishing gaze; and what thoughts in that departing spirit. . . . and the island and the ocean; life and eternity—whence and whither. Why, our life is an island in the ocean of eternity.

I also remember that wonderful book about Napoleon in St. Helena, by Lord Rosebery, *The Last Phase*, an unforgettable book. In what a gruesome manner it brings the past into to-day; how well he understands by small, unimportant details to rebuild the structure of life. What a fight this book is against death. Read it; the bitter struggle of St. Helena palpitates in every page. Well then, is not a book that we love also an island in that sea of paper that is written or printed on, and in the dimness of our ignorance what we know are but islands of light.

And besides, I remember our two poets, Pushkin and Lermontov. What beauty there is in their references to Napoleon, what spiritual detachment from all earthly considerations, what a lofty forgetfulness of wrongs even at that time, when the wounds of 1812 were scarcely healed. That was the time of youth; in the whole of history has there ever been a more attractive page of youthful enthusiasm than

"The days of Alexander's excellent beginnings."

[1] " The last days of Napoleon."

Youth knows how to forget; old age forgives, youth does not require to forgive—it forgets. The youthful muse of our eternally youthful poets forgot. Looking on Napoleon's grave, Pushkin says,

> "There the hatred of nations slumbers,
> And the light of immortality burns."

But in his poems he has forgotten the hatred and he only speaks of immortality.

Napoleon was not left on the island—his ashes were brought to France. The re-established, but very decrepit kingly power, in the absence of its own laurels, snatched at these remains of the Emperor. Louis Philippe ordered them to be exhumed and brought to Paris. It took eighteen hours to disinter the coffin.

> "The desert and gloomy granite"

would not give up its hero. At last the coffin was dug up, placed on the vessel in which the king's son had arrived to escort him to France. The island watched the departing ship, and, like the bark of faithful watchdogs, accompanied him with the parting salute of artillery from its rugged cliffs.

In Paris, under the dome of the Church of the Invalides, the King of the French, surrounded by his Court, awaited his arrival. Artillery fire announced that the remains of Napoleon had entered the capital of France. They waited . . . . The door is thrown open, the Marshal of the Court, with his staff, enters and announces in a loud voice "L'Empereur." The King and the whole Court rise from their seats. The comrades of war of the great commander bring the coffin into the church and lower it into the grave.

" Je désire que mes cendres reposent au bord de la Seine

au milieu de ce peuple français que j'ai tant aimé."[1] His wish was accomplished. There in the ocean there remained

> "Only a rock the sepulchre of glory."

But this is not the last island of my narrative. There is still another I wish to mention, and to mention with gratitude. It is not an island, but an isle, a small islet. But it is precious to me for having offered a refuge to my soul. This islet in the midst of the ocean of Bolshevistic triviality and wickedness is—that ream of paper on which for the last four months I have been writing my reminiscences.

Yes, islands have *always* had a kind of mysterious attraction for me!

---

[1] "I wish that my ashes should repose on the banks of the Seine in the midst of the French people I loved so much."

ROME

Rome has sheltered four generations of our family; and now it is sheltering a fifth.

During the first quarter of the last century the daughter-in-law of my grandfather, the Dekabrist, "Princess Zénéide" Wolkonsky, née Princess Beloselsky, settled in Rome. I did not know her, she died before I was born, but the name of Aunt Zénéide is one of my earliest childish recollections. The sound of that name has something very caressing in it, and something smiling seems to radiate from it. The smile of Zénéide Wolkonsky dwells not alone in our family; it illuminates the first half of the nineteenth century in every branch of Russian artistic life. Music, painting, literature, drama—all were dear to her, she was in contact with them all, and if not with the same creative power in all, still she brought to each the same sincerity of her nature and with the same undiminished regard for people. The most celebrated people of her time blend their rays with the radiance of her name: Pushkin, Gogol, Mickiewicz, Venevitinov, Brülow, Bruni, and Rossini. She knew how to receive, make much of a man, to place him in those surroundings—moral, physical and social— that were necessary for his work, for his inspiration. It was thus that she received and caressed Venevitinov, the poor, sick poet, who perished in the flower of his age and the blossoming of his talent, of whom Pushkin wrote to his friends: "How could you let him die?" He was madly in love with Zénéide. In Rome she warmed the difficult days of sick, morose Gogol. In the Poli Palace, which now exists no more, she arranged a literary evening in order to help him. Gogol was to read his " Inspector." The tickets were dear for those times—twenty francs—and they were all sold, but alas Gogol proved to be a very bad reader. After the first act half of the audience left the hall. After each act the listeners grew fewer, and it was only owing to the fascinating persuasion of Princess Zénéide that she succeeded in retaining a small group of her nearest friends, and mustered them round the morose reader. Thus ended Gogol's unfortunate debut. She also brought the writer Shevyrev to Rome, offering him the post of tutor to her son, Alexander, and saved him from illness in this way. The disciples of every art liked her, they felt they were at home with her whom Pushkin called " the queen of the muses and beauty." I shall never forget the story told by Princess Marie Baryatinsky, of how once in the Villa Wolkonsky she had been the witness of a meeting between Princess Zénéide and Bryulov, who had just arrived in Rome. They had not met for a long time, and their meeting was such a burst of delight, such a blending of common interests, different, higher and more special than those of others, that all who were present felt they had receded to the background, and that they were only the accidental and extraneous witnesses of another existence.

The beautiful image of Princess Zénéide is worthy of study and remembrance. Now it is of course difficult to study our past, more especially as most of it has been wiped off the face of the earth. Princess Zénéide left many letters, many albums in which she had made notes, and had pasted in remembrances. On their pages can be found scraps of thought, impressions, pictures of the surroundings of her life—rooms, portraits, views of towns where she had lived or where she had stopped in passing, and of life on her estate. Leaves and flowers, that had once been alive and plucked at different times and in various places, are dried up on these pages. I saw two of these albums not long ago in Moscow; they had been brought from Princess Zénéide's Tula estate and placed in one of the new museums where the ashes of culture are being heaped up. It is doubtful if anything could be reconstructed out of these chance fragments, besides, who would undertake such a task.

Princess Zénéide's husband, Nikita Wolkonsky, was a mild, lazy man. In the voluminous archives left me by my father, and which I had always the intention of publishing, there are only two letters written by his hand. I know but little about him. In the family he was always spoken of as " l'entiché " owing to his devotion to his wife, who was called " l'enchanteresse." I can relate one amusing occurrence in the life of Nikita Wolkonsky. In 1808, Alexander I sent him with a letter to Napoleon. The Emperor of the French received him amiably and dismissed him graciously. On the stairs Duroc caught him up and handed him a case: " This is a remembrance from his Majesty." In it was a ring with a small diamond. Wolkonsky found that this gift was unworthy of the Ambassador of the Emperor of Russia, and on his departure he gave it to the gendarme who escorted him. " Take this remembrance from a Russian officer." The gendarme boasted about it, the affair became known and reached Napoleon's ears. Napoleon instructed his Ambassador in Petersburg to complain of this disrespectful treatment of his present. Alexander summoned Wolkonsky, and asked him if he had told him all the details of his journey. Wolkonsky affirmed that he had not withheld anything, and repeated what had taken place and what had been said. " Well, and afterwards, did nothing special occur ? " the Emperor asked. Then

Wolkonsky remembered the ring, and he understood that the emperor's question referred to it, and that he knew the story of the ring. However, in Petersburg this story did not seem as terrible as it did in Paris. The Emperor only said " Il parait que vous avez manqué me brouiller avec Napoléon. C'est une imprudence de votre part. Après tout vous n'avez pas eu tout-à-fait tort dans cette affaire. N'en parlons plus."[1]

The Villa that Princess Zénéide purchased in Rome, which became afterward the very famous " Villa Wolkonsky," was situated on land that tradition said had formerly belonged to the Empress Helena, the mother of Constantine the Great. At that time it stood quite in the outskirts of the town, and was shaded from the back by the magnificent façade of the basilica of San Giovanni in Laterano, and from the distant spreading Campagna the old arches of the Roman aqueduct passed through the garden. Now all is changed. Huge dwelling-houses surround the villa on all sides, the façade of the basilica can only be seen from the second story, and instead of the misty view of the Campagna and the blue outlines of the Alban and Sabine mountains, you have the usual picture of the roofs of Italian towns ; roofs and linen hanging between the chimney-stacks, oleanders, geraniums, feathery bamboos, geraniums, oleanders and linen. Under the shadow of Italian pines and the Roman ruins, that adorned her garden, Princess Zénéide had collected material remembrances of what was dear to her in her native land and in foreign countries ; the first place was occupied by a bust of the Emperor, Alexander I. It was placed on a pedestal made of a fragment of granite from the Alexander column, which stands before the Winter Palace. All this has

---

[1] "It appears that you have almost embroiled me with Napoleon. It was imprudent on your part. However, you were not so far wrong in this matter. We need not talk of it any more."

remained; "l'allée des souvenirs" has remained, but all is not the same. It is a mistake to suppose that a place which has been dear to us for its own sake has its own face; no, it is the face of man that shines from the house and from the trees; when the man disappears the place changes its face. But Zénéide Wolkonsky is remembered. At the same time that Professor Tsvetaev in his pamphlet on the history of the Alexander III Museum, places her name at the head of the new building, as the first idea of the institution originated with her, in Rome a street adjoining her villa was given the name of "via Wolkonsky." It is quite natural that she should be remembered in Rome. She did much good there; the poor of Rome worshipped her. She died in consequence of a chill she caught one cold winter morning, when, under the gateway, she took off a warm petticoat to give it to a poor woman. Her last years were devoted to acts of faith and charity. She had been converted to Roman Catholicism. In Rome they cannot remember such a confluence of poor people as followed her to the grave. Her remains repose in the Church of Santi Vincenzo ed Anastasio, that is situated near the Trevi fountain.

During the 'thirties of the last century the elder brother of my grandfather the "Dekabrist," Prince Nicholas Wolkonsky, who, after the death of his grandfather, received the family name of Repnin, also resided in Rome. His wife, Princess Barbara, was a daughter of Count Razumovsky and a granddaughter of the famous Hetman. There is something beautiful and fairy-like in their lives, which began amid the glitter and racket of the Napoleonic wars. The wife accompanied her husband, and at Austerlitz she helped to remove the wounded from the field of battle. He was the Russian representative in Cassel to the King of Westphalia, Napoleon's brother. It is interesting to remember that at the same time the French ambassador there was Victor Hugo's father, and that the Repnin children played with the future poet. After our troops had taken Berlin, Nicholas Repnin was governor of the Prussian capital. In 1813 he became vice-King of Saxony; two years later he was governor-general of Little Russia. The Repnins lived grandly; they were as lavish as they were generous and as generous as they were careless. After they had left Cassel a pearl necklace belonging to the Princess was found in a chest of drawers. The splendour of their style of living, the legendary episodes of his career, his governorship in Berlin, his kingship in Dresden, make the Repnins appear as an echo of the eighteenth century, the last outburst of the Razumovsky fairy-tale. But this brilliancy of the early 'thirties was dimmed by a fog. A denunciation was sent in against Repnin, accusing him of having appropriated state moneys destined for a Poltava institution. This establishment was the Repnins' pet child; insulted by this calumny Nicholas Repnin sent in his resignation, and went with his whole family to Italy. In 1872 the Repnins returned to Russia and took up their abode in their estate in Little Russia. The rest of his days he passed under the weight of this denunciation, and humiliating tutorage, while awaiting the result of this protracted inquiry. But he did not wait for its conclusion. Two months after his death his entire innocence was proved and officially attested. He had a strong, straightforward and noble character.

In Italy they resided in Frascati near Rome, in the splendid Villa Muti, in which seventy years later my brother Alexander lived with his family. Here in this villa their daughter Elisabeth got engaged to Paul Krivtsov. This marriage, according to the ideas of those times, did not appear very brilliant in the eyes of her parents, especially for their favourite daughter, Lily. However they gave their consent and the marriage took place in Florence, where the Repnin family had gone owing to an outbreak of cholera, and where they resided in the beautiful Palazza Toririgani. The daughter, Olga, born of this union, married my father's cousin, Nicholas Orlov ; his mother, Catherine Raevsky, was the sister of my grandmother, Marie Nikolaivna. Olga Orlov is still living in Moscow with her daughters, Mme. Kotlyarevsky, and her unmarried daughter, Elisabeth. Mme. Orlov is 87 ; she lives with her whole consciousness in the events of to-day, while her unfailing memory goes back to the distant past. I read to her all that I have written in these pages. In a little house in a by-street of Moscow, in a drawing-room crowded with furniture, or on the half-ruined but still shady balcony ; during many evenings I read these chapters to her and to the members of her family. I count those minutes among the bright recollections of that time, and I am grateful for the welcome and attention she bestowed on me and for the assistance I received from her clear and unfailing memory. And so from the low wooden porch of the little house in a Moscow by-street I pass mentally to the lofty stone terraces of the Villa Muti and the immeasurable horizon of the Roman Campagna.

Many letters written by Princess Barbara Repnin to my grandmother, in the Petrov factory in Siberia, are dated from the Villa Muti. From time to time rays of Italian sunshine penetrated into this Siberian exile ; there were letters from Princess Barbara from the Villa Muti ; and from Zénéide from the Villa Wolkonsky—music, flower and vegetable seeds were sent ; from Naples, Marie Nikolaevna's mother, Mme. Raevsky, sent her some dried leaves gathered on Virgil's grave. There, in the Petrov factory they also received a lithographic portrait of Zénéide, it was a beautiful portrait, the work of a certain Rossi—she was in a lace cap with large, widely-opened eyes; below the portrait was the ruins of a Roman archway, and under it the Roman she-wolf.

In those years Princess Sophie Wolkonsky, the sister of the "Dekabrist" was also in Rome. She was a strange person. A characteristic episode shows her solicitude and avarice, two fundamental traits of a strange phenomenon that shows itself in our family. When she was leaving for Russia, she asked her brother Nicholas to take charge until her return of a trunk with some things she did not need in Russia. This trunk Repnin lugged about with him all over Italy for a whole year; at last it became so dilapidated that one day his valet declared that it would be necessary to open the most serene Princess's trunk. It proved to be filled with firewood. This fidgety creature, " my swiftly-flying traveller," as her father called her, did not always reside in Rome.

In the 'forties her son, my mother's father, Prince Gregory Wolkonsky, settled in Rome, as a member of the Russian mission to the Vatican. Besides this post he was the President of the Russian Archælogical Commission in Rome and the curator of the Russian artists living in Rome. My mother, who was then a little girl, and her brother Peter, five years younger than herself, came with their parents. They lived in the Palazzo Salviati on the Corso. It was here that my mother passed the whole of her childhood. She was sixteen when she returned to Russia, and at eighteen, in 1859, she got engaged. In 1908, ten years after my mother's death, when walking on the Corso with my father, we entered the Palazzo Salviati and he showed me the landing on the staircase where he met my mother for the first time.

My maternal grandfather, Prince Gregory Wolkonsky,

PRINCESS ELISABETH WOLKONSKY (*née* WOLKONSKY)

was a strange type of man, and a brilliant representative of the society of those times. Having been educated in the Lycée Richelieu in Odessa, he returned to Petersburg as a refined flower of the culture of the time. At the same time there appeared in him, and in an even more pronounced form than in most, that strange effect that education produced in Russia. With us, education has always torn a man out of his surroundings; and, according to his station, has either made him a stranger to his social surroundings or to his country. Gregory Wolkonsky, like many at that time, was in proportion to his culture all the less Russian. The celebrated Maid of Honour, Mme. Smirnov, who was a friend of Pushkin's and Gogol's, says of my grandfather in her letters that he sometimes " showed contempt for all that was called Russian literature." But she adds " Perhaps he is right regarding its present development, or, more correctly speaking, stagnation." He was a brilliant example of what we call a " bohemian." With strong artistic propensities, an exceptional talent for music, the possessor of a rarely fine voice, he was not created for anything that requires roots; he was unnecessary for his country and he remained unnecessary for his family. He was separated from my grandmother and lived far away from all the family in Odessa and Akerman. Charming in his intercourse with strangers, he was dull in the family circle. The opinions of his contemporaries are full of respect for the high qualities of his sociability and his humaneness. But at home, to live with him became every year more difficult, owing to his unbearable pedantry. Even after he had separated from his family, he continued, from a distance, to communicate his pedantic opinions and appreciations of this and the other family complication, government measures, or the political events of Europe. He wrote on large sheets of paper with a blue pencil, in a clear upright handwriting and underlined his words vigorously. Subsequently when I was looking through my parents' archives, I came upon a letter from my grandfather, Gregory Wolkonsky, and I was horrified by this accumulation of arguments, examples, quotations, and moralizings. In my childhood I can remember very well, when a large thick letter arrived by post, how wearily my grandmother raised her hand to open it, how wearily her eyes gazed at my mother as if to say " Again a letter." Of course it was more difficult to answer it than to read it, but a reply was necessary. He was a strange man.

In differentiation from his mother my grandfather was extraordinarily liberal and wasteful. He never bought single articles but always dozens. The well-known bookseller in Rome, Piazza di Spagna Spithoever, said to me with a sigh " Customers like your grandfather are no longer to be found."

During the last twenty years of his life my grandfather lived far away from his family. He fell under the influence of his mother's companion, a certain Lidia Wachsel. I saw her in 1881 in Mentone, when, after my grandmother's death, my mother and I went to visit him there. She was very plain but remarkably clever; she could be very amiable and brilliant in conversation. She took the weak old man of seventy-two into her hands, and a year after my grandmother's death she got him to marry her. He died a year after, and she inherited his estate in Bessarabia and all his movables. She lived in Odessa, and I learned much of interest about her in a strange, roundabout way. About eight miles from our former Pavlovka estate, in the Tambov government there lived the landowner, Jacob Bunin. At one time he had been chief of police in our district, in the 'eighties he was already a general, and suddenly he was appointed to the post of policemaster in

Odessa. There he and his wife became acquainted with my grandfather's widow. It appeared that she could not bear the members of her own family, and had decided that after her death the estate and all the movable property was to go back to the Wolkonsky family. She made a will leaving the property to my mother's brother Peter. But my uncle died before she died ; his sons by law could not inherit it, and by the force of circumstances the estate had to go to the legal heirs of the deceased. She had two brothers. One was a colonel and had a post in the Caucasus ; the other, a confirmed drunkard, was serving as a billiard-marker in a Vienna café. When he was discovered in the attic where he lived, he was at first alarmed at the arrival of official personages, but when the cause of this visit was explained to him, and he understood it was to put him in possession of a large inheritance he experienced such a moral shock that he died on the spot. The Caucasian colonel remained the sole heir. This is what I heard from General Bunin and his wife. At that time I was occupied in collecting relics of the family, portraits, etc. I knew that my grandfather had many things that would be valueless for a stranger, but that were very precious to me, so I wrote to the colonel asking him to let me have what he considered possible, and I offered to pay for them. My letter was returned " owing to the death of the addressee."

In the Palazzo Salviati on the Corso my mother passed her youth ; she loved Italy, she breathed Italy, and Italy always remained the breath of her life. In the winter of 1859 my grandfather, the " Dekabrist," came to Rome with my grandmother and my father. My grandfather had only returned from Siberia three years previously. Our exiles who had returned from a banishment that had lasted thirty years found themselves surrounded by relatives in Rome. Princess Zénéide was no longer living. Her son, Alexander, was the master of Villa Wolkonsky. He had inherited the attractive qualities of his mother's character—sincerity, spiritual warmth, and an unusual softness in his relations with other people. Bartenev, the editor of the *Russian Archives,* called him " one of the best men in the whole of Russia." From his mother Prince Alexander also inherited the good terms on which she was with his uncle the " Dekabrist," and his family. Thus the " Dekabrist " Wolkonsky found two nephews in Rome; Alexander, the son of his brother Nikita, lived in the Villa Wolkonsky, and Gregory, the son of his sister Sophy, lived in the Palazzo Salviati. Prince Michael Wolkonsky, the son of the " Dekabrist," married the daughter of his cousin Gregory, Princess Elisabeth Wolkonsky. They were my parents. The marriage took place on the 27th of May, 1859, in Geneva, on the birthday of my maternal grandmother, Princess Marie Wolkonsky.

Thus ended the Rome that I never saw, but which I knew from hearsay, and from the faded photographs and numerous watercolours and drawings, that are scattered in our grandmother's albums. Those were the last days of papal Rome. The Roman ruins, still not surrounded by railings, blended with the life of the street, and the sunburnt peasant women in variegated aprons and white headdresses on their black hair, sat under the shade of the ruins with their baskets of vegetables and their pitchers of water. The fountains were not enclosed and served to water both man and beast. The red cardinals still drove about in their own carriages; and from the high balcony of the cathedral of St. Peter the Pope still blessed the populace kneeling in the Piazza beneath. It was still the time when the many-coloured carnival passed through the gaily decorated streets with noise, antics, and dances;

when once a year the holiday-making crowd assembled in the Corso for the barbarous spectacle of horses being made to run the gauntlet, goaded onwards with red-hot irons. All this is past, but still remains in the recollection of even those who had not seen it, and still lives in the albums of our grandmothers. Who has them? In whose safe-keeping are they? Do you know that dome of St. Peter against the evening sky, and that sly peasant woman talking to a monk, and that cardinal reading a missal; or that shepherdess with a pipe, pasturing her goats in the midst of the ruins. . . . Charming albums. On their pages Italy is in Russia and Russia in Italy. Here we find Bryulov and Bruni painting Italian peasant women, monks and shepherdesses, here there are also Italian artists painting our grandmothers and girls. Whoever has such albums must take care of them. I had a portrait of my mother drawn by the Italian artist Canevari, a year after her marriage. A beautiful pencil drawing; it is now adorning the office of the district People's Commissar in the town of Borisoglebsk.

I mentioned in another chapter that I was twelve years old when first I came to Italy. We passed the winter of 1872–73 in Florence. At Christmas we went to our grandmother, who was living in Rome with her son, my mother's brother, Prince Peter Wolkonsky. My uncle was married to Princess Vera Lvov, a celebrated beauty. At that time their third son, Peter, had just been born; their elder children were called Gregory and Alexander. My uncle Peter was not a commonplace man. The peculiarities of three generations were concentrated by the fourth in new originality. It is curious to trace the evolution of the family peculiarities. Old Prince Gregory, the father of my grandfather, the " Dekabrist," and of his sister Sophie, was a good-natured oddity; but little cultured with a great aptitude for music—a real Russian type—a merry, generous fellow with strongly developed family feelings. His daughter Sophie had inherited nothing of her father's good nature; with the exception of his brilliant humour, though with a strong admixture of bitterness, she was quite the opposite of her father, but the originality and the picturesqueness with which this difference manifested itself were inherited from him. Another distinctive trait of that generation was the absence of self-observation and a great straightforwardness in their relations with other people. They knew nothing of that psychological probing of their inner selves which afterwards was so strongly developed in the new generation. Thanks to this, they impressed themselves on the memory of their contemporaries with great warmth and clearness. Princess Sophie's son, Gregory, my mother's and my uncle Peter's father, inherited from his grandfather his musical capacities but none of his family virtues. He exaggerated to the last degree the wandering propensities of his mother, and one may say that he squandered in a sort of cosmopolitan Bohemia all the Russian naturalness of his grandfather; but he preserved his generosity and had nothing of his mother's avarice. His son, my uncle Peter, displayed a combination of all the characteristics of the previous three generations, but added to them an exceptional capacity for mental work in the domain of philosophy.

The impression my first visit to Rome produced on me was less than might have been expected. I had become too enamoured of Florence. But I, a twelve-year-old boy, was astonished how much of Rome I already knew—from books, photographs, albums, by the reproductions of pictures that were hanging in our Petersburg house. The Colosseum, the Forum, the Triton fountain, and the

Colonnade of St. Peter were all familiar to me. Perugino's " Resurrection " in the Vatican I had seen in my mother's bedroom, and among Raphael's stanza I recognized the " Release of St. Peter from prison," that hung in my grandmother's drawing-room. And when I entered the Cathedral of St. Peter, it was in the afternoon, I exclaimed " Ah, there's that sun-ray." A beautiful water-colour, representing the interior of the Cathedral hung in my mother's drawing-room. From my childhood, although I had never been to Rome, I knew the ray of sunlight, that all, who have been to St. Peter's in the afternoon, know so well; from the high left window, in the depth of the cathedral, it falls diagonally on the altar.

The interior of the cathedral, strange to say, does not astonish by its great size. There is evidently some mathematical secret in its dimensions, but we realize this not by our imagination, but by our reason; it is only when we know how enormous it is that we feel its vastness. I remember a story my grandmother used to tell of a general who ordered his regiment to go to St. Peter's to assist at some function, and to wait for him there. He arrived at the appointed time, the church was empty; he went on, and found the whole regiment in one of the side chapels. In the middle of the cathedral, just under the dome, and just above the grave of the Apostle Peter, there is an altar, and above it a canopy supported by four twisted columns. This canopy appears to be of quite insignificant proportions in the general picture of architectural perspective; and nevertheless these twisted columns have the exact height of the Winter Palace. On my estate of Pavlovka I measured out from the porch of the entrance hall along the drive up the exact measurement of the interior of the cathedral of St. Peter. I placed a stone at the side of the road, and watched the time it would take for a carriage to drive from the centre of the cathedral to the entrance door, from the spot where, under the diagonal sun-ray, the four prelates of the church support the altar of St. Peter.

Once, many years later, I felt very acutely the enormous size of the cathedral of St. Peter. I was at the twenty-five years jubilee of Leo XIII. I do not know how many tens of thousands of people found place in the cathedral. I remember the impression of its vastness that I received not by sight but by hearing. The Pope was carried in from the inner apartments of the Vatican; he was greeted with shouts. It is the distant sound of these shouts that I remember; I remember how the sound increased in volume as if they were approaching through the streets. I remember how long they lasted, and still he was not to be seen. I remember how at last I could see in the distance the waving of peacock feather flabilla over a sea of heads, and how at last appeared, borne on the shoulders, seated on a throne, a little stooping white figure in a mitre tied on with a string, but with a joyous beaming face, spreading his blessings high and wide—it was Leo XIII. The shouts increased and were echoed under the vaults. I found myself in the midst of Slavs; around me there were shouts of " Zivio "! What a babel of tongues there was there! They were all blended together. What other idea on earth can unite so many " languages " in one feeling? Leo XIII did not only bless; he sometimes smiled and waved his hand. It is difficult to describe the charm of that movement when the blessing pastor gave place to the man thanking for the welcome. His successor, Pius X, did not like to be greeted with shouts—he ceased to bless and the shouts became silent.

After that visit I was often in Rome, and during the last ten years before the war I lived there. My father could not stand the Petersburg climate and had removed to

Rome. At first I lived with him and my sister, afterwards I took a separate lodging, which I have still retained. Much has changed in Rome, and Rome itself is changed. Many old streets exist no more, many old palaces have been pulled down, many broad new streets, that are quite unlike Italy, have been made ; the muddy yellow Tiber has been fettered by new marble quays, the ruins have been cleaned and railings have been put round them as if they had been numbered ; tramways tinkle through the narrow streets of old Rome, and new Rome is colourless and stretches out in dusty boulevards and monotonous houses with green shutters. Rome is changed, is changing and will yet change, but still it is Rome. As in the midst of the violent shocks they have experienced the seasons of the year, and the quarters of the world do not change, so in the midst of the changes that the town has experienced the Colosseum, the Forum, the Pantheon, the cupola of St. Peter's, the yellow Tiber, with the fortress of St. Angelo on its banks, all the churches, the belfries, the numerous gates that lead from the seething city to the silent deserted Campagna will still remain ; there will still remain the stern, smooth façade of the Capitol hanging perpendicularly above the Forum, there will still remain the mysterious excavated ruins, the brilliance and the plash, the noise and the spray of the fountains. There will remain on the lower steps of the high staircase of the Trinita dei Monti the odorous baskets of flowers. And of an evening from the upper steps there will always remain, spread out beyond the town, the conflagration of the sunset in the sky, and to the right, on the golden background, the umbrella-shaped line of pines. On the horizon there will remain the faint outline of Monte Mario, and the blaze of the sunset will still illumine the most beautiful cupola in the world. And there will still remain that Roman air, in which we have the steppes, the sea, the mountains, and, lastly, all that wonderful Rome in which is blended this heritage of ages.

In 1909, just before Christmas, my father died in a house situated quite in the corner of the Piazza Trinita dei Monti. We were fond of living near that place. Other Russians also liked to live in that part of the town; it was the Russian corner of Rome; my brother Sasha gave it the nickname of " Kaluga." They are still living there. My brother's wife keeps a pension and all the relations take their meals with her; it is the corner of Russian refugees. My brother had stuck in Rome in his quality of the former military agent. His wife had remained in Moscow, where she was at the time of the October revolution, and then had gone with her children to the Caucasus. There she had to suffer cold, hunger, and ruin, the invasion of their countrymen, and flight; they hid in the hills and walked barefoot in Sochi, when suddenly they were sought out by the captain of an English steamer, who gave to each of them a parcel addressed to them by my brother, which contained linen, soap, brushes, etc. The English captain took them on board, exhausted by suffering and worn out by malaria, and conveyed them to Italy.

Thus Rome played a part in the history of our family.

Casting an eye on the different generations of one family, one is involuntarily surprised how much they have travelled. The spirit of wandering, as a sort of fate, sometimes in the form of evident necessity, sometimes from inner inclination, governed their lives. My grandfather, the " Dekabrist," who passed the middle years of his life in Siberia, during his latter years travelled all over that Europe which in his youth he had traversed from one field of battle to another. His sister Sophie had been everywhere from London to Orenburg and from Kiakhta to Naples. My father was not infected in a similar degree with " the love of change," but even he, born in Siberia, had been, in his youth, in Kamchatka, and ended his days in Rome. And was not his whole life a series of wanderings? What a journey was his list of service. The son of a convict, entered at his birth as a factory peasant, he finished life as lord-high-steward and member of the Council of the Empire. My brother Gregory, who struggled twenty years with consumption, went to Madeira, Teneriffe, the Cape of Good Hope, and the Orange Republic. And my brother Alexander, who had been sent on special missions at one time to Teheran and Peking, now stretched out his hand from Rome to his wife and children in the Caucasus. However, who in Russia does not think of wandering now; but I think that I have been able to bear with such comparative ease the fate that has befallen me, thanks to our natural tendency for change, the result of the nomadic propensities of former generations.

Is it not strange that in such strongly diversified types the family resemblance should have showed itself especially in this trait—the inclination for travel, for solitude, for individualization? Why, travel is one of the forms of self assertion, it is to a certain degree the protest of the individual against the race. And is it not strange that it is especially the community of these passions that shows itself as an attribute of the race?

How strange is this gravitation to Rome? Why, is it not well known that all roads lead to Rome? No, it is *not* strange, as it is also not strange that the last chapter of my " wanderings " should be entitled " Rome."

www.ingramcontent.com/pod-product-compliance
Lightning Source LLC
Chambersburg PA
CBHW071219080526